CREATIVE HOMEOWNER®

ULTIMATE GUIDE TO

Floors, Walls, and Ceilings

BUILD ▪ REMODEL ▪ REPAIR

CREATIVE HOMEOWNER® Upper Saddle River, New Jersey

CREATIVE
HOMEOWNER®

A Division of Federal Marketing Corp.
Upper Saddle River, NJ

ULTIMATE GUIDE TO FLOORS, WALLS, AND CEILINGS

MANAGING EDITOR	Fran Donegan
SENIOR GRAPHIC DESIGN COORDINATOR	Glee Barre
GRAPHIC DESIGNER	Kathryn Wityk
PHOTO RESEARCHER	Robyn Poplasky
EDITORIAL ASSISTANTS	Jennifer Calvert, Nora Grace
INDEXER	Schroeder Indexing Services
COVER DESIGN	David Geer, Kathryn Wityk
ILLUSTRATIONS	Ian Warpole, Vincent Babak, Clarke Barre, Craig Franklin, Ed Lipinski, James Randolf, Paul M. Schumm & Ray Skibinski, Robert Strauch, Charles Van Vooren
FRONT COVER PHOTOGRAPHY	*left to right* courtesy of Shaw Industries; courtest of York Wallcovering; Anne Gummerson
BACK COVER PHOTOGRAPHY	*top* www.davidduncanlivingston.com; *bottom row left to right* John Parsekian/CH; Eric Roth; John Parsekian/CH

CREATIVE HOMEOWNER

VICE PRESIDENT AND PUBLISHER	Timothy O. Bakke
PRODUCTION DIRECTOR	Kimberly H. Vivas
ART DIRECTOR	David Geer
MANAGING EDITOR	Fran J. Donegan

Current Printing (last digit)
10 9 8 7 6 5 4 3 2 1

Ultimate Guide to Floors, Walls, and Ceilings
Library of Congress Control Number: 2006934267
ISBN-10: 1-58011-342-7
ISBN-13: 978-1-58011-342-7
CREATIVE HOMEOWNER®

A Division of Federal Marketing Corp.
24 Park Way
Upper Saddle River, NJ 07458
www.creativehomeowner.com

METRIC EQUIVALENTS

Length

1 inch	25.4mm
1 foot	0.3048m
1 yard	0.9144m
1 mile	1.61km

Area

1 square inch	645mm²
1 square foot	0.0929m²
1 square yard	0.8361m²
1 acre	4046.86m²
1 square mile	2.59km²

Volume

1 cubic inch	16.3870cm³
1 cubic foot	0.03m³
1 cubic yard	0.77m³

Common Lumber Equivalents

Sizes: Metric cross sections are so close to their U.S. sizes, as noted below, that for most purposes they may be considered equivalents.

Dimensional lumber	1 x 2	19 x 38mm
	1 x 4	19 x 89mm
	2 x 2	38 x 38mm
	2 x 4	38 x 89mm
	2 x 6	38 x 140mm
	2 x 8	38 x 184mm
	2 x 10	38 x 235mm
	2 x 12	38 x 286mm
Sheet sizes	4 x 8 ft.	1200 x 2400mm
	4 x 10 ft.	1200 x 3000mm
Sheet thicknesses	¼ in.	6mm
	⅜ in.	9mm
	½ in.	12mm
	¾ in.	19 mm
Stud/joist spacing	16 in. o.c.	400mm o.c.
	24 in. o.c.	600mm o.c.

Capacity

1 fluid ounce	29.57mL
1 pint	473.18mL
1 quart	0.95L
1 gallon	3.79L

Weight

1 ounce	28.35g
1 pound	0.45kg

Temperature

Fahrenheit = Celsius x 1.8 + 32
Celsius = Fahrenheit - 32 x ⁵⁄₉

Nail Size & Length

Penny Size	Nail Length
2d	1"
3d	1¼"
4d	1½ "
5d	1¾"
6d	2"
7d	2¼"
8d	2½"
9d	2¾"
10d	3"
12d	3¼"
16d	3½"

safety

Although the methods in this book have been reviewed for safety, it is not possible to overstate the importance of using the safest methods you can. What follows are reminders—some do's and don'ts of work safety—to use along with your common sense.

▌ Always use caution, care, and good judgment when following the procedures described in this book.

▌ Always be sure that the electrical setup is safe, that no circuit is overloaded, and that all power tools and outlets are properly grounded. Do not use power tools in wet locations.

▌ Always read container labels on paints, solvents, and other products; provide ventilation; and observe all other warnings.

▌ Always read the manufacturer's instructions for using a tool, especially the warnings.

▌ Use hold-downs and push sticks whenever possible when working on a table saw. Avoid working short pieces if you can.

▌ Always remove the key from any drill chuck (portable or press) before starting the drill.

▌ Always pay deliberate attention to how a tool works so that you can avoid being injured.

▌ Always know the limitations of your tools. Do not try to force them to do what they were not designed to do.

▌ Always make sure that any adjustment is locked before proceeding. For example, always check the rip fence on a table saw or the bevel adjustment on a portable saw before starting to work.

▌ Always clamp small pieces to a bench or other work surface when using a power tool.

▌ Always wear the appropriate rubber gloves or work gloves when handling chemicals, moving or stacking lumber, working with concrete, or doing heavy construction.

▌ Always wear a disposable face mask when you create dust by sawing or sanding. Use a special filtering respirator when working with toxic substances and solvents.

▌ Always wear eye protection, especially when using power tools or striking metal on metal or concrete; a chip can fly off, for example, when chiseling concrete.

▌ Never work while wearing loose clothing, open cuffs, or jewelry; tie back long hair.

▌ Always be aware that there is seldom enough time for your body's reflexes to save you from injury from a power tool in a dangerous situation; everything happens too fast. Be alert!

▌ Always keep your hands away from the business ends of blades, cutters, and bits.

▌ Always hold a circular saw firmly, usually with both hands.

▌ Always use a drill with an auxiliary handle to control the torque when using large-size bits.

▌ Always check your local building codes when planning new construction. The codes are intended to protect public safety and should be observed to the letter.

▌ Never work with power tools when you are tired or when under the influence of alcohol or drugs.

▌ Never cut tiny pieces of wood or pipe using a power saw. When you need a small piece, saw it from a securely clamped longer piece.

▌ Never change a saw blade or a drill or router bit unless the power cord is unplugged. Do not depend on the switch being off. You might accidentally hit it.

▌ Never work in insufficient lighting.

▌ Never work with dull tools. Have them sharpened, or learn how to sharpen them yourself.

▌ Never use a power tool on a workpiece—large or small—that is not firmly supported.

▌ Never saw a workpiece that spans a large distance between horses without close support on each side of the cut; the piece can bend, closing on and jamming the blade, causing saw kickback.

▌ When sawing, never support a workpiece from underneath with your leg or other part of your body.

▌ Never carry sharp or pointed tools, such as utility knives, awls, or chisels, in your pocket. If you want to carry any of these tools, use a special-purpose tool belt that has leather pockets and holders.

contents

6   Introduction
7   Guide to Skill Level

CHAPTER ONE
10 TOOLS
12 Demolition Tools
14 Layout Tools
18 Hand Tools
22 Power Tools
26 Drywall Finishing Tools
28 Painting and Papering Tools
30 Tile Tools
32 Specialty Tools

CHAPTER TWO
34 MATERIALS
36 Drywall
38 Wall Paneling
40 Tile
42 Paint
43 Wallcovering
44 Wallcovering Alternatives
45 Trim
46 Flooring

CHAPTER THREE
52 STRUCTURAL
54 Removing a Partition
55 Building Walls
60 Framing with Steel Studs
61 Installing Wood Furring
62 Soundproofing
64 Windows and Doors
70 Installing Windows
76 Building a Glass-Block Wall

CHAPTER FOUR
84 DRYWALL AND PANELING
86 Drywall Basics
88 Installing Drywall
90 Installing Backer Board
92 Resurfacing a Wall
94 Finishing Drywall Seams
97 Inside and Outside Corners
98 Sheet Paneling
102 Solid-Wood Paneling
104 Installing Wainscoting

CHAPTER FIVE
108 WALL FINISHES
110 Wall Prep
112 Preparing Plaster for Painting
113 Preparing Woodwork
114 Painting a Wall
118 Wet-Stripping Wallcovering
126 Installing Tile
132 Installing Trimwork
138 Installing Window Trim
142 Installing Door Trim
144 Installing Baseboard Trim

192 Installing Wood Strip Flooring
196 Carpeting

CHAPTER EIGHT
202 REPAIRS
204 Patching Drywall Holes
206 Repairing Corner Beads
207 Patching Plaster
208 Repairing Solid-Wood Paneling
209 Repairing Plywood Paneling
210 Refinishing Wood Trim
212 Replacing a Broken Tile
214 Reinforcing Joists
216 Installing Attic Stairs
218 Fixing a Leaking Skylight

CHAPTER NINE
220 LIGHTING
222 Lighting Options
223 Fixture Types
226 Lightbulbs
226 Installing a Ceiling Fixture
228 Recessed Lights
228 Installing a Recessed Light Fixture
230 Installing Track Lights
232 Chandeliers
233 Installing a Chandelier
234 Indoor Lighting Design

CHAPTER SIX
146 CEILINGS
149 Framing a Ceiling Opening
150 Installing Framing for a Skylight
152 Building a Deadman Brace
154 Installing a Suspended Ceiling
157 Installing a Wood-Paneled Ceiling
158 Installing a Tin Ceiling
160 Building a False Ceiling Beam
162 Installing a Wood Cornice
163 Installing Plastic Cornice
164 Installing Built-Up Cornice
167 Installing a Ceiling Medallion

CHAPTER TEN
236 VENTILATION
238 Ventilation Basics
239 Roof Vents
240 Installing a Ventilating Fan
242 Wiring a Ventilating Fan
244 Wiring a Ceiling Fan
246 Installing a Whole-House Fan

CHAPTER SEVEN
168 FLOORING
170 Flooring Layout
174 Installing Underlayment
176 Installing Vinyl Tiles
178 Installing Vinyl Sheet Flooring
180 Installing Ceramic Floor Tile
182 Installing Slate Flooring
186 Installing Radiant-Floor Heat
188 Routine Tile Cleaning
190 Installing a Laminate Floor

248 Resource Guide
250 Glossary
252 Index
255 Photo Credits

sensational surfaces

Many people tend to think of the walls, floors, and ceilings in their homes as separate elements—that's a mistake. Interior designers consider all three when designing a room because a weak link among the three will ruin the overall look. The same is true when repairing or improving these surfaces: each deserves attention, but not at the expense of the others. The *Ultimate Guide to Walls, Floors, and Ceilings* covers all three areas for the do-it-yourselfer.

WHOLE-HOUSE HOME IMPROVEMENT

Floors, walls, and ceilings are among the most basic components of any building. They provide strength and shelter, of course, but there is a lot to consider about these basic house parts because there are many different ways to build them, and countless ways to finish them.

There are window walls, walls with pass-throughs that join adjacent rooms, walls covered in nearly indestructible sheets of fiberglass, and specially built double walls filled with insulation so you don't hear any noise from the next room. When it comes to flooring, the old standbys of ceramic tile, solid wood, and carpeting are joined by laminate flooring, a newer material that can provide any style or color floor you wish. *Ultimate Guide to Floors, Walls, and Ceilings* covers all the different materials and types of construction in detail.

RIGHT Carpeting is still king in many homes. Learn about the different types available to you.

Building

It's a rare do-it-yourselfer who builds a home from scratch. But many tackle repairs and improvements, particularly in older homes that may need damaged surfaces removed before remodeling can begin. In fact, the secret to any remodeling project often lies within the preparation work necessary. That's why you will find major sections and illustrated how-to projects on stripping wallcoverings, removing walls, and refinishing floors.

When it comes to construction, you'll find the ins and outs of the stick-building approach to construction used in most homes, as well as steel framing and other systems. The *Ultimate Guide to Floors, Walls, and Ceilings* also contains sections on making repairs to sagging floor joists and damaged subflooring. And if your plans call for installing large lighting fixtures or ceiling fans, you will learn how to make the structural changes to your home that can support these heavy items.

Even if you are not an experienced do-it-yourselfer, you'll be able to follow along with step-by-step photo sequences that show how to build bearing and partition walls, and how to frame new window and door openings. The steps show the details of cutting, nailing, assembling headers, and more, and include many useful tips on using tools and materials.

GUIDE TO SKILL LEVEL

 Easy. Even for beginners.

 Challenging. Can be done by beginners who have the patience and willingness to learn.

 Difficult. Can be handled by most experienced do-it-yourselfers who have mastered basic construction skills. Consider consulting a specialist.

Surfacing

Over the solid framing you'll learn how to build, you can install drywall, paneling, wood planking, and other surface materials. Drywall, the most popular wall facing, can also be used to re-cover problem walls.

The flooring sections deal with the latest trends in flooring materials—everything from practical, easy-care vinyl tiles and sheet flooring to trendy natural stone. There are also sections on refinishing old floors. These techniques can revive what looks like a worn-out surface and make it look new again. Think of a refinished floor as recycling of a natural resource.

You'll also find resurfacing solutions for old ceilings, including complete photo sequences for installing embossed tin panels and suspended acoustical ceilings that you can use to finish off a basement without permanently blocking access to pipes, ducts, and other utilities. And for pure decoration, you can find out how to build and install elegant ceiling beams and false beams that allow you to box-in wiring and lights.

ABOVE Walls and windows go together. Find out how to install new windows and doors.

BELOW Learn the ins and outs of refinishing old wood floors to make them look new.

ABOVE Lighting plays an important part in the design of a room and how you perceive the surfaces in your home. Install track lighting, ceiling fixtures, and other types of lighting.

Finishing

You may not need a lot of help with painting, the project do-it-yourselfers tackle more often (and generally more successfully) than any other. But you'll find plenty of application and tool tips on painting just in case. And don't forget the secret to a good paint job is the preparation that goes into sanding surfaces and fixing holes and other damage in walls and ceilings.

Wallcoverings are a little more challenging, even though most modern papers come prepasted: you just dunk them and hang them. Planning the job and making the right cuts are often the keys to a successful project, and those details are covered in photo sequences.

In some rooms, particularly kitchens and baths, the durability of ceramic tile is in order. And that's a job most homeowners can handle with the how-to help found in

Ultimate Guide to Floors, Walls, and Ceilings. It covers the basics, as well as the tools and techniques that make the installation go faster and the completed project last longer.

Most flooring does not require any additional finishing: however, solid-wood flooring does. But the effort you put into doing the job right will help the flooring last for years.

Finally, there's the finishing touch that adds architectural detail to all the surfaces—trim. You'll see how to handle baseboards and cornices, and find the tricks of trimming casings around windows and doors. There are also major improvement projects, such as installing traditional beaded wainscoting and chair rails.

And if you're more interested in fixing what you've got instead of adding new features to your surfaces, every section contains information on the best way to make the most common repairs.

12 DEMOLITION TOOLS

14 LAYOUT TOOLS

18 HAND TOOLS

22 POWER TOOLS

26 DRYWALL FINISHING TOOLS

28 PAINTING AND PAPERING TOOLS

30 TILE TOOLS

32 SPECIALTY TOOLS

1 tools

Many of the tools you will be using to repair or improve the walls, floors, and ceilings in your home are likely already part of your basic tool collection. If you do need to buy new basic tools, select quality products that are easy to use and feel good in your hand. Well-made tools tend to be more durable than cheaper models and pay for themselves over the long haul. Some jobs will require specialty tools. For example, a crosscut saw won't be of much use if you need to cut an opening in drywall for an electrical receptacle box. For that job, a utility, or keyhole, saw is better. And many jobs will go much faster if you have the right power tool. Confusing? The best course of action is to decide which tools you need and purchase what you can. For big-ticket items, consider renting and using before committing to a purchase.

DEMOLITION TOOLS

When a home improvement project begins with demolition work, some do-it-yourselfers begin to salivate. Finally, a chance to vent frustrations over every leak, squeak, and repair that didn't pan out and to pound part of the house into oblivion.

Before you start any demolition work, consider these two points. First, remember to protect yourself with safety goggles, gloves, a respirator mask, and other appropriate gear. If you're digging into exterior walls, you may want to wear a long-sleeved shirt to help prevent possible skin irritation from fiberglass insulation. Second, don't break through a wall with a sledgehammer or slice through it with a saw unless you are sure it does not hold pipes and wires. Take the time to peel away a section of drywall for a good view of the wall cavities underneath. Remember that in older homes you may find materials such as lead-based paint or asbestos insulation that require special handling.

As you work, stop periodically to remove debris and clear the work area of materials and tools you don't need. To prevent accidents, it's wise to bend over any nails in boards or sections of drywall.

Protect yourself first, of course, but also take the time to protect the surrounding area of the house. Demolition makes such a mess that you'll want to spread heavy dropcloths over nearby finished floors and hang plastic sheeting over doorways to prevent the spread of dust.

● AVOIDING BINDING

When you cut through an old stud, the wood can close on the blade and cause binding or kickback.

If the blade starts to bind, you can tap a wooden wedge into the cut to keep the kerf open.

stripping walls safely

1. Strip away surface materials first. Wear gloves and safety glasses or goggles during demolition work.

2. Once you gain a foothold in a surface material such as tile, use a pry bar to pry off the pieces.

Demolition Tools: **A**–shop vac, **B**–spray bottle (for suppressing dust), **C**–push broom, **D**–tarp or drop cloth, **E**–crowbar, **F**–sledgehammer, **G**–2-lb. hammer, **H**–pry bar, **I**–cat's paw (for pulling buried nails)

3. Strip away a section of drywall by pulling any protruding nails and digging in next to one of the studs.

4. As you break out larger sections of drywall, pull nails so that you'll be able to cut safely through the studs.

LAYOUT TOOLS

A basic collection of rulers, squares, and levels should serve on most home improvement projects. But it always helps to follow the adage "Measure twice and cut once," particularly when it can save an extra trip to the lumberyard for more wood.

For measuring, you can use a classic folding carpenter's ruler or a measuring tape. Both are available in several lengths. The fold-out variety takes a little time to open and close, but some models have a handy pullout extension that makes it easy to take accurate inside dimensions—for example, between two wall studs.

For squaring up measurements for cutting, use a combination square on smaller boards. On larger boards and over larger areas—for example, to check the corner of a room—use a 2-foot-long framing square.

But there are a few carpentry tricks that work as well as any tool. One is to check for square by measuring the diagonals of a piece of plywood or a room. If the room is square, the diagonals should be equal.

Another trick is to use the proportions of a 3-4-5 triangle. If one leg is 3 feet long, another is 4 feet long, and the hypotenuse is 5 feet long, the angle between the two legs will be 90 degrees. Triangulation is practical in construction and remodeling work because it works at any scale. You can measure the sides of the layout triangle in inches, feet, or yards and in multiples of 3-4-5 (6-8-10, 9-12-15, and so on).

MEASURING

A long measuring tape is handy for layout work on walls. Most have 16-in. centers marked in red.

The extension bar on a folding ruler makes it easy to take accurate measurements between studs.

step-ahead layout

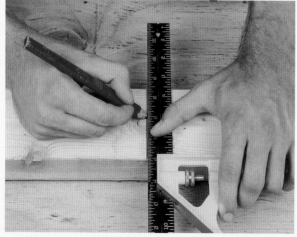

1. When you draw layout lines to mark the locations of studs, use a combination square to mark one side.

2. Mark a large X where the stud will go, and stick to the same step-ahead layout to maintain even spacing.

Layout Tools: A—measuring tape, **B**—electronic distance finder, **C**—framing square, **D**—stud finder, **E**—chalk-line box, **F**—contour gauge, **G**—speed square, **H**—sliding T-bevel, **I**—compass, **J**—folding carpenter's ruler, **K**—combination square

Levels

For odd jobs around the house such as leveling a shelf, a 2-foot-long spirit level will do. On larger projects where you have to level and plumb longer distances, a 4-foot level offers more accuracy. Keeping the bubble between the centering lines produces good results on straight timbers three and four times the level's length, which is enough for most home projects. Small levels and gadget tools that include a small bubble vial generally are not accurate enough for remodeling work.

To check for level over very long areas, you could use a line level—a small bubble vial suspended on a string stretched tightly between two points. Even more accurate is a water level—a flexible plastic tube filled with water, which works because water always seeks its own level. Attach each end of the tube upright against a wall stud on opposite ends of a large room—20, 40, or more feet apart if you have a long enough tube—and the water level at one end will be level with the water level at the other end. You can make your own version of this basic, time-tested tool (adding colored dye to the water for easier reading). Some models include an electronic sensor that helps establish level marks.

To make sure large areas, such as two-story walls, are plumb, the best bet is another simple, old-fashioned tool—a plumb bob, which is a weight (with a pointed bottom) attached to a string. Suspend the plumb bob string on a nail, and give the bob time to steady. The point will indicate a spot that is plumb with the nail above.

LEVELING

Use a 4-ft. spirit level to check furring strips and other jobs where you read the bubble.

Also use the level as a straightedge, to check for depressions in a wall surface.

using a layout stick

1. To mark a repeating layout on a wall, such as the spacing on a tile grid, start by making a layout stick.

2. With the layout mark captured on a straight board, you can transfer a series of marks to the wall.

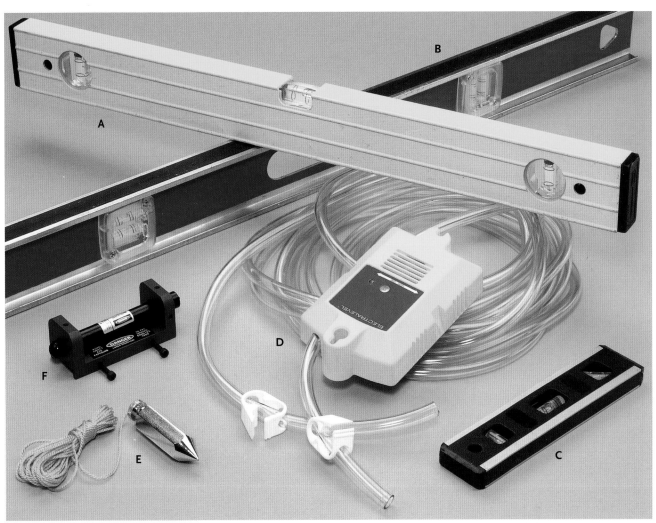

Levels: **A**—2-ft. spirit level, **B**—4-ft. spirit level, **C**—6-in. spirit level, **D**—water level with electronic level sensor, **E**—plumb bob and string, **F**—laser level, which can be attached to a standard level

3. After transferring a series of vertical and horizontal marks, you can establish level and plumb lines.

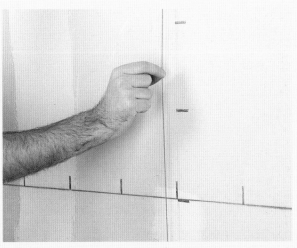

4. On large areas, establish marks at the top and bottom of the wall, and snap a chalk line between the marks.

HAND TOOLS

Many do-it-yourselfers already own the basic hand tools required for building and remodeling walls and ceilings. Unless you plan a special application, such as installing ceramic wall tiles, you won't need any specialty tools.

But if you are in the process of accumulating tools, consider these general buying guidelines. Naturally, the selection that's right for you depends not only on the work you want to do but also on how often you'll use the tools, how expert you are at handling them, and how much money you want to spend.

Durability. Buy better-quality tools when you purchase those that you use often, such as hammers and saws. It's worth a little extra to have a set of screwdrivers with comfortable handles or chisels with steel-capped heads that stand up better than plastic heads. But don't pay top dollar for heavy-duty contractor tools you'll use occasionally. Many have features you don't need. And the truth is that inexperienced do-it-yourselfers don't get professional results just by using top-notch tools. Skill is in the hand that holds a tool, not in the tool itself.

Precision. Stick with basic tools designed to do one job well, and avoid multipurpose gimmick tools that are loaded with bells and whistles. That 9-in-1 wrench and hammer may be handy in the car glove compartment but not so much on home improvement projects.

Strength. Look for hammers, wrenches, pry bars, and other mainly metal tools that are drop-forged instead of cast metal. Casting can trap air bubbles in molten metal, creating weak spots. Drop-forging removes more bubbles and makes the metal stronger and safer. In general, when manufacturers take the time and money to drop-forge a tool and machine-grind its surface, they leave the fine-grained metal in plain view. Inferior cast tools are sometimes disguised with a coat of paint.

Price. If in doubt, avoid the most and least expensive models. The top end often has more capacity than you need, and the bottom end often has fundamental flaws that make work difficult—even for a professional. There are some exceptions, of course. For example, a throwaway brush is fine for slapping some stain on a rough landscape timber or fence post. But if you're a practiced how-to painter looking for a pristine finish on your trim, by all means invest in high-quality brushes.

Also, be sure to wield the tool in the store: check the feel and comfort, whether it seems controllable, too heavy, or too light. If you shop in a large outlet where there are several brands of the same tool, try one against another. It can be difficult to compare tools such as power saws, which you can't normally test on the spot. But some tools you can test—for example, levels. Before you buy one, check three or four on the store floor or counter, and stack them on top of each other to catch the one whose bubble may be out of line with the others.

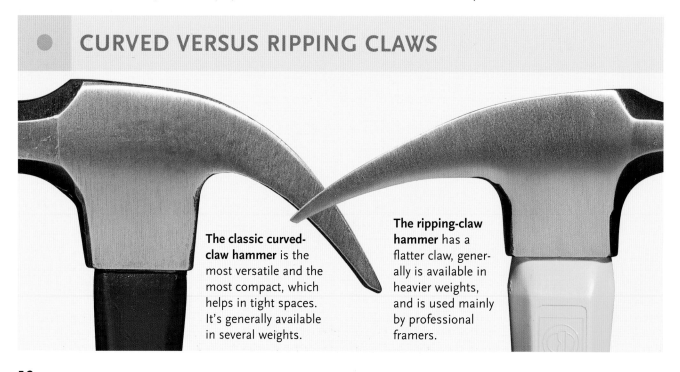

● CURVED VERSUS RIPPING CLAWS

The classic curved-claw hammer is the most versatile and the most compact, which helps in tight spaces. It's generally available in several weights.

The ripping-claw hammer has a flatter claw, generally is available in heavier weights, and is used mainly by professional framers.

Hand Tools: A–rasp, **B**–needle-nose pliers, **C**–sandpaper and sanding block, **D**–block plane, **E**–shaver/shaper, **F**–chisels, **G**–nail set, **H**–flat-blade screwdriver, **I**–Phillips screwdriver, **J**–utility knife, **K**–pliers, **L**–aviation snips

Trim Blade

Crosscut Blade

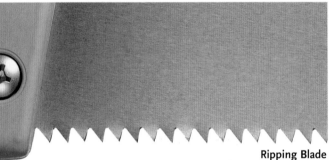

Ripping Blade

Handsaws

Many production-type sawing jobs are best suited to a power saw. But the trusty handsaw still is an indispensable tool. There are many types, and most have some factors in common that are worth a close look.

Saw Style and Teeth. For special jobs, there are hacksaws and utility saws, but for general carpentry you have three choices: a rip saw, a crosscut saw, and a trim saw. The difference is in the number of saw teeth per inch, measured in points. More teeth make a finer cut but work more slowly; fewer teeth cut through wood faster but leave rougher edges.

Rip saws have 5½ points per inch. They're designed to cut quickly with the grain—reducing a 6-inch pine shelf to 4 inches, for example. But it's easier to buy stock lumber in the right width and just trim it to length. At the other extreme is a trim saw with ten or more teeth per inch that's good for fine work such as cutting molding. But the best choice is a compromise—a crosscut saw with seven or eight teeth per inch that can handle the most common cuts efficiently.

No-Set Saws. If most of your projects require only fine cuts, consider a backsaw. It has 12 or 13 teeth per inch and a short 10- to 16-inch blade reinforced along its top edge. Unlike full-size saws, most backsaws and other short, fine-toothed saws are available with no-set teeth, which means there's no side-to-side splay to clear a path for the cut. They won't move as freely as set crosscut teeth, but you'll cut a finer line perhaps smooth enough that you won't need sandpaper.

using saws

A full-size crosscut saw is handy for making cuts against other boards where a power saw wouldn't fit.

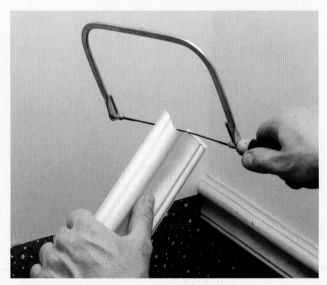

A coping saw has a very narrow blade that is maneuverable enough to make curved cuts in molding.

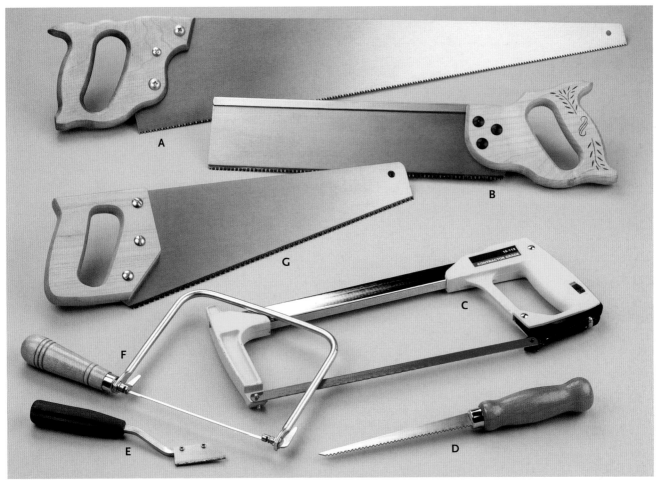

Hand Saws: **A**—full-size trim saw, **B**—reinforced backsaw with no-set teeth, **C**—hacksaw, **D**—utility saw, **E**—grout saw (for tile work), **F**—coping saw, **G**—short crosscut saw

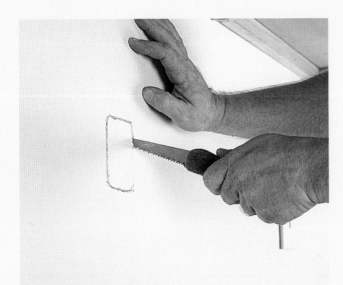

A utility saw has a pointed tip that you can force through a drywall surface and sharp teeth to cut gypsum.

A hacksaw cuts through metal and through some types of face brick and other hard materials.

POWER TOOLS

Among the many power tools on the market, most people get the most use from two: a circular saw and a drill.

Circular Saws

You can buy a functional circular saw for less than $50, and a very good one with more than enough power for home repairs and remodeling for about $100. There are dozens of models, including huge heavy saws with 10-inch-diameter blades that can slice through landscaping timbers, and midget models with 4-inch-diameter blades. But two basic types offer the kind of overall versatility most DIYers need: the standard, 7¼-inch corded saw, and the smaller, cordless version with a blade diameter of 5 to 6 inches.

If price is important, forget about cordless saws. They are compact, easy to handle in tight spaces, and decidedly slick. But they're expensive. While a good-quality 7¼-inch corded saw rated at 13 amps with 2½ horsepower might cost under $100 (including a carbide-tipped blade), a comparable 18-volt cordless model with charger, two battery packs, and blade might cost $200 and up.

You don't get any extra power for the extra price. In fact, you generally get less. Corded saws can keep cutting until your arm turns to putty. But cordless models have a limited fuel supply, although a good 18-volt-or-better model should be able to crosscut about 100 2x4s on a single charge, depending, of course, on the hardness of the

USING NAIL GUNS

These air-powered tools, used mainly by contractors, load with multiple framing or finishing nails.

Before a pneumatic nail gun will fire, you have to set the safety head against the nailing surface.

edging and joining boards

The electric version of a block plane is a power planer, which makes it easy to smooth the edges of boards.

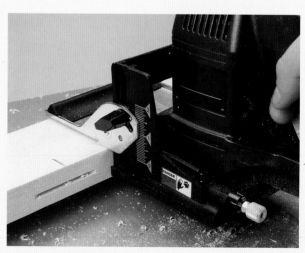

To join true edges, use a biscuit joiner to cut opposing slots that are bridged with wood wafers and glue.

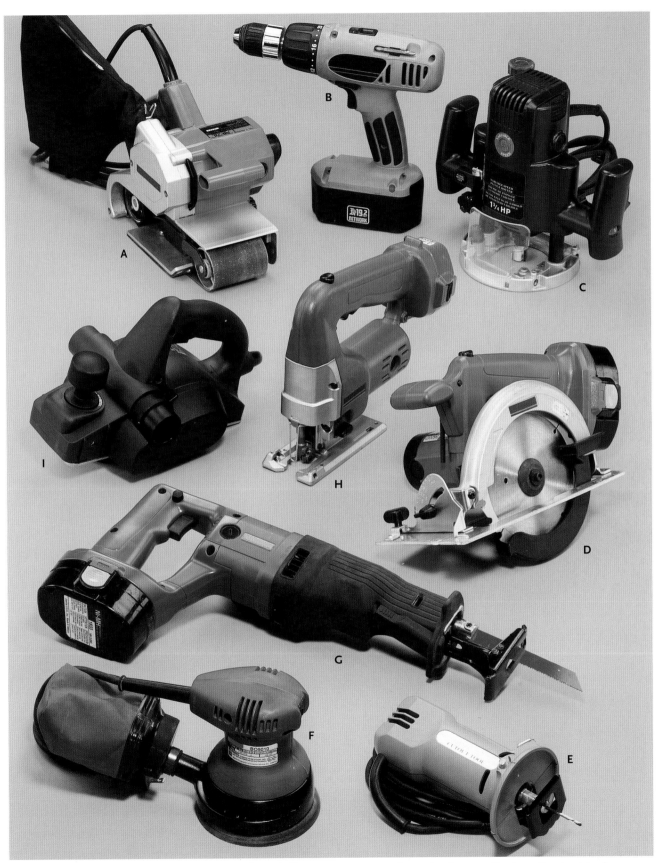

Portable Power Tools: **A**—belt sander, **B**—cordless drill, **C**—router, **D**—cordless circular saw, **E**—drywall cutout tool, **F**—random-orbit sander, **G**—cordless reciprocating saw, **H**—cordless saber saw, **I**—planer

Crosscut Blade

Ripping Blade

Plywood Blade

wood. And even with a full charge, most cordless models just don't turn as fast as comparable corded models. The blade on a corded saw may spin at 5,000 rpm, while the blade on a cordless model may turn at a mere 2,500 to 3,500 rpm.

Capacity and power won't matter much, though, if you can't use the saw comfortably and safely. So after you check the performance numbers, heft several saws in the store to check weight and balance and test the hand holds, trigger, blade guard, and other controls.

There are many types of blades for circular saws. Most models come with a standard crosscut blade. You'll get more use from a crosscut that's carbide tipped, although you can't touch up these blades with a file the way you can a standard steel blade.

Drills

Among a slew of features and a wide range in capacity, you should not be disappointed with a $3/8$-inch model that reverses, with variable speed and a keyless chuck. A torque-limiter is handy, not essential, because it keeps you from ruining screwheads and surrounding wood. Although power keeps increasing, even a 12-volt drill has more than enough power for household use.

A keyless chuck is particularly handy. These tighten by hand so you don't have to go looking for a chuck key. Most new drills have a keyless chuck—an improvement in convenience because in the past keys that attached to the drill cord were often lost. Among many handy accessories, consider a combination pilot bit and countersink that saves time drilling and driving screws.

Bench Power Tools

If you have the room and the budget, it might be nice to accumulate a full line of stationary power tools, such as table saws and drill presses. But there is another less costly and sometimes more practical option: bench-top power tools. These large table saws, drill presses, planers, and such have more capacity than handheld power tools, but they are portable. You can build a bench platform out of plywood and 2x4s, bolt on the bench-top tool, and clamp the setup securely on sawhorses near your work area.

Wherever you keep and use power tools, remember to start by going over the operating instructions and safety features. The work area should have ample space for you to operate the tool safely, a lot of light, and grounded electrical outlets.

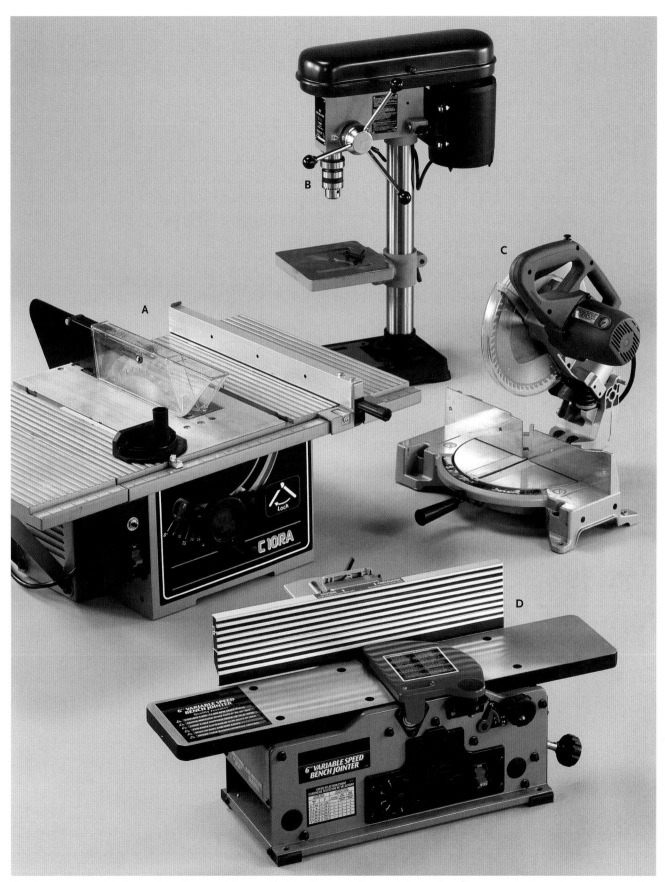

Stationary Power Tools: A—bench-top table saw, **B**—bench-top drill press, **C**—power miter saw, **D**—bench-top jointer

DRYWALL FINISHING TOOLS

To finish new gypsum drywall or repair damaged panels on existing walls, you need a pair of drywall knives and a larger blade for spreading and smoothing compound over wide seams between panels. The basics will do for most projects, although there are specialized drywall tools such as corner blades and swiveling sanding blocks attached to long poles so that you can sand joint compound more easily.

Nailholes, dents, scratches, and other minor blemishes are easy to fix with a little compound and a pair of blades because there is $\frac{1}{2}$ inch of solid gypsum under the surface. To bridge a small puncture through drywall, you'll probably need to add some type of reinforcing material, such as fiberglass mesh tape. When you tackle deep scars, use a base coat to bond against the reinforcement and fill most of the opening. Once the base coat hardens, add one or two top coats to fill up the hole. You may want to add a very thin skim coat, too.

One type of finishing knife isn't much better than another. But no matter what type or combination of blades you use, be sure to keep them clean. Drywall compound dries quickly, and even a short pause in work can allow a thin layer of compound to harden. And once you introduce a hard crumb to a smooth mix on a wall seam, the blade will drag it along the wall, creating a trough that needs more finishing and sanding.

● BASIC WALL REPAIR

1. Fill depressions with a base coat, let it dry, and add one or more top coats to build up the damaged area.

2. When the patch compound dries, smooth the surface using a sanding block and a sheet of fine sandpaper.

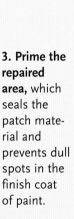

3. Prime the repaired area, which seals the patch material and prevents dull spots in the finish coat of paint.

4. Use a nearly dry roller to feather paint on and away from the patch, blending it with the adjacent surfaces.

Drywall, Paint, and Wallcovering Tools: **A**—sanding pole, **B**—screen sander, **C**—wallcovering trough, **D**—smoothing blade, **E**—paste brush, **F**—smoothing brush, **G**—seam roller, **H**—paintbrush, **I**—angled sash brush, **J**—foam brush, **K**—paint tray, **L**—roller, **M**—putty knife, **N**—4-in. taping knife, **O**—10-in. finishing knife, **P**—inside corner knife

PAINTING AND PAPERING TOOLS

Painting is a job do-it-yourselfers tackle more than any other, and the one where, for a modest investment, they can use the same high-quality tools professionals use: a basic roller and a good-quality brush. If you have a lot of wall area to cover, consider using a 5-gallon paint bucket with roller screen instead of a pan. You won't need to keep refilling the pan, and the bucket allows you to douse the roller (covering it with paint quickly) and flick off the extra against the screen.

The basic papering tool kit consists of a brush or blade for smoothing out paper, a utility knife for trimming seams, and a narrow trough for soaking paper. Most papers used today have adhesive on the back, which eliminates the messy and time-consuming step of brushing on paste. You simply dunk and book the sheet, place it on the wall, and smooth and cut it to fit.

● PAINT SPINNERS

Mount a brush in the end of a spinner, dip the bristles in water, and pump the spinner handle: the brush whirls fast enough to spin clean.

This paint-mixing spinner has a long stem that fits into the chuck of a drill. Pull the trigger, and the blender thoroughly mixes a can of paint.

Brushes

There are two basic choices to make when you buy a good brush. First, get the right type of brush for the paint: nylon bristles for latex paint that cleans up with water and natural bristles for oil-based paint that cleans up with mineral spirits. Second, get the right size brush for the job. Most people find it easiest to cover large areas with a roller and use a brush for corners and trim. This means you don't need a huge brush that holds a lot of paint. The best compromise for all-around use is a 3-inch wide, long-handled brush.

Some people prefer a brush with angled bristles. But once you get the feel of a straight-ended brush, you'll be able to flex it to suit the job at hand, and you won't need an angled model or several different sizes. The best brushes are flagged and tipped. When bristles are tipped, the ends are slightly tapered, which helps to release an even, controllable amount of paint. When bristles are flagged, the tapered ends are slightly split, which helps the brush hold more paint and spread it more smoothly.

Rollers

Some high-end varieties, such as mohair, are used to apply clear sealers without introducing air bubbles. But for painting, standard rollers are fine. For many projects, both 9-inch and 3- or 4-inch models are handy. A large roller covers unobstructed surfaces most efficiently. You can load it up with paint, apply several horizontal swaths of paint, and spread them evenly across the wall with vertical strokes.

To spread paint evenly close to trim and in confined areas, a smaller roller offers more control. Roller sleeves with a short nap produce the flattest finished surface, but they don't hold much paint. Models with a thick nap hold a lot of paint, but their woolly texture leaves a pronounced stipple pattern on smooth drywall.

Sprayers and Power Painters

Another option is to use a power painter, which feeds a constant supply of paint to a roller, or a sprayer, which dispenses paint through an adjustable nozzle under pressure from a compressor. Both types get a lot of paint to the wall in a hurry and save you the trouble of returning a roller to the pan for more paint. But the increased capacity isn't really necessary on projects that involve only one or two walls—and most do-it-yourselfers can use a few breaks to refill pans or buckets.

BRUSH, ROLLER, AND SPRAYER CHECKLISTS

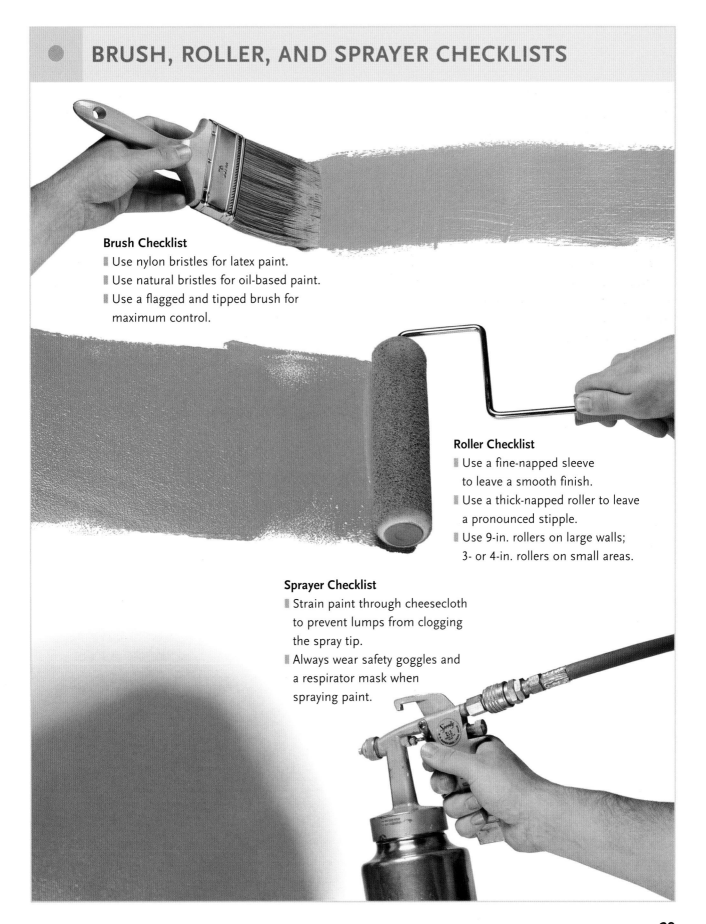

Brush Checklist

▌ Use nylon bristles for latex paint.
▌ Use natural bristles for oil-based paint.
▌ Use a flagged and tipped brush for maximum control.

Roller Checklist

▌ Use a fine-napped sleeve to leave a smooth finish.
▌ Use a thick-napped roller to leave a pronounced stipple.
▌ Use 9-in. rollers on large walls; 3- or 4-in. rollers on small areas.

Sprayer Checklist

▌ Strain paint through cheesecloth to prevent lumps from clogging the spray tip.
▌ Always wear safety goggles and a respirator mask when spraying paint.

TILE TOOLS

You probably own most of the tools needed for tile work, including basic equipment used for preparing new and existing walls and laying out the job. But you will need a notched trowel to spread tile adhesive; nippers to cut small, odd shapes (for example, where a tile must fit around a plumbing pipe); and either a snap cutter or a wet saw to handle straight cuts. A power wet saw is normally used by contractors, but you can rent one (and other tile equipment) for large home projects.

The most basic tool is a snap cutter, which scores and snaps tile. This tool comes in several sizes and variations, but most versions consist of a metal frame that holds the tile in position and a carbide-tipped blade or wheel that travels along a guide rod so that you always get a square cut. Most also have a built-in ridge and a handle that you can use to snap the tile once it's scored. After positioning the tile, draw the carbide blade or wheel across the surface to score it. Then you can press down on the handle until the tile snaps.

Some snap cutters may not work on large, thick tiles, such as quarry tiles or pavers. If you have many tiles to cut that prove troublesome in a snap cutter, use a wet saw. This power tool is basically a stationary circular saw with a water-cooled diamond blade. A reservoir below the work surface holds water that lubricates and cools the cutting action. The saw component stays put, and you guide the tile into it on a sliding table.

● USING TILE NIPPERS

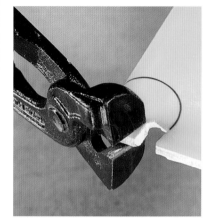

Start with very small bites along the edge of the tile, and work along your cut marks gradually.

The teeth of a nipper will leave a slightly ragged edge. Where appearance counts, you can clean up the nipped edges using a file.

using a snap cutter

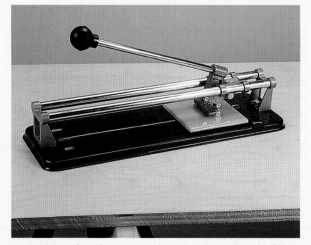

1. Position the tile against the stop at the head of the tool, and draw the scoring wheel across the surface.

2. After you score the surface, press down on the handle to split the tile along the score line.

Tile Tools: **A**–snap cutter, **B**–sponge, **C**–wet saw, **D**–rubber float for applying grout, **E**–carbide-tipped scoring tool, **F**–nippers, **G**–notched adhesive trowel

using a wet saw

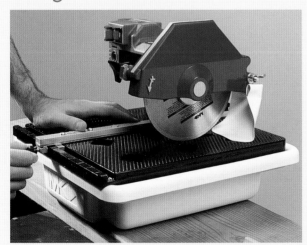

1. A reservoir in the base supplies water that circulates onto the cutting area to lubricate the blade.

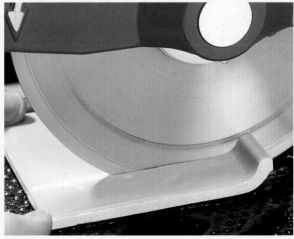

2. Rest the tile on the sliding table. Feed the tile into the blade instead of pulling the blade into the work.

SPECIALTY TOOLS

Almost every trade has several specialty tools that you may not find in the local hardware store. Some of the tools increase comfort, productivity, or capacity. Most of them are for contractors who handle the kind of project you're tackling day in and day out.

For example, tile contractors often invest in a set of heavily cushioned knee pads because they spend a lot of time on their knees. But for a small, one-time tile project, you may not want them. If you feel some discomfort, you could kneel on a rolled-up towel.

There are many specialty tools, such as a drywall panel lifter, that you can rent for a one-time project. This gangly piece of equipment allows you to set full sheets against ceiling joists, and nail them off safely and securely without teetering on a ladder with one end of the sheet balanced on your head. This kind of tool is quite expensive, but it can make sense on a major home remodeling project that you plan to tackle by yourself.

And remember to include basic safety gear in your assortment of tools, whether you use only a basic collection or an elaborate mix that includes special equipment such as panel lifters and scaffolding.

● SAFETY EQUIPMENT

On most surface remodeling work such as finishing drywall and painting, safety isn't much of an issue. But when you're breaking through walls, using power tools, and handling other jobs on walls and ceilings, you should wear appropriate safety gear. Pay particular attention when you use high-speed power tools such as a circular saw, which can throw out chips of wood, or striking tools such as a cold chisel and hammer, which can throw off chips of masonry. Gloves and other gear are important, but eye protection is crucial.

A–rubber gloves, **B**–ear protectors, **C**–hard hat, **D**–knee pads, **E**–work gloves, **F**–filtered respirator, **G**–safety glasses, **H**–safety goggles, **I**–ear plugs, **J**–particle mask

Specialty Tools: **A**—drywall panel lifter, **B**—fiberglass stepladder, **C**—two-by planking material, **D**—sawhorses

36   DRYWALL

38   WALL PANELING

40   TILE

42   PAINT

43   WALLCOVERING

44   WALLCOVERING ALTERNATIVES

45   TRIM

46   FLOORING

2 materials

Whenever you attempt a major remodeling project, or even a minor one for that matter, you will be making a number of decisions that affect the floors, walls, and ceilings of your home. And you have a lot from which to choose, starting with commodity-type products, such as drywall and plywood, to more exotic materials, such as imported hardwoods for flooring and trimwork, and engineered-wood products for paneling and floor coverings. As you go through this chapter, you will find that floor, wall, and ceiling systems usually consist of two parts: the underlayment, or support system, and the finish material. While the finish may get most of your attention, don't forget about the importance of the drywall or subfloor underlayment. A well-installed underlayment is the secret to a successful project.

DRYWALL

The standard for new construction and remodeling is a ½-inch-thick panel. Some suppliers don't stock anything else. Bulkier ⅝-inch-thick panels are not usually used in houses due to the extra cost and weight. And what seems like a minor addition, only ⅛ of an inch, makes these panels surprisingly heavier and much harder to handle. Lighter, ⅜-inch-thick panels are good for resurfacing work when a wall is so scarred that spackling can't save it. One-quarter-inch-thick panels would be even more economical. They can be specially ordered, but aren't used much because the sheets are very whippy and snap too easily during handling.

Standard sheets are 4 x 8 feet. Like plywood and many other building materials, it's a modular size that works with both 16- and 24-inch-on-center residential framing. Two common variations of standard panels are manufactured with qualities that improve drywall performance in key areas: drywall impregnated with fire-retardants, referred to as FC or fire code panels, and panels treated to resist moisture, known as WR or water-resistant panels.

From the standpoint of handling, smaller sheets are best; they are easier to carry and install. But from the standpoint of taping and finishing joints, larger sheets are better because they cover more wall area. The best approach is to use the biggest sheets practicable—large enough to eliminate some seams and taping time, but not large enough to create major handling problems.

Drywall Types: A–¼ in., **B**–⅜ in., **C**–½ in., **D**–⅝ in. fire code, **E**–½ in. water-resistant

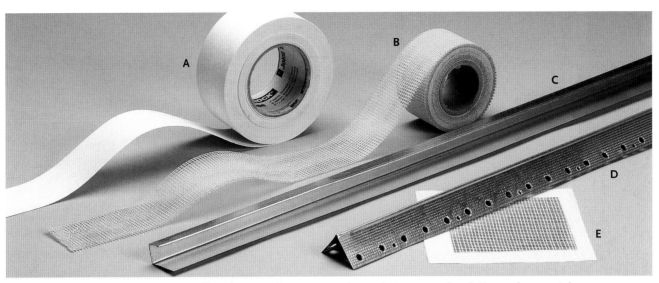

Drywall Supplies: A–paper tape, **B**–fiberglass mesh tape, **C**–J-channel, **D**–corner bead, **E**–patch material

DRYWALL OPTIONS

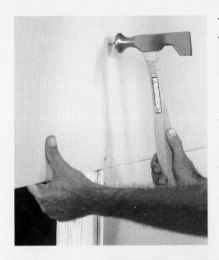

This is the old-fashioned but still workable fastening system: driving nails with a drywall hammer. (Use it very carefully because of the hatchet end.)

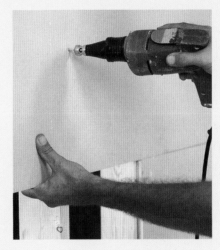

This is the modern method used by most pros: driving screws with a power screwdriver (or drill with a screw bit), which leaves a small dimple.

Use a drywall corner clip to support the panel edge when corner studs support only the adjacent sheet.

One side of the clip holds the panel, and the other has a tab that is nailed into the adjacent stud.

WALL PANELING

Wood paneling is available in many configurations, ranging from inexpensive sheets with photo-printed wood surfaces to varieties of real and even exotic hardwoods. You can combine plain or grooved panels with prefab trim pieces to cover a wall quickly or use veneer sheets as the backdrop for elegant paneled walls.

Paneling also is a good choice for resurfacing old walls. Even thin panels are rigid enough to bridge cracks and other flaws in a wall, and they are lightweight, making them easy to handle. And with paneling, you don't have to tape, finish, and paint the surface seams and fastener holes. You can install thin panels quickly with adhesive and nails, often tucking them against existing trim around windows and doors.

● TYPES OF WALL PANELING

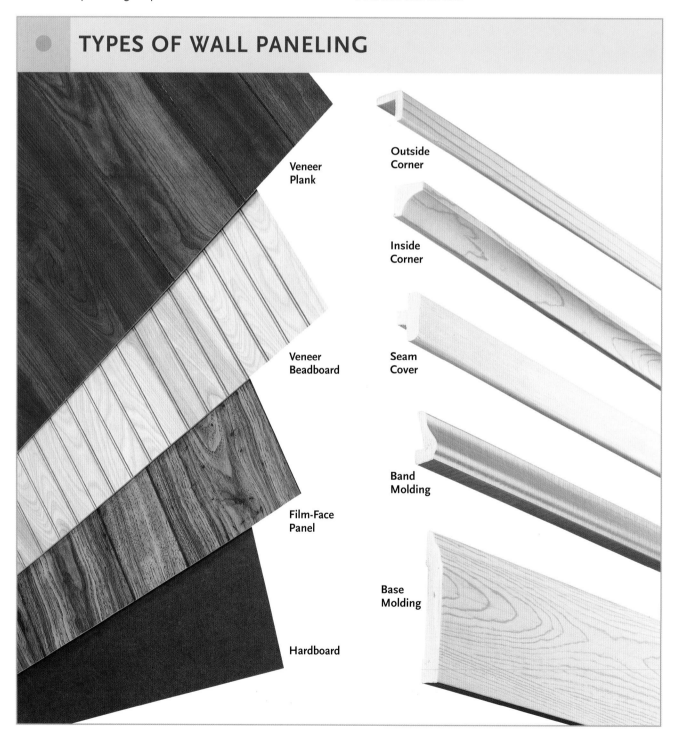

Veneer Plank

Veneer Beadboard

Film-Face Panel

Hardboard

Outside Corner

Inside Corner

Seam Cover

Band Molding

Base Molding

Beadboard Tongue and Groove   Shiplap   Cedar Tongue and Groove   1x6 Pine

PLANK PANEL OPTIONS AND HIDING FASTENERS

Tongue-and-groove boards that tuck one against the other are the most common type of plank paneling.

Planks with square edges can be set close together with the joints covered by narrow boards called battens.

Conceal fasteners in sheet paneling by driving color-matched nails into the grooves over the studs.

Conceal fasteners in solid paneling by driving angled nails into the tongue area that will be covered by the next board.

TILE

Modern ceramic tiles are manufactured to consistent sizes, surfaced with sturdy glazes, and hardened in temperature-controlled kilns. Combined with a dense grout in the seams, ceramic tile resists wear better than most building materials and should last as long as the surfaces that support it.

The traditional setting method (on floors as well as walls) is to lay tiles in a thick bed of cement mortar. This time-consuming system has given way to a more efficient method using thinset adhesive. You spread this mix with a notched trowel that leaves uniform ridges on the wall, and press the tiles into the ridges.

Many thinset adhesives are on the market, but you will probably wind up using either a cement-based mortar or an organic mastic adhesive, and in some cases an epoxy-based mortar.

These materials allow you to set tile directly on gypsum drywall with only minimal preparation because the adhesive will bridge the kinds of small scars you would otherwise have to fill and sand smooth before painting.

In some situations you may want to apply a special substrate called a cementitious backer unit, or CBU. This rigid, heavy cement-based panel makes a stronger and more durable supporting surface than drywall in wet areas such as kitchens and baths. Water will not damage it, and the dense, dimensionally stable material will not shift or deteriorate under the tile.

● CEILING TILE

Acoustical ceiling tiles do deaden noise somewhat—and even more so if you install batts of insulation between them and the old ceiling above. But most homeowners use them to cover exposed framing quickly and inexpensively, particularly where ducts, plumbing pipes, or wires run below the floor joists. A typical installation consists of edge pieces, main runners that are held in place by wires connected to the ceiling joists, and crosspieces that form a grid for the tiles.

Ceiling tiles hide pipes and ducts from view. You can easily remove the panels to gain access.

ceramic tile shapes and patterns

The most basic tile shape is a square that forms a symmetrical grid, such as this 12 x 12-in. terra-cotta.

Large squares, small squares, and very small tiles are sheet-mounted to set in groups.

● CERAMIC TILE TRIM OPTIONS

Many ceramic tiles are available in sets with complementary colors or special patterns you can use for trim.

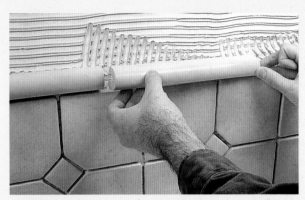

Combine tiles by trimming the corners and installing small squares under half-round trim.

Cap off combinations of sizes and shapes with special trim strips, such as this large ogee shape.

Use many elements in one wall, including complementary colors, patterns, half-rounds, and cap pieces.

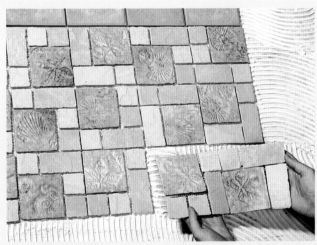

Sheet-mounted tiles also come in a variety of patterns, including random combinations of color and size.

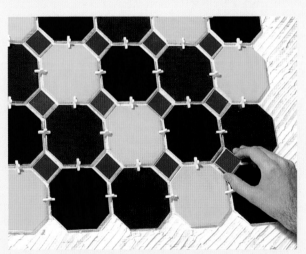

Make your own pattern using different shapes and colors—set here with spacers to maintain grout lines.

PAINT

The trend with modern paint is a promise of long-lasting one-coat coverage over almost any material in any condition, inside or outside the house. To be competitive, manufacturers outpace one another with claims of needing only the most minimal prep work.

But a clean, smooth wall and two thin coats are almost always better than one thick coat, which is more likely to drip or sag before it dries. And no paint is immune to dull-spotting and eventual peeling where repair patches on walls pull excess moisture from the fresh paint as it dries.

Of the two basic choices, water-based (latex) or oil-based, latex is the clear choice today, mainly because of the easy cleanup. Total sales for some major paint suppliers are only about 5 percent oil-based paint. But you may want to use a pigmented white shellac stain killer to cover blemishes and prevent color bleeding on old walls.

There are special priming paints, but in most cases a layer of your top-coat paint thinned by about a third will do just as well. Priming provides the most uniform surface for the top coat, particularly on older walls that required a lot of scraping, sanding, and patching. If you don't want to paint everything twice, at least prime filled patches to avoid isolated appearance and maintenance problems. You can cover unsealed areas with a quick sweep of a roller or brush, and feather out the primer over adjacent sealed areas so that you don't leave a ridge.

Flat

Eggshell

Semigloss

Gloss

surface-prep materials

Pigmented white shellac hides discolorations under one coat, and makes a good primer for metal.

To clean stubborn mold and mildew stains on paint, you may need to use a 4:1 water-to-bleach solution.

WALLCOVERING

Wallpapering used to be a messy project that required a huge brush and pails of gooey paste. Now both do-it-yourselfers and professionals generally use prepasted papers that are available in a wide array of colors and patterns. A prepasted sheet makes wallpaper work a lot easier. You just dunk it and hang it.

Laying out the job, measuring, and cutting still take time and thorough planning. But the alternative to prepasting—mixing and brushing on your own adhesive—increases the potential for problems, including premature drying, lumps under the paper, and air pockets that are difficult to fix. If you want to use an exotic paper like grass cloth that isn't available prepasted, it's wise to have a contractor handle the project.

Also check the paper for defects and to be sure the pattern aligns sheet to sheet. Using patterned papers economically can be tricky, so you may want to dry-match patterns by laying out sheets on the floor, or by sketching on graph paper how the sheets will fall.

After soaking, some papers should be set aside for a short time specified by the manufacturer. Keep the interval consistent from sheet to sheet because the paper may expand or shrink a little once it's wet. If you hang one strip right away next to a sheet that had a long soak, you could get enough of a mismatch to notice. Overworking or stretching the paper into position can cause the same problem.

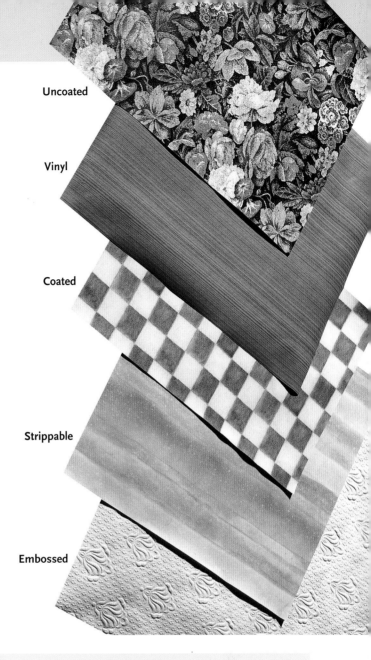

Uncoated

Vinyl

Coated

Strippable

Embossed

adhesive versus prepaste

This is the old system: mixing up a batch of sticky paste and brushing it onto the wallpaper.

This is the modern system: dunking a sheet of prepasted paper in a small trough of water.

WALLCOVERING ALTERNATIVES

No wallcovering is strong enough to hold together a crumbing surface. But several coverups, including mirrors, masonry veneers, and specialty wallcoverings, can solve widespread cosmetic problems. One unusual type is made of thick fiberglass strands that can bridge cracks to create a solid surface for painting, even over rough-faced concrete blocks. Most are sold as semirigid sheets with weaves that vary from coarse burlap patterns to finer, linenlike surfaces. You apply them with adhesive, and once they are set you can paint them. Scratch-resistant fiberglass won't erode in damp conditions the way plain wallpapers often do.

MASONRY VENEERS

Brick is normally a heavy exterior-grade material, but you can install thin veneer brick on inside walls, too.

Stone veneers are often made of lightweight synthetics that you can add to the surface of a standard wall.

Mirror walls are a good option in bathrooms and any small space where you need more light. You can mount mirrors on wooden ledgers or screw special L-shaped clips into wall studs.

Heavy-duty fiberglass weaves look like standard wallpaper. But the sheets are strong enough to span cracks in the wall and resist scratching and other surface deterioration.

Tin panels used on ceilings are another traditional covering making a comeback. Embossed panels and matching trim pieces can completely cover a problem surface.

Large cornice moldings set at an angle along the ceiling and wide trim nailed around doors and windows add a traditional look of architectural detail to rooms.

Ceiling medallions and other decorative details were previously made on-site by forming and shaping fresh plaster. Today you can buy reproductions made of foam that you can paint.

Chair-rail and picture-rail moldings can separate and frame areas of a large wall for painting or covering with wallpaper.

TRIM

There are hundreds of different wall and ceiling moldings, although you would never know it from seeing the few stock types such as basic clamshell used in many new houses today. But you can create more detailed and architecturally interesting surfaces by combining stock lumber and trim, building up complex shapes. Another option is to add decorative details yourself by cutting grooves, ogees, and other shapes into stock boards with a router. And although purists generally prefer wood, several companies produce lightweight prefinished synthetic moldings such as ceiling medallions and cornices that are easy to install.

● BUILT-UP TRIM

Use a combination of stock trim to build up a decorative windowsill, predrilling to avoid splits.

Use a stock 1x4 or 1x6 with a decorative cap and shoe molding to build up detailed baseboards.

FLOORING

Floor coverings fall into two broad categories: resilient flooring, which has some resiliency, or bounce; and hard flooring, with no flex whatsoever. Resilient floors are less tiring to stand on than hard-surface floors and less likely to produce instant disaster for dropped glasses or chinaware. But the flooring you select plays more than a practical role in your kitchen.

Before replacing an old surface, make sure the subfloor is in good condition. Subflooring that is in need of repair will eventually ruin any new flooring material that you install.

Resilient Vinyl Tile and Sheet Flooring. Vinyl flooring wears fairly well to very well, needs only occasional waxing or polishing (in some cases none at all), and is easy to clean. It comes in a wide variety of colors and patterns, and is an economical alternative among flooring choices.

These products are available in individual tiles or in large sheets. (The sheets can look like individual tiles as well as a wide range of designs.) Installing vinyl tile is a popular do-it-yourself project. Installing sheet goods is a bit more complex but well within the skills of an experienced do-it-yourselfer.

ABOVE An individual tile look, complete with grout lines, is only one of the designs possible with vinyl sheet flooring.

BELOW Wood and tile are not the only styles produced in laminate. In this sunroom, laminate imitates brick.

TOP Real linoleum fell out of favor during the 1970s. New manufacturing methods are making it popular again.

ABOVE In tight quarters, go with a smaller grid, as shown, or with a simple textured pattern.

Vinyl does have disadvantages, however. It dents easily when subjected to pressures such as high-heel shoes or furniture legs. Vinyl surfaces may also scratch or tear easily, and high-traffic areas are likely to show wear. You can control some degree of wear by the type of vinyl flooring you choose. Look for a minimum 10-mil thickness up to the most expensive 25-mil-thick flooring. Inlaid vinyl flooring is solid vinyl with color and pattern all the way through to the backing. This most expensive vinyl flooring is designed to last 20 to 30 years.

Hard-Surface Flooring. Ceramic tile, stone, and slate floors are hard, durable, and easy to clean, especially when you use grout sealers. Because these floors are so inflexible, anything fragile dropped on them is likely to break. Also, they are tiring to stand on and noisy, and they conduct extremes of temperature. For those who love the look of this kind of flooring, however, the drawbacks can be mitigated with accent and area rugs that add a cushion.

Ceramic tile makes an excellent kitchen floor when installed with proper grout and sealants. The tiles range from the earth tones of unglazed, solid-color quarry tile to the great array of colors, patterns, and finishes in surface-glazed tiles. Grout comes color-keyed, so it can be either inconspicuous or a design element. Ceramic and quarry tiles are best suited to a concrete subfloor, though you can lay them over any firm base. Cost ranges from moderate to expensive. Installation is hard work but straightforward if the subfloor is sound. This is a great project for do-it-yourself remodelers who want to create special designs with the tiles.

Stone and slate are cut into small slabs and can be laid in a regular or random pattern. Materials are inexpensive or costly, depending on quality and local availability. Even if you find these materials more expensive than other floor coverings, don't dismiss them because of price. They will never need to be replaced, making

ABOVE Ceramic tiles provide beautiful, long-lasting floors. Notice how the counter material complements the tiles.

RIGHT Tile pavers provide a rustic, natural feeling to this family kitchen.

OPPOSITE TOP Laminate in a slate style is far easier to install and costs much less than the real thing.

your initial investment your final one. Because stone and slate are laid in mortar and are themselves weighty materials, a concrete slab makes the ideal subfloor. In other situations, the subfloor must be able to carry a significantly heavy load. Installation is a complex do-it-yourself job.

Laminate. This type of flooring consists of laminate material, a tougher version of the material used on counters, bonded to a fiberboard core. The decorative top layer of material can be made to look like just about anything. Currently, wood-grain patterns are the most popular, but laminates are available in many colors and patterns, including tile and natural-stone designs.

Available in both plank and tile form, they are easy to install, hold up well to normal traffic, and are easy to clean. Most laminates can be installed directly over any other floor finish with the exception of carpeting. Some products simply snap together, others are glued.

LEFT Bamboo is at home in contemporary and minimalistic settings, such as this kitchen area.

BELOW The look of hand-scraped wood floors is back in vogue and available in both solid and engineered-wood products.

OPPOSITE Wood flooring is obtainable in more species than ever, including merbau, shown here.

Wood. Thanks largely to polyurethane coatings that are impervious to water, wood flooring has made a comeback—even in kitchens. You already may have a wood floor buried under another floor covering. If this is the case, consider exposing it, repairing any damaged boards, and refinishing it. Or install an all-new wood floor. Wood can be finished any way you like, though much of the wood flooring available today comes prefinished in an assortment of shades.

Hardwoods such as oak and maple, are popular and stand up to a lot of abuse. Softwoods such as pine, give a more distressed, countrified look. Flooring comes in 2¼-inch strips as well as variable-width planks. Parquet flooring, another good option for the kitchen, consists of wood pieces glued together into a geometric pattern. These prefinished squares can be installed in a way similar to that used for vinyl tiles.

CORK FLOORS

Although cork flooring has been around since the late 1800s, it is only recently that designers have rediscovered it for homes. Cork is a truly sustainable product because only the bark of the cork tree is used. Once the bark is harvested, the tree grows new bark in about 15 years. Cork floors are resilient, easy on the feet, and can reduce noise and vibration. They are available in dozens of colors. The material is available in 12 x 12-inch blocks that is adhered to the substrate by a troweled-on adhesive. Engineered-cork flooring consists of a cork veneer that is attached to a fiberboard core. These products measure 12 x 36 inches and can be floated over an existing floor.

Alternate dark, solid, and striated cork tiles to add punch to a floor. Sample patterns are shown at left.

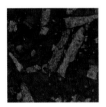 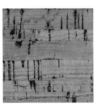 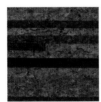

54 REMOVING A PARTITION

55 BUILDING WALLS

60 FRAMING WITH STEEL STUDS

61 INSTALLING WOOD FURRING

62 SOUNDPROOFING

64 WINDOWS AND DOORS

70 INSTALLING WINDOWS

76 BUILDING A GLASS-BLOCK WALL

78 INSTALLING A DOOR

82 SPECIAL OPENINGS

3 structural changes

What we see when we look at floors, walls, and ceilings is usually the finish material that defines the outside surface of these structures. That's what everybody else who comes to visit sees too, and why we spend so much time with paint, and furniture. But behind all these eye-catching components is the backbone of your house: its framing. And sometimes you have to make alterations to it to get the results you want. Common examples are moving or building partitions, installing windows and doors, and even changing the location of plumbing fixtures in a bathroom or kitchen. Fortunately, dealing with framing isn't very difficult, but it usually does require some demolition to make the framing accessible. And this is where you'll get a good dose of dust, sweat, and tears.

REMOVING AN OLD PARTITION

project

Although removing a partition is not difficult, it certainly makes a mess. The drywall (or plaster) dust gets everywhere, and you end up spending almost as much time cleaning up as doing the work. Making the cleanup easier just takes a couple minutes. First, open at least two windows, and put a floor fan next to one to get the air moving out of the house. Then cover the entry door with a piece of plastic sheet and tape it to the door trim. Also, make sure to cover the furnace duct grilles with plastic and tape.

TOOLS & MATERIALS
▮ Work gloves and dust mask
▮ Plastic sheeting, tape, and water mister
▮ Reciprocating saw
▮ Shims or wedges
▮ Pry bar and hammer

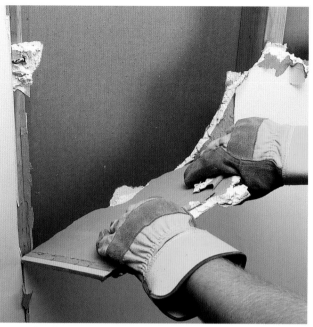

1 The first step in tearing down a partition wall is to remove the drywall from the studs. To make the job go faster, score the drywall along the studs using a sharp utility knife. Then poke a hole through the surface using a hammer; reach into the wall cavity; and pull. The panels will break apart and leave remnants attached to the studs by screws or nails.

2 The best way to remove the wall studs is to cut them in half using a reciprocating saw. To prevent the blade from binding in the cut, drive a scrap wood wedge into the blade kerf before continuing the cut. The wedge will just drop out when the cut is completed. Pull the two parts of the stud away from the wall plates.

3 Remove the bottom plate from the floor and the top plate from the ceiling using a flat pry bar. Slide the tool between the board and the floor or ceiling and lift. Pry at every nail location; then pull the board up and out. Make sure to remove all the nails from the board to prevent accidentally walking on them.

BUILDING A TEMPORARY SUPPORT WALL

project

While removing partitions is messy work, it doesn't have much impact on the structure of your house. These walls just divide up space and usually don't need to support anything more substantial than five or six sheets of drywall. But if you need to make alterations to walls that support structural weight, such as outside walls or interior bearing walls, then you have to temporarily support this weight with a support wall. These are easy to build, and once you're done with them you can remove them.

TOOLS & MATERIALS

- Hammer and 8d common nails
- 4-ft. level
- Circular saw
- Drywall or cardboard scrap
- 2x6 and 2x8 lumber

1 To achieve a tight fit for a support wall, it's a good idea to build it in place. Start with the bottom plate. Use a 2x8, and place it on a piece of drywall or heavy cardboard to protect the floor finish from damage. Don't nail the 2x8 to the floor. It will be wedged in place by the studs and top plate.

2 The top plate must align with the bottom plate. Use a level and straight board to establish this location. Then tack-nail the plate to the ceiling using a couple of 8d nails. Drive the nails into the ceiling joists.

3 Measure the distance between the top and bottom plates, and cut a 2x6 stud $1/16$ in. longer than this measurement. Slide the stud between the plates, and toenail it into the bottom plate.

4 Push the stud against the top plate, and check it for plumb using a level. Toenail the top of the stud to the top plate. Add the remaining studs to this support wall, spacing them 24 in. apart.

BUILDING PARTITIONS

There are two ways to build partition walls: in place (shown below) or preassembled. When you build a wall in place, you nail the wall plates to the floor and ceiling and then fill in the studs between, toenailing each to both plates. The great advantage of this approach is that it makes for a tight wall in rooms where the floor and ceiling aren't parallel, which is often the case in older houses. Preassembling a wall, on the other hand, is easier because you cut all the studs to the same size and nail the plates to the ends of the studs before the wall is tipped up.

TOOLS & MATERIALS
- Hammer and 10d common nails
- 4-ft. level, circular saw, and chalk-line box
- 2 x 4 lumber ▌ Measuring tape
- Safety glasses

1 Building a partition in place is often the best way to create a small wall in a room where the floor and ceiling are not parallel. The first step is to lay out the location of the wall on the floor and snap chalk lines for the bottom plates. Nail the plates to the floor, hitting as many floor joists as possible.

2 Once the bottom plates are installed, establish the location of the top plates so they will be plumb with the bottom plates. To do this, hold a stud on the bottom plate so the edges of both are flush. Then hold a level to the side of the stud, and move the stud until it's plumb. Mark the ceiling at this point.

3 Add a stud between the bottom and top plates until the wall is framed. Preassemble a 3-stud corner, and nail it between the plates. This corner post should be plumb in both directions. (See the drawing on the facing page.)

NAILING TECHNIQUES

Face-nailing through the top or bottom plate into a stud makes the strongest connection. It's also easier and faster than toenailing, where the angled nail sometimes can cause splits or miss most of the stud altogether. Either way, lay out stud locations on both the bottom and top plates at the same time.

Keep the frame from shifting by standing on the stud as you nail.

Start a toenail at a shallow angle, and steepen it once the point grabs.

WALL FRAMING BASICS

Overlapped Corner

Double Plate

Cripple Stud

Header

Corner Nailing

Blocking

Stud

Two-By Board

Plywood Filler

Jack Stud

Siding

Full Stud

Air-Barrier Paper

Drywall (Back)

Drywall

Cavity

Sheathing

3-Stud Corner

Insulation

Vapor Barrier

Drywall

Sill

Sill

Stud 16" O.C.

Plywood Decking

FRAMING A WINDOW OPENING

Building partitions is one thing, but cutting an opening for a window or a door in an outside wall is another thing altogether. To begin with, you'll have to build a temporary support wall to carry the load from above when you are working. (See page 55.) Then you'll have to cut a hole through the wall and expose the interior of your house to outside weather. And once you have this hole cut and properly framed, you'll still have to modify the exterior siding (and sometimes trim) to make a watertight seal around the window or door.

TOOLS & MATERIALS
▌ Hammer and 10d common nails
▌ Circular saw, drill-driver, and ¾-in. spade bit
▌ Safety glasses ▌ Measuring tape
▌ 2x4 and 2x8 lumber, and ½-in. plywood

1 Establish the location of the window on the outside wall, and remove any studs that fall within this opening. Then mark the height of the rough sill, following the specifications that came with the window. Nail a cripple stud to support the rough sill on the two full studs that define the rough opening.

3 A substantial header must be installed to support the weight above the window in a load-bearing wall. And this header must be supported by a jack stud on both ends. These can either extend all the way down to the bottom plate or stop at the rough sill, if the sill was installed first as shown here. Nail the jack stud to the full stud every 12 inches.

4 A typical outside wall header is constructed of two 2x8s with a piece of ½-in. plywood sandwiched between. These components are glued with construction adhesive and nailed together. This arrangement fills a 2x4 wall that is actually 3½-in. thick. For a 2x6 wall, assemble three 2x8s and two pieces of plywood.

2 Measure the distance between the two studs that define the rough opening, and cut a 2x4 to fit between. This will be the rough sill that supports the window. Nail this board into the cripple studs.

● **STUD SIZES**

Wall studs in old houses built generally around or before 1950 measured close to a full 2 x 4 inches. Studs used in the 1960s and 1970s often measured $1\frac{5}{8}$ x $3\frac{5}{8}$ inches. Today many studs are a hair smaller and measure $1\frac{1}{2}$ x $3\frac{1}{2}$ inches. The difference doesn't matter if you're using all new studs in a room addition. But if you're using new, smaller studs against older studs—in a wall opening, for example—you can set one edge flush for nailing or pack out the stud with furring.

$1\frac{1}{2}$" x $3\frac{1}{2}$" Stud

2" x 4" Stud

5 Place the header on top of the jack studs, and attach it with nails driven through the full stud into the header. Make sure the header is level before nailing it in place. If it isn't, shim the ends accordingly, and then nail it in place.

6 Lay out the sill and the header for cripple studs to maintain regular 16-in.-on-center nailing surfaces below and above the window. Cut and nail cripple studs in place on these marks.

7 Once all the framing is complete, drill a reference hole at each corner of the rough opening. It's easier to cut out the plywood from inside the house. But it's usually better to cut and remove the siding from outside first.

FRAMING WITH STEEL STUDS

Steel studs, joists, and rafters are old hat to most high-volume carpentry contractors. Using them may have started on the west coast, but now steel framing is used throughout the country. It has many advantages over wood. It's lighter, doesn't shrink with age, resists water damage, and is impervious to insects. Most do-it-yourselfers still prefer working with wood. But knowing a few steel work basics is a good idea for everyone, especially those who live in a new house where steel components were used throughout the building.

TOOLS & MATERIALS
- Safety glasses
- Aviation snips, clamps, and 4-ft. level
- Drill-driver and sheet-metal screws
- Steel studs and tracks

1 Cut a U-shaped steel channel to length for the top and bottom plate. Make the cuts using tin snips or a saber saw outfitted with a metal-cutting blade. Wear gloves when making these cuts to avoid being hurt by the sharp edges. Mark the correct location of the plates on the ceiling and floor; then hold the plates in place; and fasten them using screws.

2 Once the plates are installed, lay them out for studs spaced 16 in. apart. Then cut the studs to length, and slide each one into both channels. Hold the end of each in the correct spot with a clamp; then join the two with a sheet-metal screw. Use self-tapping screws so you don't have to drill a pilot hole in the steel parts.

3 Horizontal parts, such as non-load-bearing headers, need to be modified so they can be attached to the studs. Cut the piece 2 in. longer on both ends, and snip a 45-deg. angle on all the edges. Bend the ends down, and attach them to the studs using screws.

INSTALLING WOOD FURRING

project

Furring is an indispensable building material for any number of jobs. It's usually one of the cheapest things a lumberyard or home center sells, so it's the first choice for temporary fencing, holding roofing felt until the shingles are installed, and for straightening out walls that aren't flat, like the one shown here. This is often the case with basement walls that you want to cover with drywall or wood paneling. It takes a while to install the furring like this, but the flat walls are well worth the time. The hardest part is driving nails into a masonry wall.

TOOLS & MATERIALS
▌ Hammer and 10d masonry nails
▌ Circular saw and 4-ft. level
▌ Safety glasses ▌ Measuring tape
▌ 1x4 lumber and shim

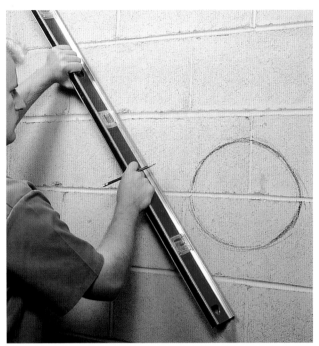

1 Before nailing any furring in place, locate the high and low parts of the wall by pressing a 4-ft. level every 6 to 12 inches against the surface. If the level rocks, the wall is high, and you should make a straight mark. If there's a gap under the level, the wall is low, so mark this with a circle to easily differentiate it from the high areas.

2 Don't install furring over the high areas, but do run it over the low areas. Then add shims to fill the low area, using inexpensive cedar shimming shingles. Push the shingles together until the furring is flat. Check this using a level.

3 Fill the gaps with smaller pieces of furring to suit the material you are putting on the wall. The best nails to use are standard masonry nails because they are the easiest type to drive straight. But traditional cut nails penetrate the concrete faster, if you have experience driving them.

BUILDING A SOUNDPROOF WALL

There's a lot of noise around these days, both inside and outside the house, and most of us would like to turn down the volume a bit. Fortunately, the truck rumbling by doesn't sound as bad as it could because some of the sound is blocked by the insulation in the exterior walls. Unfortunately, interior walls aren't insulated. In fact, these walls sometimes seem like amplifiers, especially when the kids are watching TV in the next room. While it may be impractical to soundproof an existing wall, as shown here, it does make sense if you're remodeling.

TOOLS & MATERIALS
- Hammer and 10d common nails
- Drill-driver and 2-in. drywall screws
- Safety glasses and gloves Measuring tape
- 2x4 and 2x6 lumber, insulation, and drywall

1 There are several good ways to reduce the sound transmission through a wall. One of the best is to build a 2x6 wall with staggered 2x4 studs. Begin by cutting and nailing a 2x6 plate on the floor and ceiling. Then cut studs to fit between these plates, and begin nailing them in place along one edge of the plates.

4 If you can sacrifice the room, attach ¾-in.-thick polystyrene foam boards to the studs before installing ½-in.-thick drywall panels. The foam boards will improve the soundproofing of the wall.

5 Finish up the soundproofing by installing a second layer of drywall over the first, staggering the joints between layers. The best way to do this is to install the first layer vertically and the second layer horizontally. Once all the panels are in place, finish the seams and joints using drywall tape and joint compound.

2 When you've nailed one row of studs in place, nail studs along the other edge. Center them in the open space between the studs in the first row. Make sure the studs fit tightly between the plates. If they are loose, the toenails won't hold as well.

3 Weave fiberglass insulation batts between the stud rows, beginning at the bottom of the wall and working up. Pack the insulation together so there are no air gaps between batts. Using batts that are enclosed in plastic reduces the spread of fiberglass fibers, but wear a dust mask or respirator anyway.

● SOUND-DEADENING DETAILS

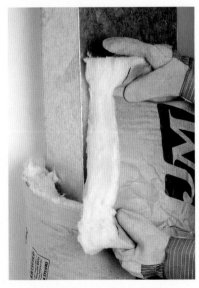

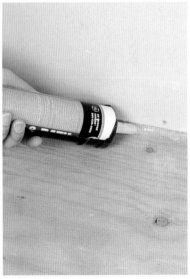

Reduce the sound of plumbing noises by wrapping supply, vent, and especially drainpipes in walls with insulation.

A spiral wrap of insulation batts around in-wall ducts reduces the noise of air movement and saves energy.

Sound can seep around the edges of a wall, as well as through it. Applying caulk along the edges will help.

WINDOWS & DOORS

Sunlight brings cheer and sparkle to any room. All you have to do is welcome it inside with windows, glass doors, or a skylight. When you shop for window and door units, make energy conservation a prime consideration. Double glazing is now standard, but most manufacturers offer windows with low-emissivity (low-e) glazing. These windows have films that reflect heat but let in light. The film also blocks ultraviolet light that can fade fabrics. Look for energy ratings that reflect the entire window unit, not just the glazing. You can also add exterior awnings to shade the windows from unwanted heat gain. Because a house loses more heat at night than during the day, drapes can provide privacy and minimize nighttime heat losses from windows.

ENERGY-EFFICIENT WINDOWS & DOORS

Choose windows, doors, and skylights based on your local climate. Products that meet the following requirements earn the Department of Energy's Energy Star Label. Look for windows, doors, and skylights tested by the National Fenestration Rating Council, an independent testing group.

Northern States

▌Windows and doors must have a U-factor* of 0.35 or below.

▌Skylights must have a U-factor* of 0.45 or below.

Middle States

▌Windows and doors must have a U-factor* of 0.40 or below and an SHGC** rating of 0.55 or below.

▌Skylights must have a U-factor* of 0.45 or below and an SHGC** of 0.55 or below.

Southern States

▌Windows, doors, and skylights must have a U-factor* rating of 0.75 or below and an SHGC** of 0.40 or below.

* U-factor is a measurement of heat loss. The lower the number, the less heat lost.
* * SHGC stands for Solar Heat Gain Coefficient and is a measurement of how well a product blocks heat caused by sunlight. It is a number between 0 and 1. The lower the number the more heat the product blocks.

Window Types

Before you decide that your kitchen needs more or bigger windows, take down the curtains from your existing windows—the change in light levels may amaze you. If that's not the answer, consider adding or enlarging the windows. Place them wherever they work best. Sometimes

an above-cabinet soffit space provides an excellent site for awning-type windows. Or you may install traditional-style windows. These needn't be the same width as the old ones, but they usually look better if the top edges line up with other windows in the room.

If you want a window to provide natural task lighting for a kitchen sink or work surface, its sill should be 3 to 6 inches above the countertop. For safety reasons, most building codes don't permit windows over ranges or cooktops.

Don't overlook style when selecting a window. If your house is a colonial, for example, stick with a traditional double-hung window instead of the contemporary casement type that may not blend with your home's overall architecture. Also check for other desirable features. A tilt-in unit, for instance, makes cleaning easier. Optional grilles simply pop in and let you create a divided-light window.

For purists, manufacturers fabricate true divided-light windows in standard sizes. There are five common types of windows. They can be used individually or combined in various ways.

LEFT Counter-to-ceiling windows will maximize natural light but take up cabinet space.

BELOW Speciality windows add a dramatic touch.

Fixed Windows. Fixed windows are the simplest type of window because they do not open. A fixed window is simply glass installed in a frame that is attached to the house. Fixed windows are the least expensive, admit the most light, and come in the greatest variety of shapes and sizes. However, they can't be used to provide ventilation.

Double-Hung Windows. Perhaps the most common kind used in houses, double-hung windows consist of two framed glass panels, called sash, that slide vertically on a metal, wood, or plastic track. The glass can be a single pane of glazing or divided into smaller panes, called lites. One variation, called a single-hung window, is made using an upper panel that cannot slide and a lower, sliding panel.

Casement Windows. Casements are hinged at the side and swing outward from the window opening as you turn a small crank. Better casement windows can be opened to a 90-degree angle, providing maximum ventilation.

Sliding Windows. Sliders are similar to double-hung windows turned on their side. The glass panels slide horizontally and are often used where there is need for a window opening that is wider than it is tall.

Awning Windows. Awning windows swing outward like a casement window but are hinged at the top. Awning windows can be left opened slightly for air even when it rains.

RIGHT Windows let in light, but they can also make the view part of the design.

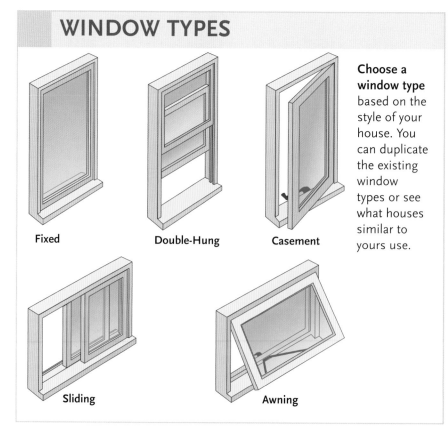

WINDOW TYPES

Choose a window type based on the style of your house. You can duplicate the existing window types or see what houses similar to yours use.

Fixed

Double-Hung

Casement

Sliding

Awning

WHICH WAY SHOULD WINDOWS & SKYLIGHTS FACE?

Orient a door, window, or skylight to take best advantage of breezes and seasonal sunlight. Also take into account trees, neighboring structures, and the potential view.

• **South light** will pour into windows with a southern exposure in winter because the sun's path is low in the sky. But in the summer, when it rides high in the sky, the sun will beat down on the southern roof instead. Southern exposure is an ideal placement for a window because it gains heat through the window in winter but not in summer, especially if it's shielded by a deep overhang. A skylight on a southern or western exposure will capture solar heat during the winter—and the summer, too. Be careful about this placement.

• **East light** brightens the morning yet rarely heats up the room. Skylights on north- and east-facing roofs lessen heat gain in the summer.

• **West light** subjects a room to the hot, direct rays of late-afternoon sun, which can make a room uncomfortable until far into the night. If a west-facing window is your only option, shade it with overhangs, awnings, sun-stopping blinds, or broad-leaf plantings.

• **North light** has an almost consistent brightness throughout the day. Because it's from an open sky, without direct sun, the light doesn't create glaring hot spots or deep shadows in work areas. North light lacks the drama of other exposures, but room design and colors can compensate for that.

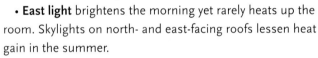

Summer Sun

Winter Sun

W N
S E

Replacement Windows

When buying new windows you'll have two important concerns: the type of window to install and the type of installation.

Replacement Installations. You can install your own windows, of course, or buy the units and hire someone to install them. Or you can shop at one of the increasing number of retailers who offer package deals including installation. If you don't do the job, watch out for the common problem of downsizing, or installing windows that are much smaller than your originals. Downsizing windows by excessively packing out the old frame can change the scale of the facade and create clumsy-looking trim details inside and out.

There are a few installation methods available. For double-hung windows, you can remove and replace the sash while leaving the window frame in place. It's a good option for replacing damaged or inefficient sash if the overall frame is still in good condition.

Complete replacement is much like installing windows in new construction. But you have the extra work of removing the old units to start with, and after the windows are in, you need to piece-in siding and drywall and reinstall the exterior trim.

Skylights. In a single-story house or one with a vaulted ceiling, a properly planned and located skylight can provide five times more natural light than a window of equal size located in a wall. It's important to plan for the seasonal angle and path of the sun to avoid unwelcome heat gains and losses from skylights. It's usually better to locate a skylight on a north- or east-facing surface, for example, to prevent overheating and provide diffuse light. Venting models, placed near the roof ridge, can also greatly improve natural ventilation. Seek advice from an architect or designer if you're not sure how a skylight will affect your room's climate.

Door Types

Interior and exterior doors are offered in dozens of shapes, sizes, and materials. Most units are made of wood or wood by-products, but many are made of metal and stamped or embossed to look like wood. Exterior doors often incorporate glass panels. French and sliding patio doors are almost all glass. Most interior wood-based doors are fabricated in one of three ways: as individual panels set in a frame, as a hardboard facing molded to look like a panel door and secured to a frame, or as a thin sheet of plywood secured to each side of a wood framework.

Panel and Panel-Look Doors. Panel door styles offer a variety of choices. They can be constructed with as few as three to as many as ten or more solid panels, in all sorts of shapes and size combinations. Sometimes the bottom is made of wood and the top panels are glass.

Flush Doors. Generally less expensive, flush doors come in a more limited range of variations. You can enhance their simple looks with wood molding for a traditional appeal.

Sliders. Sliding doors consist of a large panel of glass framed with wood or metal. Usually one of the doors is stationary while the other slides. Replacing an existing wood door with one that's all or mostly glass can double its natural lighting potential. For safety and security, be sure that the new door has tempered glass and has a secure locking mechanism. Enlarge an existing door or window opening, or cut a new one, to gain access to a deck

TOP Skylights allow in five times more light than windows. Used over a sink, they provide task lighting.

LEFT Set near the ridge of a roof, skylights provide general lighting to the room.

or patio outside. The frame may be wood, aluminum, or wood covered with aluminum or vinyl.

French Doors. Traditional French doors are framed-glass panels with either true divided lites or pop-in dividers; usually both doors open. Manufacturers also offer units that look like traditional hinged doors but operate

like sliders. If space is limited, consider out-swing patio doors. These units open outward rather than inward like other doors. So you can open them without taking up valuable floor space.

Dutch Doors. Made in two parts, Dutch doors have independently operating sections, top and bottom. Locked together, the two halves open and close as a unit. Or you can open just the top section for ventilation.

Sunrooms, Greenhouses, and Bays

If a full-scale addition just does not make sense for your house, you might wish to enhance your existing space, at less cost, with a "mini-addition," in the form of a sunroom or greenhouse-like bump out.

Prefabricated Sunrooms. Prefabs usually have double- or triple-glazed glass panels and come in prefit pieces that can be assembled by amateur carpenters, although this isn't a simple project by any means. For a sunroom, you'll need a foundation, which is usually a concrete slab over a perimeter wall that goes below the frost line.

A sunroom should face within 20 degrees of due south to take greatest advantage of solar heating in colder climates.

Window Greenhouses. Also called box windows, these units provide a site for year-round indoor gardening. All you need to do is remove a window and hang a prefabricated unit or a home-built greenhouse outside. Fill it with flowering plants or greenery; grow herbs or vegetables; or use it to give your outdoor garden a jump on spring. This window treatment is also an excellent way to replace a poor outside view with your indoor garden while keeping the window open to light.

As with sunrooms, window greenhouses work best with southern exposures. You might also have sufficient light from an eastern or western exposure if no trees, buildings, or other obstructions cast shadows. You might as well rule out a northern exposure; a north-facing greenhouse loses great amounts of heat in winter, and many plants don't grow well in northern light.

Bay Windows. Bay units allow you to add a foot or two of sunny space without having to construct a foundation. In this case, you would cantilever the bay window from your home's floor joists. Most window manufacturers sell bays in a variety of widths and configurations, ranging from simple boxes to gentle bows. Installing one is a job best left to a skilled carpenter.

INSTALLING NEW WINDOW SASH

project

You can replace worn sash without replacing the entire window. The first steps are to measure the window openings carefully and order your new sash. Then remove the old ones, and fill the window-weight cavities with insulation. Cut the liners to size, and install them. Then slide the sash into the liners. Finish up by installing window stops to hold the sash in place.

TOOLS & MATERIALS

▌ Wood chisel or pry bar
▌ Utility knife ▌ Hacksaw
▌ Sash-replacement kit
▌ 8d (2½-in.) finishing nails
▌ Loose-fill insulation (vermiculite)
▌ Cup and cardboard guide for insulation

1 Using a sharp utility knife, cut the paint seal that runs along the sash stop boards and the window jambs. Then carefully push a flat pry bar under the stops and pry them off. Pull the nails from the backside of these trim boards.

4 Carefully measure the jamb opening, and cut the new jamb liners to fit, using a hacksaw or a power miter box. Then attach them to the old jambs following the directions that came with the kit. In many cases, you simply screw the liners to the jambs.

5 Install the top sash first by angling one corner of it into the outermost track on one of the liners. Make sure the pin on the corner of the sash (inset) engages in the track channel.

2 Pull the bottom sash away from the window opening, and remove the cords or chains that are connected to the sash weights. Set the bottom sash aside, and pry away the parting strips that separate the top and bottom sash from the grooves in the side jambs.

3 Remove the sash weights, cords, and pulleys from the side jambs; then enlarge the pulley opening using a drill and a sharp spade bit. Using a piece of scrap cardboard and a cup, pour loose-fill insulation into the weight cavities.

6 Slide the other sash corner into its channel, and push the sash down to the sill. Then lift the sash and push the bottom into place.

7 Install the bottom sash in the inside liner tracks. Push the bottom against the sill, and then force the top into place.

8 Finish up the job by installing window stop trim boards. If you removed the old ones carefully, you can reuse them.

INSTALLING A NEW WINDOW

project

If you are working on a new addition or just adding a new window to a room, the process is the same. You have to expose the sheathing on the outside of the house so the window can rest against it. On new work, the sheathing is exposed already. But on old work, you have to remove the siding before you can proceed. Use a circular saw, with a straight guide board nailed to the house, to cut the siding boards. Set the saw depth so it cuts just through the siding; then remove the boards with a pry bar.

TOOLS & MATERIALS
▮ Tape measure and safety glasses ▮ Level
▮ Circular saw ▮ Window and shims
▮ Caulking gun and caulk ▮ Hammer
▮ Staple gun and staples ▮ House wrap
▮ 6d common and 8d finishing nails

1 Remove the siding from the outside of the house, and mark the rough opening of the window according to the manufacturer's specifications. Draw all four lines on the sheathing, and make sure they are level, plumb, and square.

5 Set the window onto the rough sill, and tip the top into the opening. Avoid touching the caulk on the backside of the flange. Have a helper hold the window from the outside, while you go inside to position the window.

6 Begin adjusting the window position by centering it in the opening from side-to-side. Check the level on all the sides, and shim the window so it is level and plumb. Once it properly shimmed, change places with your helper.

2 Measure the thickness of the sheathing; then set the depth gauge on a circular saw $1/16$ in. deeper than this thickness and cut along the lines.

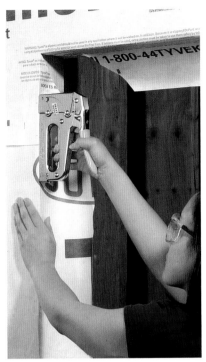

3 Install house wrap over the sheathing, and cut out the window opening. Fold the house wrap around the framing members, and staple it in place.

4 Before putting the window into the opening, run a bead of silicone caulk around the backside of the nailing flange to create a tight seal.

7 Install the window by driving galvanized roofing nails through the holes in the nailing flange that surrounds the window. Fill all the available holes, and make sure the nails are flush with the flange surface.

8 Fill the gap between the window jambs and the wall framing with fiberglass insulation. Push the fiberglass into the opening, but don't compact it because this will reduce its insulating effectiveness. A shimming shingle (or a putty knife) works well for this job.

REPLACING A WINDOW

project

Installing replacement windows is a great way to reduce energy use while getting a window that works and looks better at the same time. There are two basic types as discussed in "Surface vs Drop-In" on the facing page. The drop-in units are the easiest to install, while the surface-mount units usually have better energy performance features. The photos here show installing a surface-mount unit. Over half the job is devoted to removing the old window.

TOOLS & MATERIALS

- Work gloves, pry bar, and crowbar
- Reciprocating saw with metal-cutting blade
- 1x4 lumber(for shimming between window and framing)
- Replacement window, house wrap, and shims
- 4-ft. level, hammer, and 6d common nails

1 Start removing the old window, on the inside of the house, by prying off the casing boards. If you work carefully, you may be able to use these boards for the new window. This can save a lot of work later if these boards have a distinctive design that you want to use for the new window.

3 Once the nails are cut, pry out the window using a flat bar or a crow bar. Work slowly, starting at the top of the window. Make sure that your ladder is standing on firm soil, and have a helper close by to support the window once it is free of the opening.

4 Compare the old rough opening with the rough opening specified for the new window, and make any necessary modifications. If possible, use full-width lumber, like 1x4s or 1x6s, to fill in the space. Be sure to cover these shims with strips of sheathing the same thickness as the existing sheathing.

2 Remove the casing boards on the outside of the house. Because exterior trim boards should fit tightly between the window and the siding, you probably can't reuse the old boards for the new window. Cut any nails that hold the jambs to the framing using a reciprocating saw and a metal blade.

5 Apply house wrap or roofing felt to the sheathing around the opening. Then tip the window into the opening, and center it from side-to-side. Check the window for level and plumb; then nail the window flange to the sheathing with galvanized roofing nails.

SURFACE VS DROP-IN

Most replacement windows have a nailing flange that fits over builder's felt or house wrap.

Drop-in replacements are designed to provide modern glazing inside your old window casing.

divider options

One-piece clip-on dividers make cleaning easy but look less like true divided lites than two-piece units.

BUILDING A GLASS-BLOCK WALL

project

Design your installation so it makes use of only full blocks, which makes the job much easier. Begin by mixing some mortar and adding an expansion strip and joint anchors to the wall; then spread a bed of mortar on the floor. Lay each block in this bed; then start the next course. Finish up by smoothing the joints using a jointing tool.

TOOLS & MATERIALS
- Lumber for curb forms, blocking and extra joists
- 10d nails (3 in.)
- Mortar mix for curb (optional)
- Glass block
- Glass block mortar mix
- Masonry trowel
- Plastic tub
- Foam expansion strips
- Metal wall anchors
- 1/4-in. plastic joint spacers
- Wire joint reinforcement
- Jointing tool
- Silicone caulk and caulking gun
- Rubber gloves

1 When you are ready to start laying up the blocks, mix the white-colored glass block mortar in a plastic tub or a wheelbarrow. Use as little water as possible to make a stiff mix. You have the consistency right if you can form a "baseball" out of the mortar.

BELOW Glass-block walls and windows not only add a distinctive design element to this room, they also allow filtered light in without sacrificing privacy. These blocks aren't difficult to install, but the framing in the room may need to be beefed up to support the additional weight. Check with an engineer or architect for what's required.

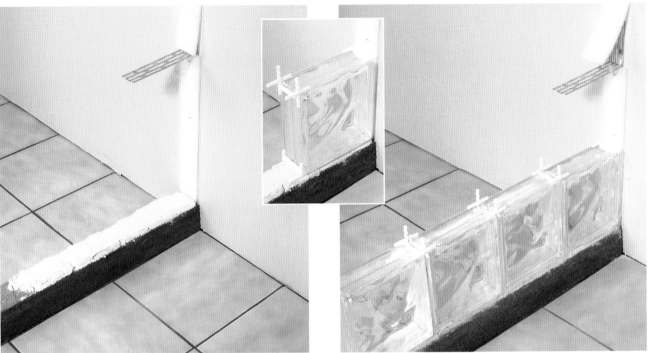

2 Staple an expansion strip and a joint anchor to the wall above the curb (optional) or the floor. Then spread ½-in. bed of mortar on top of the curb or the floor. Set the first block in place, and add plastic mortar spacers to the outside corners (inset).

3 Complete the first coarse of blocks by adding mortar to both sides of each block and spacers to one side. Tap them in place carefully with a rubber mallet. If you push too hard, you may force too much mortar from the bed. Check each block for level.

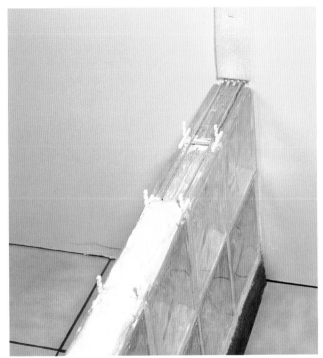

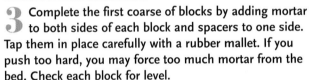

4 Once a course of block is complete, cover the top of the blocks with a new bed of mortar. Embed any wall anchors in this mortar. Then add lengths of wire joint reinforcement on top of the mortar, and carefully push them into place.

5 When the wall reaches the ceiling, carefully slide the blocks on the last course in place so that the mortar joints on the sides and bottom are not distorted. Twist off the end of the spacers; then smooth the joints using a jointing tool (inset).

77

INSTALLING A DOOR

Installing a new interior door can be easy or not, depending on the type of door you buy. While it is certainly possible to hang an individual door, these days the most popular doors are prehung units where the door panel is mounted on the jambs, holes for the lockset are predrilled, and in some cases, molding is attached to one side of the jambs. Many different door designs are available this way, so prehung models are the default units for professionals and do-it-yourselfers and are the type we show here.

TOOLS & MATERIALS
▌ Safety glasses ▌ Tape measure
▌ Drill-driver and drywall screws
▌ Framing square and scrap bracing material
▌ Prehung door, shims, and 10d finishing nails
▌ 4-ft. level ▌ Hammer ▌ Screwdriver

1 Check the rough door opening for level and plumb, and make sure the drywall is firmly attached to the framing. Use drywall screws to tighten any gaps. You can finish the drywall either before or after installing the door. Here, the walls will be finished afterwards.

3 Tip the door unit into the rough opening so the ends of the diagonal braces bear against the wall. Then slide wood shingle shims between the doorjambs and the wall framing to hold the door in place.

4 Check the side jambs for plumb and the head jamb for level. Install shims where needed to keep these boards properly aligned. Install the shims in pairs so you can make fine adjustments.

5 Once the jambs are all shimmed, nail them to the framing using 10d finishing nails. Set the nailheads; check the jambs with the level again; then fill the nailholes with wood filler.

2 Usually prehung doors come with diagonal bracing nailed in place to keep the doors square during installation. But if these braces are missing, install new ones. First check where the top of the door meets the head jamb with a framing square. When the parts are square, nail two braces in place.

6 Once the door is hung in the opening, remove the diagonal braces and check for proper operation. When satisfied, attach casing trim boards to the jambs. Cut miter joints at the top corners. Install a lockset in the predrilled hole following the manufacturer's directions.

ADJUSTING BYPASS DOORS

Tighten mounting screws in the overhead door tracks—even those carrying light, hollow-core interior doors. The tracks can work loose and cause sagging.

Most bypassing hardware has an adjustment screw on the back for raising or lowering the door.

STRENGTHENING DOORS & FRAMES

Exterior doors need to be versatile. They provide both easy access for occupants and security against intruders. Doors must also be resistant to cracking and warping caused by exposure to the elements and the differences in air temperature due to repeated opening and closing.

If you are installing a new door or want to beef up one you already have, you can take some extra steps during and after the installation to make both the door and the frame more durable.

Frame Strengtheners

To strengthen the connection between an existing door-jamb and house wall, start by removing the door stop trim. Score the seam with a sharp utility knife to break the paint seal. If you pry it away gradually, you should be able to reuse it. Then drive several screws through the doorjamb into the nearest studs, particularly around the hinge and lock locations. This reinforcement increases security by making it harder to pry the frame and release a latch or bolt from its keeper. It also makes the frame less likely to twist and keeps the door better aligned.

Use screws at least 3 inches long that can reach through the doorjamb, the shimming space around the frame, and well into the studs. Drive the screws flush. (It will help if you drill countersunk holes for the heads.) If you drive them too deeply, the jamb is likely to bow. Once the doorjamb is joined more securely to the house wall, you can reinstall the door stop trim over the screws. You probably will need to do a bit of touch up painting along the stop.

With many hinges and strike plates, you can accomplish a minor version of this reinforcement simply by using long screws in place of the relatively short screws often sold along with the hardware. Don't use a screw so large that its head does not sit flush with the face of the hinge or plate, however. This can cause the door to bind.

There are many add-on products that increase exterior-door security, including dead bolts and cover plates for key cylinders. But many of these don't help in what's called a kick-in burglary, where the door and frame are broken away from the house frame. Beefing up the frame increases security and helps to keep the door from sagging or shifting out of alignment.

● VINYL AND METAL DOORS

Purists may insist on real wood instead of synthetic substitutes. But both metal- and vinyl-clad exterior doors offer several advantages. They don't have directional grain, for one thing, so they are less likely to warp. The surfaces normally don't need periodic sanding and refinishing the way wood often does. And most synthetic-skin doors have a dense foam core that reduces temperature transfer. Of course, it's hard to find one that really does look like wood when you take a close look.

Vinyl-clad doors often are embossed to simulate a wood-grain surface.

Metal-clad doors can have better fire ratings than wood doors.

POCKET DOORS

Pocket doors save space by sliding sideways on a track into a cavity in the adjacent wall. They save floor and wall space—for example, on a small bath off a narrow hallway where a swinging door would be an obstruction. Installation is complicated because you need to replace standard studs with a double-sided frame that creates a cavity in the wall. The frame is normally sold as part of the door assembly and includes a sliding track and hardware. Fasten drywall to the frame with short screws that won't reach into the cavity.

A pocket door looks like other doors when it's closed but slides open sideways into a cavity in the wall.

DOOR AND FRAME CONSTRUCTION

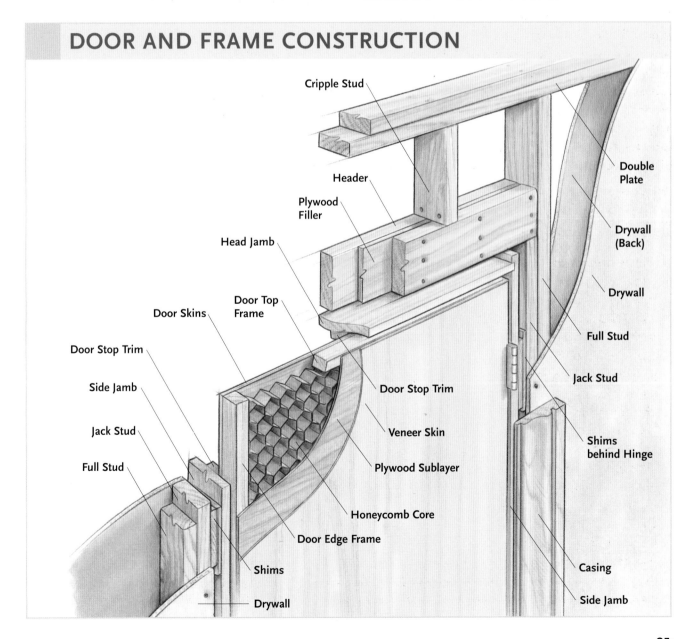

Cripple Stud

Header

Plywood Filler

Head Jamb

Door Top Frame

Door Skins

Door Stop Trim

Side Jamb

Jack Stud

Full Stud

Double Plate

Drywall (Back)

Drywall

Full Stud

Jack Stud

Door Stop Trim

Veneer Skin

Plywood Sublayer

Shims behind Hinge

Honeycomb Core

Door Edge Frame

Casing

Side Jamb

Shims

Drywall

INSTALLING A WALL NICHE

The space between the studs on interior walls is the greatest untapped supply of storage space in your house. In a typical wall, this space is 14½ inches wide by 3½ inches deep. Just about every medicine cabinet is designed to fit inside this space. And many fold-up ironing boards fit nicely between studs. But the practical storage supplied by these fixtures is not the only possibility. A wall niche, like the one shown here, for displaying collectibles and other keepsakes is another good option.

TOOLS & MATERIALS

- Foam niche ∎ Template
- Tape ∎ Utility saw
- Caulking gun and construction adhesive
- Hammer and 8d finishing nails
- Wood filler

1 Most preformed niches come with a template for laying out the rough opening on the wall. Just tape this template to the wall so its centerline falls in the middle of the space between studs. Then trace the inside of the template using a pencil to define the cutout.

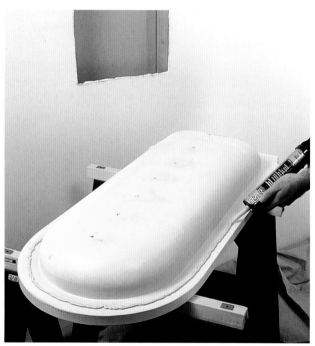

2 Niches always come with some sort of flange for overlapping, and hiding, the cut in the wall. This flange also provides a good surface for applying construction adhesive to the niche. Squeeze out a healthy bead of adhesive, and spread it smooth with a putty knife.

3 Carefully lift the niche, while avoiding the adhesive on the back of the flange, and push it into the opening. Move it up and down slightly to make sure the adhesive makes full contact. Then drive a couple finishing nails into the studs on both sides, and fill the holes with wood filler.

MAKING A FALSE HEADER

There are several ways to separate rooms. The most privacy is achieved with a door. Another option is a dropped header between rooms that divides the space without closing off the rooms visually. The last option is to simply install full partitions to separate rooms and leave an opening, from floor to ceiling, to allow passage between rooms. This last option is popular in modern design, but it isn't always attractive. Installing a dropped header is a good way to dress up this treatment.

TOOLS & MATERIALS

▌ Tape measure ▌ Framing square
▌ 2x4 lumber and galvanized corner brackets
▌ Hammer and 10d common nails
▌ Drill-driver and 1⅝-in. drywall screws
▌ Drywall, joint compound, and tape

1 To build a false header, first measure the distance between partitions and cut two pieces of 2x4 stock to match this measurement, minus about ¹/₁₆ in. to make fitting the boards easier (inset). Also cut the short end studs that fit between these plates, and join them to the plates using corner brackets.

2 Lay out the stud positions every 16 in. on center. Then cut the studs to size, and nail them in place using 10d nails driven through the plates.

3 Screw a support cleat to the side of the opening; then lift up the frame, and rest it on this cleat. Screw the fame to the ceiling joists and the jack studs on both sides of the wall opening.

4 Cut drywall pieces to cover the framework on the bottom and both sides. Screws these panels in place; then finish them using joint compound and drywall tape. Sand the joints smooth, prime, and paint.

86   Drywall Basics

88   Installing Drywall

90   Installing Backer Board

92   Resurfacing A Wall

94   Finishing Drywall Seams

97   Inside and Outside Corners

98   Sheet Paneling

102 Solid-Wood Paneling

104 Installing Wainscoting

4 drywall and paneling

These days there are many wall finish materials available, from centuries old plaster to modern metallic laminates. But the default material, on inexpensive tract houses and high-end custom models alike, is drywall. This material is usually installed directly over the framing members and is finished with paper tape and a plaster-like material called joint compound. Drywall is inexpensive, relatively easy to install, and a great surface for paint and wallpaper. It's also easy to repair if it suffers damage after installation. Other popular wall finishes are plywood and solid-wood paneling. Both can be installed directly over the wall studs and over existing drywall or plaster. Paneling is not as easy to repair as drywall, but the solid-wood type can develop a very warm patina over the years.

DRYWALL BASICS

Gypsum drywall is used to cover walls and ceilings in almost all new buildings, both residential and commercial, because it's strong, fire resistant, relatively easy to install, and readily accepts a wide variety of finishes, including paint and wallpaper.

The easy installation and finishing process is mainly responsible for drywall's success in replacing plaster as the interior wall and ceiling finish in most homes. Instead of applying a scratch coat and a paste of plaster that is difficult to spread smoothly, you simply nail or screw large solid panels to the framing. Then you add tape and layers of joint compound over the seams to create a smooth, unbroken surface.

Handling Drywall

Panels are available in a variety of sizes, from the standard 4 x 8-foot sheet that is widely available, to special-order lengths that can reach across a typical room. Handling large sheets can be taxing for do-it-yourselfers, even when working with a helper. But using larger sheets means taping and finishing fewer seams.

All drywall panels come in modular sizes that match up with residential framing set either 16 or 24 inches on center. It's smart to use the largest sheets that you can maneuver safely and without damage before you get them on the wall. That often means you need to order different sizes for different areas of a large drywall project.

But before you sketch out a plan with minimal seams, remember that even a 4 x 8-foot sheet of $\frac{1}{2}$-inch drywall weighs about 60 pounds. Maneuvering one up a staircase or through twists and turns in a narrow hallway can be tricky.

You can handle one sheet at a time by gripping the lower edge of the panel at its balance point and resting it against your arm and shoulder. If you're not used to handling that kind of weight, try a panel holder that grips the edge. On large projects, inquire about delivery services. Some suppliers with special boom-extension trucks can deposit many sheets where you need them, even through second-floor windows.

Fastening Systems

As you apply and finish panels, most of the trouble do-it-yourselfers encounter is along nailed seams. The best solution to a host of problems—from bent nail scars to hammer gouges from off-center hits—is to use screws instead of nails.

In fact, specs generally call for nail spacing of about 7 inches on ceilings and 8 inches on walls. But when you shift to drywall screws, specs call for fewer fasteners because they have more holding power, generally 12 inches apart on ceilings and 16 inches on walls. But the main benefits are that you can drive screws easily with a drill-driver, and save time on taping because screws leave a small, uniform dimple that's easy to hide under joint compound.

making cutouts for electrical boxes

1. Measure horizontally to the edges of the box from the corner or edge of the adjacent sheet.

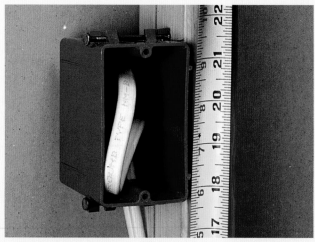

2. Measure vertically as well, noting the outside dimensions of the box, including any molded protrusions.

DRYWALL CONSTRUCTION

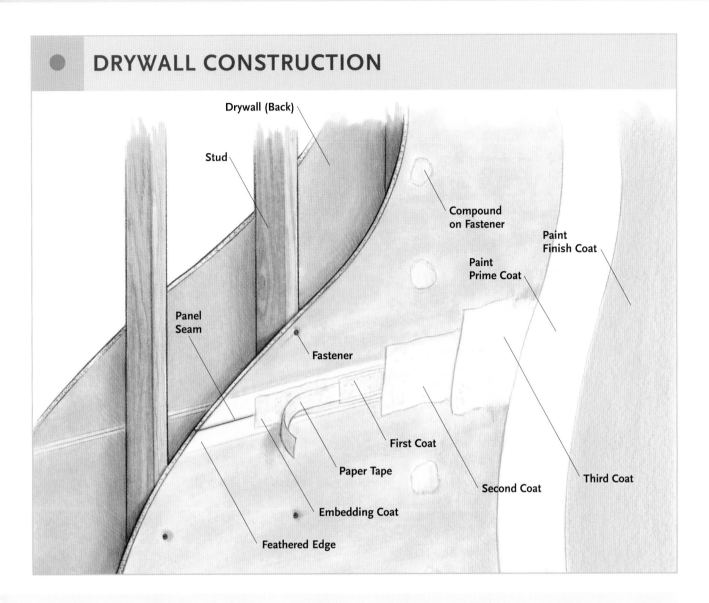

Drywall (Back)

Stud

Compound on Fastener

Paint Finish Coat

Paint Prime Coat

Panel Seam

Fastener

First Coat

Paper Tape

Second Coat

Third Coat

Embedding Coat

Feathered Edge

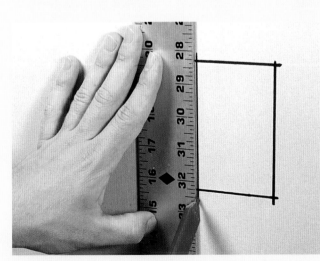

3. Duplicate your measurements on the face of the sheet, making sure you measure from the correct edge.

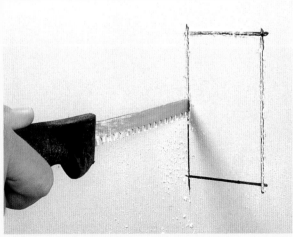

4. You can cut with a utility knife, but it's easier and safer to use a drywall saw with a plunge point to start the cut.

INSTALLING DRYWALL

The hardest part of hanging drywall is installing it on the ceiling. The panels are heavy and unwieldy, so be sure to line up some help for this job. If you have to work alone, rent a drywall lift from a tool rental store. It costs about $40–$50 a day, and it's hard to find a better bargain. Once the ceiling is done, you can also use the lift to install the top row of panels on the wall. Remember, you can install these panels either vertically or horizontally. But the latter makes finishing the joints much easier.

TOOLS & MATERIALS
▪ Tape measure ▪ Utility knife ▪ Hammer
▪ Drill-driver and drywall screws
▪ Drywall nails ▪ Drywall
▪ Caulking gun and construction adhesive
▪ 4-ft. T-square ▪ Panel lifter

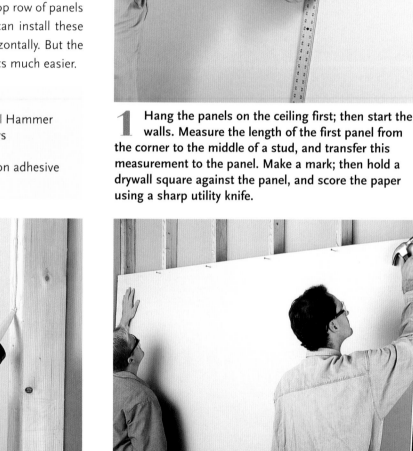

1 Hang the panels on the ceiling first; then start the walls. Measure the length of the first panel from the corner to the middle of a stud, and transfer this measurement to the panel. Make a mark; then hold a drywall square against the panel, and score the paper using a sharp utility knife.

3 To improve the joint between the panels and the framing members, use construction adhesive. Apply it to the edge of the studs and ceiling joists using a caulk gun. Then install the panel. This adhesive is very sticky and has a way of getting on every tool in sight, so apply it carefully.

4 Get some help to lift the panel; tip it in place at the top of the wall; and press its top edge against the ceiling to get the tightest joint possible. Attach the panel using drywall nails or screws.

2 Once the paper is scored, hold the board on one side of the cut; then snap the board on the other side of the cut. The panel should break cleanly. If it doesn't, move behind the panel; put your knee behind the cut line; and pull the board against your knee. Cut through the backing paper using a utility knife and separate the pieces.

● SETTING SCREWS

If screws chew through drywall paper, you may have trouble covering them with joint compound. That can happen if you overdrive the screw or use the wrong bit. The screw should leave a smooth, shallow dimple, shown below. Drywall screwguns (and some standard drills) have a torque setting that stops the screw at the right point.

Torn Edge   Smooth Dimple

5 Drywall screws hold better than nails, and they are easy to install if you have a cordless drill/driver. Just drive the screws until the head stops just below the surface of the paper. Nails should be spaced about 6 in. apart, and screws should be installed 8 in. apart.

6 After the top row of panels has been installed, start with the bottom sheets. Stagger the butt joints, and keep the long tapered joints tight. An inexpensive panel lifter helps raise the sheets off the floor. You can do the same thing with a simple fulcrum and lever made of two pieces of scrap lumber.

INSTALLING BACKER BOARD

In wet areas, cement-board is better backing for ceramic tile than regular or water-resistant drywall as it will not degrade if it should get wet. Although it's usually $\frac{1}{2}$ inch thick and is installed much like drywall, it is heavier and harder to cut.

Begin by marking the cutline on the panel and cutting the panels to size using a utility knife. Then snap the panel, and cut through

the fiberglass mesh on the back of the panel. Cut faucet holes using a carbide-tipped hole saw in an electric drill. When making these cuts, it is best to make the holes slightly oversized to allow for minor adjustments when you place the panel on the wall.

Screw the panels to the studs using special cement-board screws. These should be driven $\frac{1}{2}$ inch from the edges, and spaced every 4 or 5 inches. In the field of the panels, 12-inch spacing is fine, but make sure you drive the screws into a stud. To finish the joints, all that's required is to apply self-sticking fiberglass tape that you press into place over the seams of the panels. No joint compound is needed because the entire surface will be covered with tile and grout.

TOOLS & MATERIALS
- Tape measure ▌ T-square ▌ Utility knife or cement-board cutter ▌ Masonry drill bit
- Power drill with screwdriver bit and carbide-tipped hole saws ▌ Saber saw (optional)
- Fiberglass mesh tape ▌ Thinset adhesive
- Cement-based backer board
- 1½-in. galvanized cement-board screws

smart tip

FRAMING PREP

BECAUSE CEMENT BOARD IS MUCH LESS FLEXIBLE THAN DRYWALL, IT CAN CRACK WHEN SCREWED TO UNEVEN STUDS. SHIM ANY PROBLEM WALL STUDS.

1 Backer board is cut the same way as drywall. First mark the panel; then score this line using a sharp utility knife and a straightedge guide. Break the panel against your knee or over a piece of scrap wood placed on the floor.

2 Once the panel is broken, place it on its edge and cut through the fiberglass mesh on the back using a utility knife. This cut is generally rough and can be smoothed to fit using 80-grit sandpaper.

ESTIMATING QUANTITIES FOR DRYWALL

Quality drywalling requires accurate estimates of material quantities. Nothing breaks your stride like having to run out to the store for materials once you've started a job. Here are some tips on how to estimate materials.

▌**Joint Compound:** You'll need roughly a gallon for every 100 square feet of drywall.

▌**Joint Tape:** To finish 500 square feet of drywall, figure on using 400 feet of tape.

▌**Nails/Screws:** This figure can vary depending on stud spacing (walls framed 16 inches on center require more fasteners than those framed at 24 inches) and on your nail or screw schedule (panels attached with adhesive require fewer fasteners). Figure on one fastener for every square foot of drywall on your job. For example, an 18 x 18-foot ceiling (324 square feet) will require about 320 screws or nails. Because 1 pound of 1¼-inch drywall screws contains about 320 screws, you'll need a pound of screws for every 320 square feet of drywall.

▌**Drywall Panels:** Estimating how much drywall you'll need to cover a room is a matter of square footage. Calculate the wall surface of the room, and divide that figure by the square footage of the panels you intend to use. For instance, a 4 x 8-foot panel measures 32 square feet. If you have a 1,000-square-foot room, you'll need just over 31 panels. Because they come in units of two, order 32 panels.

▌**When estimating square footage,** don't subtract the door or window areas (except for bay windows or unusually large doors), because you'll need extra for mistakes.

3 Faucet holes can be cut in backer board with an electric drill and a carbide-tipped hole saw. Mark the location using a center punch, and drill slowly.

4 Attach the panels to the wall framing with 1½ in. cement-board screws. Drive them every 5 in. around the perimeter and every 12 in. in the field.

5 Cover all the joints with fiber-glass drywall tape. No joint compound is needed underneath because the tape is self-sticking.

RESURFACING A WALL

Resurfacing walls and ceilings with drywall is a great way to give a facelift to an old room. Instead of gutting a room, you just cover everything with thin drywall, usually ¼-inch-thick panels. These are special order items and can be hard to handle without breaking. But they are well worth the trouble. You can either remove the room trim before installing these panels. Or install the panels, without removing the trim, if the drywall will butt against the trim boards instead of running over them.

TOOLS & MATERIALS
▪ Hammer ▪ Pry bar ▪ Work gloves
▪ Stud sensor ▪ Tape measure ▪ Caulking gun
▪ Adhesive ▪ Drywall panels
▪ Drill/driver and drywall screws
▪ Joint compound ▪ Tape ▪ Taping knives

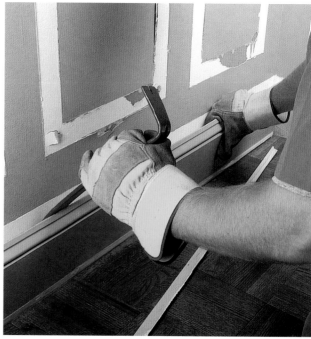

1 If you decide to remove the trim, start with the baseboard and shoe molding. Work carefully so this trim can be reinstalled later. Depending on how your trim is installed, you may be able to run the new drywall behind the baseboards and against the window and door casing boards, which would make the job much easier.

4 Press the new panels against the wall to spread the adhesive over a wider area. Then attach the panel using drywall screws, driven in a 6- to 8-in. grid. Locate butt joints over the middle of the joists and studs.

5 Finish the joints on resurfacing drywall the same way you finish standard drywall. Begin with a base coat of joint compound. Then embed paper tape in this base coat. Smooth the surface using a 6-in.-wide knife. When the compound is dry, add two more coats of compound with a 10-in. knife, letting it dry between coats.

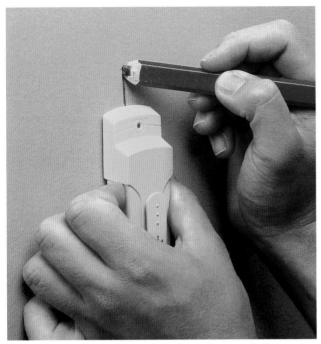

2 Use an electronic stud finder to locate all the studs and joists that will fall under the new drywall. Mark the floor, ceiling, and walls where appropriate to indicate where the framing members are.

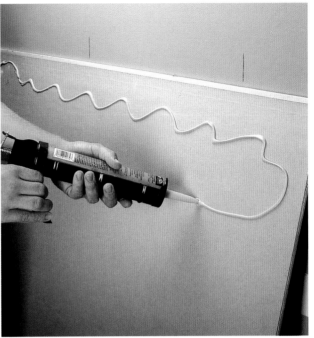

3 Apply construction adhesive to the back of the panels to improve the bond with the ceiling and walls. Use a wavy bead in a 8- to 12-in. grid. Once this glue is in place, handle the panel with care to avoid smearing the glue on your tools, yourself, and other surfaces.

● ELECTRICAL BOX EXTENDERS

1. Bring existing switch and outlet boxes flush with new drywall by adding extensions. Start by turning off the power and removing the device.

2. Add a code-approved extension to the existing box; screw the outlet or switch back in place; and turn on the power.

FINISHING DRYWALL SEAMS

project

Finishing drywall is one of those jobs that get easier with practice. The more comfortable you become with the tools and materials, the faster the finishing will go and the better results you'll get. For the beginner, the biggest problem is keeping the knives clean and the compound free of any debris. The goal is to get the smoothest possible surface after the compound is applied. So any impurities that are dragged across the surface will create deep grooves that need to be sanded out once the compound is dry.

TOOLS & MATERIALS
▌ 4-in., 6-in., and 10-in. taping knives
▌ Joint compound, tape, and compound pan
▌ 120-grit sandpaper, wood block, and sanding pole ▌ Safety glasses

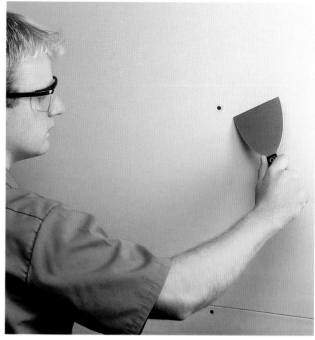

1 Begin finishing by running a taping knife over all the fasteners. If you hear a click as the knife passes over the wall, the nail or screw is too high. The goal is to be able to cover the head of the fastener with joint compound that can be sanded flush with the surrounding surface.

4 Roll out the joint tape, and press it into a corner. Then place it in the compound using your lead hand, and follow with the 4-in. knife in the other hand. Once you're comfortable with the knife and tape, you should be able to embed the tape as fast as you can walk along the wall.

5 Smooth the tape and compound with a 6-in. knife, using firm pressure to smooth out any wrinkles. Don't press too hard and risk forcing all the compound out from under the paper. If this happens, the tape will not stick to the wall when the compound dries.

2 Fill the compound pan with premixed joint compound. If you see any dried pieces of compound around the rim of the pail, remove them and throw them away. Do not try to mix these back into the pail. Use a 4-in.-wide knife to apply compound over the fastener heads. Wipe off the excess using the same knife.

3 Finish all the tapered joints first; then do the butt joints. Use a 4-in. knife to spread a base coat on the tapered joints. The goal is to fill the depression with compound and to create a bed for the paper joint tape. Scrape away any excess compound to yield a smooth surface.

6 When the tape is smooth, run the 6-in. knife along both sides of the joint to remove excess compound. The smoother you make the surface now, the less sanding you'll have to do later. Remember, it's much easier to get the compound on the wall smoothly than it is to sand it smooth after it's dry.

7 While the tapered joints are drying, sand the dried compound over the fastener heads. Use 120-grit sandpaper wrapped around a wood block. Be sure to wear eye and breathing protection when doing this job, and vacuum off the dust when you're done.

(continued on page 96)

(continued from page 95)

8 When the tapered joints are dry, use a 10-in. knife to apply the first topcoat of compound. Apply the compound so it's as smooth as possible. Then remove the excess in a couple of smooth strokes.

9 After the first topcoat is dry, lightly sand it to remove any ridges. Use a sanding block or a pole sander to cover more area faster. Don't worry about filling any gaps, the next coat of compound will take care of them.

10 Apply compound for the second and final topcoat. Your goal is to spread a 12-in.-wide coat over the joint. Smooth the middle first, then smooth each edge. Clean the knife on the edge of the pan after each pass.

11 When dry, sand all the joints using 120-grit paper. Use either a wide pole sander or a small sanding block. For best results, go over the joints one more time with 100-grit paper wrapped around a sanding block.

PREVENTING JOINT CRACKS

The main ways to prevent joint cracks that disrupt taped seams is to use stable studs that won't twist or warp. That means bypassing (or returning) unusually heavy studs that are overloaded with moisture. As the wood dries out, which may not happen until the first heating season, wet lumber can shrink and twist enough to pop nails and break open joints.

You also need to set framing carefully so that drywall panels will lie flat. Even small misalignments between standard studs or the extra framing installed around window and door openings can create ridges in the edges of drywall panels that rest on them. You could cover these errors with extra joint compound. But that can lead to cracking as thick coats dry unevenly. The best bet is to align all studs, if need be, by driving a few extra nails to shift the studs slightly one way or another before installing drywall.

Standard ½-inch-thick panels can bridge the spaces between studs. But they need full support along the panel edges. Typical framing provides continuous support along the floor and ceiling, but not always at corners. Several types of drywall clips are designed to reduce wood use and construction time by holding unsupported drywall edges together. Sometimes they work. But sometimes they don't and the corner shifts, cracking the tape and joint compound. So it's best to provide solid-wood support on all drywall edges. The time to do this, of course, if when the framing is exposed.

INSIDE AND OUTSIDE CORNERS

Standard procedure is to use paper tape where the walls form an inside corner and metal guard on corners that protrude into the room. The rationale is simple. You probably won't bang into drywall recessed behind chairs and tables but may well collide with a corner that sticks into living space. To set tape, smooth on an embedding coat, fold the tape down the center, and smooth it onto the compound with a taping knife.

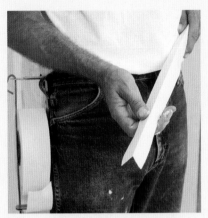

Cut a length of tape to fit, and crease it down the middle.

Set and smooth the tape into an embedding coat of compound.

A metal corner guard reinforces the corner and provides a divider so that you can easily add compound on each side. You can set the guard in plumb position and nail through both flanges. On large projects, consider renting a clincher. Frequently used by contractors, this L-shaped tool automatically positions the guard and clinches small parts of the metal strip into the drywall when you hit the tool with a mallet.

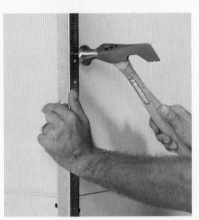

Plumb the metal corner guard before nailing it home.

Use the metal bead of the guard to guide your knife on each side.

CURVES

Almost every cut in drywall is a straight line. But some houses have a few curves—for example, over an arched pass-through. You can make these cuts in two ways. One is to measure the opening carefully, find the center of the arch on the sheet, and use a string and pencil to swing an arc. The other approach is to cut the panel in place. This is more reliable and often easier if you use a drywall saw because you can use the arch itself as a cutting guide. Drywall suppliers also offer special trim pieces to cover the cut edges of curves.

Screw a full sheet in place over the curved opening, and use a drywall saw to cut off the overlapping section.

SHEET PANELING

Many manufacturers offer a wide variety of sheet paneling including real-wood veneers bonded over sheets of plywood for easy installation, generally in $3/16$- or $1/4$-inch thickness. There are light woods, such as birch and maple, that keep a room bright as well as more traditional, darker hues, all with a subtle appearance and patina that can't be duplicated in simulated finishes. Other panels with a synthetic wood finish can't be stained or refinished, but they do look like wood if you stand far enough away from the wall.

Paneling for New Projects

Many firms that sell 4 x 8-foot sheets of paneling also offer expensive solid-wood planking. But if you want to use solid wood to create some version of a classic, raised-panel wall, it pays to use a combination of materials: thin panels (without grooves) as the main wall covering and plank paneling with different molding components to create raised frames. Manufacturers provide an array of styles but nothing even close to the depth and detail you get with solid-wood raised panels.

Prefinished real-wood veneers, sold in a wide range of wood species, are used in most paneling projects. When working with solid wood, you should stack the sheets in the work space (separated by spacers for air circulation) for two or three days before installation. This way the

ABOVE Some sheet products have molded grooves and even beaded edges that give the appearance of wood planking.

wood adapts to the surrounding temperature and humidity, reducing the chance of movement on the wall. It also helps to install panels with room for expansion at the top and bottom of the wall where gaps will be covered by strips of molding.

Working down the ladder in cost and quality of appearance, there are simulated wood grains mounted on plywood or fiberboard. These are fake wood surfaces printed, embossed, or overlaid with grain-printed paper. You install them the same way as you install real wood.

Most paneling is available in 4 x 8-foot sheets that will reach from floor to ceiling on most walls. But longer 10- and 12-foot lengths are available from some manufacturers by special order. To buy the right amount, measure the perimeter of the room, rounding out the length to the next highest 4-foot increment. Then divide by four to figure the number of panels. Usually large amounts, over 10 to 15 sheets, need to be ordered in advance.

ABOVE Standard sheet paneling with real-wood veneers generally has a grooved pattern to look like strips of solid wood.

PANELING OVER STUDS

project

High quality sheet paneling is made of good plywood that is strong and durable. When nailed directly to the wall studs, as we show here, you'll have a stable surface that looks like solid wood, at least from a couple feet away. But if you are using cheaper, fiberboard paneling, keep in mind that this product is much less substantial. To get a good job, install a layer of drywall underneath. If you'd like to include some sound-deadening in a sheet-paneled wall, then hang fiberglass batts between the studs; install drywall over the studs; and finish up by nailing the paneling over the drywall.

TOOLS & MATERIALS
▪ 4-ft. level ▪ Tape measure
▪ Saber saw ▪ Hammer ▪ Nail set
▪ Caulking gun and construction adhesive
▪ Paneling and paneling nails

1 Start in one room corner with a full sheet of paneling. Measure from the corner to the top and bottom of the stud that is 48 in. or less away. Transfer these measurements to the back of the panel, and connect the marks with a straight line. Cut along the line using a circular saw.

2 Carefully measure the location of obstructions, like this electrical outlet, and cut out the hole with a saber saw. Check the panel for proper fit, remove it, and apply construction adhesive to the studs.

3 Press the cut sheet against the wall, making sure it fits over the outlet box. Attach it using nails colored to match the paneling. Drive these into the wall studs, but don't set the nail heads below the surface.

4 Finish the paneling job by installing trim that's stained to match the paneling. Add baseboards and shoe molding to the floor and casing boards around any windows and doors.

PANELING OVER FURRING STRIPS

project

O ne of the classic remodeling jobs is to cover basement walls with wood paneling; this helps convert unfinished space into livable space. To do this job almost always requires installing furring strips on the foundation walls. Nailing wood strips to a concrete (or concrete block) wall is hard work but it can go surprisingly fast once you get started. Use 1x4 No. 2 pine boards for furring instead of the rough 1x2 material that's usually called furring. These boards are almost impossible to work with. The 1x4s provide plenty of nailing surface.

TOOLS & MATERIALS

- Furring, shims, and 10d common nails
- Hammer ▮ 4-ft. level ▮ Tape measure
- Caulking gun and construction adhesive
- Paneling and paneling nails ▮ Rubber gloves

1 The furring strips can be installed either vertically or horizontally. For this job we chose the horizontal approach for the main strips and filled in between these with shorter strips, spaced 16 in. apart. Use a level to align the strips, and attach them using masonry or cut nails.

touch-ups

Use a color-matched repair stick (available at most paneling suppliers) to conceal minor surface scars in paneling.

On deep scars, trim away any frayed wood fibers, apply wood filler, smooth the surface, and touch up with stain to blend the repair.

2 If a strip goes over a hollow spot on the wall, support the strip using shimming shingles inserted between the strip and the wall. Use a level to align the shimmed furring with the furring above or below.

SCRIBING TO AN UNEVEN SURFACE

Hold a compass in a fixed position, using one end as a guide against the wall, and draw a line to trace the irregularities of the wall on the panel.

To trace complicated cuts where panels fit around cabinets and other fixtures, use a contour gauge. Its movable pins align with the shape.

3 Complete the furring job by installing the small strips between the main horizontal strips. Leave a little space between all the furring boards to allow for expansion caused by high temperatures and humidity.

4 Apply construction adhesive to the furring; then press a sheet against the wall. Flatten it; then pull it away partially to help spread the adhesive. Press the sheet back into place.

5 Nail the panels in place using colored nails that match the surface veneer. Start in a corner, and make sure the first panel is plumb before nailing.

SOLID-WOOD PANELING

Most sheet paneling is designed to simulate individual wood planks. But nothing looks quite like the real thing. Although planking is more expensive and takes longer to install than sheets, you can use hardwoods such as birch, maple, and oak, or softwoods such as pine, cedar, or cypress. There are several styles of planks and different ways to apply them. For example, you can use shiplap planks or tongue-and-groove boards, installed horizontally, on the diagonal, or vertically over horizontal furring strips.

Plank Grades and Appearance

There is a dramatic difference in the appearance and cost of planks, depending on the grade you buy. Lumber grading can be confusing and can vary somewhat from one source to another. For softwoods, such as pine, there are three general categories for good-quality panel boards. Select lumber ranges from B or better, which has almost no flaws, to C, which has some natural flaws, and D, which has more flaws. Finish lumber is the next category, followed by common board lumber.

For hardwoods, the grading system ranges from extremely expensive woods suitable for fine furniture called first and seconds, through common grades, which generally are fine for plank paneling.

All the grading systems have the same bias. They assume that clear wood without knots and grain variations is best. It's certainly more expensive than other grades but, to some, lacks the character of a grainy birch or knotty pine that is less clear and less expensive.

ABOVE You can install solid-wood planking with tongue-and-groove seams, and stain or paint to finish.

smooth versus rough sawn

This clear grade of cedar has a smooth surface, straight grain that is easy to work, a uniform color throughout, and no visible knots or other defects.

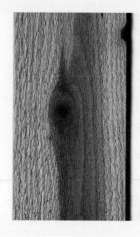

This lesser grade has a rough surface, wavier grain, distinct variations of color, and knots. But even low-cost grades have the strength required.

INSTALLING SOLID-WOOD PANELING

project

Installing solid-wood paneling, like we show on this wainscoting project, is an easy way to add real distinction to any room. And solid boards can fit any decorating scheme because they look good when painted, stained, or covered with a clear finish. The boards are usually nailed to surface-mounted horizontal furring strips. If the combined thickness of the furring and the boards extends too far into your room, you can remove the drywall or plaster from the wall and nail the furring either across the studs or between them.

TOOLS & MATERIALS
- Furring, shims, and 10d common nails
- Hammer ▪ 4-ft. level ▪ Compass
- Tape measure ▪ Saber saw
- 1x6 planking ▪ Cap molding
- Finishing nails

1 Nail horizontal furring strips to the wall, and fill any hollows behind the strips with shimming shingles. Start in one corner by placing the first board, with its tongue side against the adjacent wall, and scribing it to fit with a compass (inset). Nail it to the top and bottom furring strips.

2 Slide the groove of each succeeding board over the tongue of the previous one, and tap them together until the joint is tight. Drive a nail through the corner of the tongue into the furring.

3 Carefully measure for electrical box cutouts, or other obstructions, and mark the board accordingly. Then make the cuts with a saber saw; test fit the board; and when satisfied, nail it in place.

4 On wainscoted walls like this, where the boards don't extend all the way from the floor to the ceiling, the exposed tops of the boards must be covered with trim. Cut a piece and nail it in to the studs.

INSTALLING FLAT-PANEL WAINSCOTING

project

Y ou can choose from many different wood species when planning a flat panel wainscoting job. If you want a high-end clear or stained finish, pick the best plywood stock and chose hardwood lumber of the same species to go with it. But if you plan to paint, as we did here, you can opt for less expensive materials and still achieve a top-drawer result. We used ½-inch-thick birch plywood for the flat panels and 1x4 and 1x6 poplar for the rails and stiles.

TOOLS & MATERIALS
▌ Hammer ▌ Nail set ▌ Level
▌ Nail gun and nails (optional)
▌ Saber saw ▌ Square ▌ Power miter saw
▌ Plate joiner ▌ Power drill and bits ▌ Clamps
▌ 1x4 and 1x6 stock ▌ ½-in. birch plywood
▌ Wood glue ▌ Finishing nails ▌ Joining plates

1 Begin by installing the plywood panels on the wall. You are bound to confront some electrical boxes on this part of the job. Just carefully measure their position, and trace around a spare box (inset) to define the hole. Drill blade access holes at the corners; then cut out the waste with a saber saw.

3 Once the layout is done, remove the clamps and separate the rails. Then, using a plate joiner, cut the plate slots in the rail edges using the layout lines as a guide. Work on a firm surface, and press the board down flat so the joiner cuts the groove in the right spot. You can also join the frame parts with dowels and a drill.

4 Place the bottom rail against the plywood panel, and support it with short scrap blocks. Check the rail for level. If it needs some adjustment, slide shims under one of the blocks until it is level.

2 After the plywood is nailed to the wall, cut the top and bottom rails to size and clamp these two boards together. Lay out the position of the frame stiles on these rails, using a combination square. Also mark the location of the joining plates that are used to hold the frame parts together.

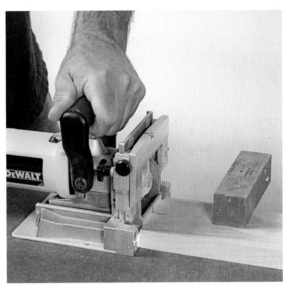

Clamp a stile to the worktable before using the plate joiner to cut slots in the end-grain. End-grain cuts are particularly liable to kick back, and this technique keeps hands far from the spinning blade.

5 Nail the bottom rail in place. We used a pneumatic nailer because it makes the work easier and faster. But hand nailing produces good results too. Drive two nails every 16 in., and set the heads below the surface with a nail set.

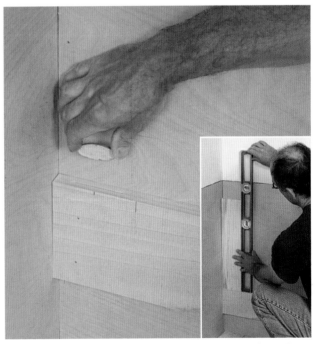

6 Spread carpenters glue in the plate slot in the rail and the matching stile. Then cover the plate with glue, and slide it into the rail slot. Place the first stile above the plate, and push it down until it is tight to the bottom rail. Check the stile for plumb (insert), and nail it in place.
(continued on page 106)

(continued from page 105)

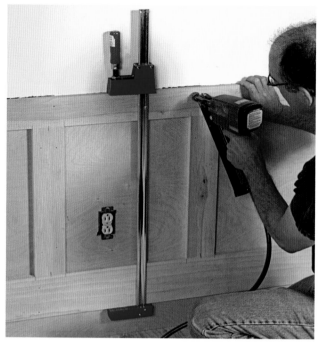

7 After all the stiles are nailed in place, apply glue to the plate slots in these stiles and in the bottom edge of the top rail. Then spread glue on the plates, and insert them in the stiles. Place the top rail onto the plates, and push it down until it is tight to the top of the stiles. Wipe away any excess glue.

8 Clamp the top rail to the bottom rail until the glue dries. Nail the rail to the plywood panel every 16 in. If you are hand nailing, set the nail heads with a nail set.

smart tip

IF YOU PLAN TO DO EXTENSIVE TRIM WORK, THE ADVANTAGES OF A PNEUMATIC NAIL GUN ARE OBVIOUS: INCREASED SPEED AND NO HAMMER MARKS. BUT EVEN FOR SMALL JOBS, THERE ARE REASONS TO CONSIDER A NAIL GUN. FIRST, THE NAILS USED IN A FINISHING NAIL GUN ARE THINNER THAN THOSE THAT YOU DRIVE BY HAND, SO THERE IS LESS CHANCE OF SPLITTING THE WOOD WHEN NAILING NEAR AN EDGE. YOU CAN ALSO ADJUST THE PRESSURE THAT DRIVES THE GUN, SO YOU CAN SET THE NAIL JUST BELOW THE SURFACE OF DIFFERENT DENSITY MATERIALS. THIS ELIMINATES THE NEED FOR DRILLING PILOT HOLES THAT ARE OFTEN NECESSARY WHEN HAND NAILING HARDWOOD BOARDS. TO DRIVE ONE OF THESE GUNS, YOU WILL NEED A COMPRESSOR. LOOK FOR AN ELECTRIC MODEL IN THE 1.5–2.5 HORSEPOWER RANGE.

11 Use the same lumber for the baseboards as you did for the rails and stiles. Cut each board to length; then nail it to the rail and the furring at the bottom of the wall. After all the baseboards are nailed in place, install the cap molding on top of the baseboards.

9 When you reach an outside corner, one of the stiles must be ripped so it's ¾ in. narrower than the mating stile. This way both walls will appear to have a full-width stile at the end. Install the rails and stiles on the second wall the same way you did on the first. And glue and nail together the corner stiles.

10 Furr out the bottom of each wall by nailing scrap strips to the plywood panel. Rip these strips from material that is the same thickness as the rail board.

12 The wainscoting cap is assembled in two pieces. First install a cove molding along the top edge of the top rail. Keep the top of the molding flush with the top of the rail. Then nail a cap molding over the rail and the cove.

13 The wainscoting can be complete at this point if you like the look of the square frames around the flat panels. You can also miter molding strips to fit inside the frame parts, and nail them in place. When you're done, lightly sand the whole installation with 120-grit sandpaper; then prime and paint.

110   WALL PREP

112   PREPARING PLASTER FOR PAINTING

113   PREPARING WOODWORK

114   PAINTING A WALL

118   WET-STRIPPING WALLCOVERING

126   INSTALLING TILE

132   INSTALLING TRIMWORK

138   INSTALLING WINDOW TRIM

142   INSTALLING DOOR TRIM

144   INSTALLING BASEBOARD TRIM

5 wall finishes

Now for the fun part. You may have spent weeks removing old walls, altering framing, and hanging new drywall. But now you can put all that dust and mess behind you. It's time to start painting and papering. This is when the new room starts to come alive. Once the walls, woodwork, and ceiling are properly prepared, you can paint just about any room in less than a day. And if you want to install wallpaper, you can wrap up a typical room in less than two days. This isn't much time to make such a dramatic difference, especially when you consider that neither painting nor papering is difficult. In fact, the hardest part of the job has nothing to do with work. The real difficulty is picking a color or pattern that you like when you choose it and when you see it on the finished wall.

WALL PREP

As is the case with many painting projects, preparation work on existing walls is the key to overall job quality.

Wash Dirty Paint. Sound but dingy paint often can be rescued by washing with mild soap or detergent and a sponge. If not, it will probably expose weak spots and clear away some of the loose chips and flakes. It's not wasted effort in any case, because after a thorough cleaning, a relatively thin roll-on coat of the same color may suffice instead of two coats, and the paint will adhere better on a clean surface.

Kill Mildew. When dinginess lingers as grey-green dots of mildew, add bleach to the cleaning solution—up to a third of the mix to handle dark areas. (Don't add bleach to detergents containing ammonia. The combination can produce hazardous fumes.) Stubborn stains may need a scrub brush instead of a sponge.

Cover Deep Stains. Surface blemishes that won't wash away can bleed through fresh paint unless you seal them under a coat of pigmented white shellac. Improve this quick-drying cover-up by first lightly sanding slick stains, such as oil paint drips from nearby trim.

Fill Deep Cracks. One thin swipe of joint compound takes care of hairlines, but to avoid repeat cracking under fresh paint, fill deep scars in stages with adequate drying time in between. On plaster, first dig out loose material, and brush the crack free of dry debris. Do the same on drywall, and trim away rough or loose edges of surface paper around the scar.

Fill Surface Cracks. Save a lot of sanding by patching with soupy, well-mixed compound. Applied from the edge of a clean putty knife, the soup will spread more evenly and lie flatter than stiff compound. You'll need to keep cleaning the knife with water.

Prime Patches. Left raw, repairs can cause the new paint film to dry unevenly by drawing in more moisture than surrounding areas. This sometimes causes adhesion problems, and almost always causes dull spots. To even up the surfaces, thin some of your paint by about a third (you don't need a special primer), and coat the patches using a brush or roller, feathering the paint edges with light strokes.

Do a Preliminary Cleanup. Wipe down walls to get rid of sanding dust that can ball up in a roller or brush and leave blemishes in the painted surface. Brush or vacuum along windowsills, tops of baseboards, and other dust

ABOVE Popular wall treatments today have random patterns and two or more overlaid colors or glazes.

collectors. If you've done a lot of sanding, also fold up the drop cloths, shake them outside, and reset them before continuing.

Complete the Setup. Remove switch and outlet cover plates, doorknobs, and other wall- or ceiling-mounted fixtures. This saves you the job of masking them and creates unobstructed surfaces that you can paint without leaving lap marks or changes in stipple. Lastly, flood the room with extra light to reveal any areas that may need more preparation work. A halogen work lamp should do the trick. When surfaces are prepared this thoroughly, slight surface imperfections you can see under bright light will disappear after you paint.

PREPARING WALLS

project

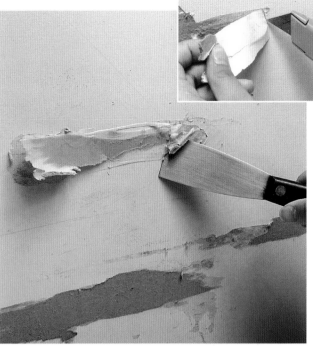

Repairing wall damage is not the only thing that needs to be done before painting. You should also remove all the light switch and receptacle cover plates, doorknobs, wall- and ceiling-mounted light fixtures, and wall-mounted heat registers. Then wash the walls (and ceilings) using a mild detergent and warm water. This will remove any dust and dirt, and make the paint stick better. If some stains still remain, cover them with a stain blocker like pigmented shellac.

TOOLS & MATERIALS
▮ Putty knife and utility knife
▮ Palm sander and dust mask
▮ Joint compound and safety goggles
▮ 10-in. drywall knife, paint, and paintbrush
▮ Stepladder (if needed)

1 Use a putty knife to scrape off any loose or flaking paint until you have a solid, smooth wall surface. Avoid digging the knife blade deeply into the gypsum core of the drywall. If the outside paper is torn (inset), cut it using a sharp utility knife so the remaining paper has a solid edge.

2 Lightly sand any damaged areas to smooth the edges; then cover the damage with joint compound. Use a 10-in. knife to get the widest and smoothest patch.

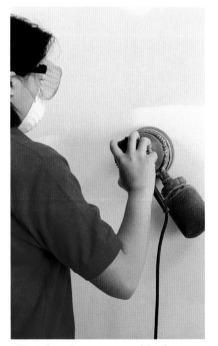

3 After the compound is dry, sand it smooth using a sanding block or an orbital sander with 120-grit sandpaper. Sanding generates a lot of dust, so be sure to wear a dust mask or respirator.

4 Wipe away any sanding dust from all the patches. Then prime each spot using primer or thinned paint. When this coat is dry, prepare the rest of the room for painting.

PREPARING PLASTER FOR PAINTING

project

Traditional plaster isn't installed in many new homes these days, but there are still a lot of old houses that have this premium finish. Serious plaster problems, such as big sagging sections of ceiling, are better left to an experienced plasterer. But smaller troubles, such as cracks in otherwise sound plaster, are easy to fix and require just a couple of common tools. Because sanding is involved, make sure to tape plastic sheeting over doorways and heat registers to keep dust from spreading around the house.

TOOLS & MATERIALS
- Utility knife or can opener
- 6-in. and 12-in. drywall knives
- Drywall joint compound
- Fiberglass mesh drywall tape

1 To fix small plaster cracks, first clean out the crack and slightly undercut both sides using a sharp tool, such as a utility knife or a can opener. Brush any dust out of the crack; then fill it with patching plaster. When the plaster is dry, sand it smooth to the surrounding surface.

2 Fix wider cracks by cleaning them out first, and then filling them with patching plaster. Let the plaster dry, and sand it smooth. Then cover the crack with self-sticking fiberglass mesh tape. Flatten the tape using your fingertips.

3 Cover the mesh tape with two or three coats of patching plaster. Feather the edges of each coat away from the tape to make a gradual transition to the rest of the wall. Sand each coat smooth before adding another.

PREPARING WOODWORK FOR PAINTING

project

The way to prepare wood trim for painting depends on the condition of the trim. If you are reusing old boards that have nicked or deeply scratched paint, you'll have to fill all holes and cracks with wood filler. Then sand the boards smooth so the filler won't be apparent when the boards are repainted, and clean up all the dust. If you are working on new boards, proceed as shown in this project.

TOOLS & MATERIALS
▌ Hammer and nail set
▌ Putty knife
▌ Wood filler
▌ Caulk and caulking gun
▌ Primer
▌ Narrow paint brush

1 Set all nailheads below the surface of the trim boards using a hammer and nail set. Fill the depressions above the set nails with wood filler. If you plan to use a clear finish, choose a colored filler that matches the wood. If you plan to paint, any type of wood filler can be used.

2 Once all the nailholes are filled, caulk all the joints between the trim boards and the walls and ceilings. Use latex caulk, and try to apply a smooth bead. Finish the caulk by running a wet finger over the bead.

3 After the caulking is done, apply a latex or alkyd primer. Use smooth brush strokes to achieve the best surface. After the primer is dry, lightly sand any rough areas. Then wipe up the dust and apply a topcoat of paint.

PAINTING A WALL

Unless you are painting a very small wall, using just a brush takes a long time. The better approach is to use a brush to paint around the perimeter of the wall; then cover the bulk of the area with a roller. The best brush for trim work is a 2½-inch-wide model. And the best roller is a 9-inch-wide unit with a threaded handle so an extension pole can be screwed into the end. If you use latex paint for interior work, water is all that's required for cleanup. A good paint pan and a sturdy 6- or 8-foot-high stepladder are other essentials.

TOOLS & MATERIALS
- Drop cloths and work lamp
- Screwdriver ▪ Paint and trim brush
- Paint roller and extension pole
- Paint roller and paint pan

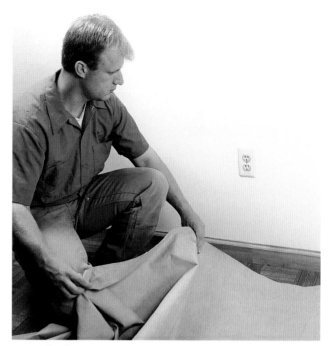

1 The first step in painting any room is to protect the things inside. Small items should be taken out and stored elsewhere. Larger pieces of furniture should be moved to the middle of the room and covered with plastic sheeting. Then cover the floor space under each wall with disposable drop cloths.

4 Start applying paint by cutting-in around the ceiling and trimwork using a 2½-in.-wide sash brush. Load the brush full; then wipe off the excess paint; and apply it with slow, smooth strokes.

5 Once the first strip of paint is applied around the trim, brush it out using strokes made at right angles to the first. Your goal is a smooth strip that's about 3 to 4 in. wide. This will provide plenty of room for a roller to work without smearing paint on the side of the trim.

2 Remove all receptacle and light-switch cover plates before starting to paint. Be sure to turn off the power to these circuits at the service panel before taking off the plates. Also remove wall-mounted heat registers and any wall- or ceiling-mounted light fixtures.

3 Having plenty of light in the room while you are painting makes it easier to apply paint smoothly. Brush and roller marks are more apparent and can be blended together before they dry. If you are using house lamps, be sure to remove the shades to get the brightest light. Or use work lights if you have them.

6 Once all the cutting-in is done, start rolling paint onto the wall. To do this, fill the well of the paint pan; then load the roller so it's full of paint. Run it over the pan ridges to force paint into the nap and spread the paint evenly onto the roller cover.

7 Begin rolling at the top of the wall and move down. By using an extension pole, as shown, you can roll a typical wall by standing on the floor instead of on a stepladder. Roll slowly so the cover doesn't spray paint onto any adjacent surfaces. *(continued on page 116)*

(continued from page 115)

8 Reload the roller and apply a second strip of paint, about 12 in. away from the first one. This time, start at the bottom of the wall and roll to the top. By working in pairs of strips, each section of wall will have about the same amount of paint at the top, middle, and bottom.

9 Spread the paint from these two strips into the unpainted areas by rolling from side to side. This should cover all the blank areas. But if some spots are still bare, add a little paint to the roller and cover these spots, blending in the adjacent strokes.

10 Finish up the general rolling by using an empty roller in long smooth strokes from the top of the wall to the bottom. Work from one side of the wall to the other. Shine a bright light on the wall to check that the roller laps aren't visible.

11 If a final inspection shows bare spots that are still coming through, partially load the roller with paint and cover the spot. Make sure to feather the roller strokes into the adjacent paint. Then reduce the pressure, and gently lift the roller off the wall.

DECORATIVE PAINT TECHNIQUES

Many decorative painting techniques offer more depth and interest than a plain painted wall. Some involve glazes and other materials that take time to master. But several, including the five shown here, are easy to do, particularly if you take the time to test the application on a sample piece of drywall to see how much of the secondary color you want to apply. In a nutshell, you can use a natural sea sponge to create a dappled finish, a rolled up rag to lay on a second or third coat for extra texture, or a combing tool to drag lines in a second coat to reveal the undercoat. Stippling blends one tone with another with a wide brush, while spattering adds dots of color to a top coat as you tap on the brush.

Sponging

Ragging

Combing

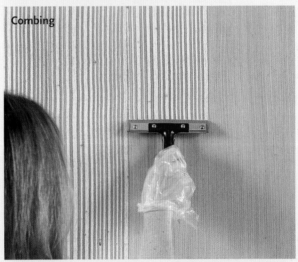

Stippling

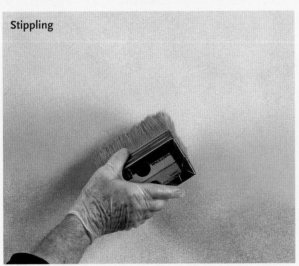

Spattering

WET-STRIPPING WALLCOVERING

Although some people paint and paper over old wallpaper, it's generally considered an inferior approach. The better idea is to remove the existing paper. To do this, first score the paper; then wet the surface with a steamer. Pull loosened paper off the wall with your hands or a paint scraper. Finish up by cleaning the walls with a sponge soaked in cleaning solution.

TOOLS & MATERIALS
▌ Scoring tool ▌ Rubber gloves
▌ Safety goggles ▌ Utility pail
▌ Steamer (may be rented or purchased)
▌ Wallpaper scraper
▌ Sponges or rags
▌ Phosphate-free trisodium
▌ Wallcovering remover

1 The first step in removing wallpaper is to score the surface using a scoring tool. This tool is usually shaped like a triangle with round disks at each corner. These disks have toothed wheels that perforate the wallcovering without damaging the drywall or plaster underneath.

3 Once the wallpaper starts to loosen, grab one corner and pull it down the wall at a shallow angle. Don't try to pull the paper off quickly because it will tear. A slow steady motion will yield better results.

4 Some stubborn papers will not pull cleanly from the walls. Help to loosen these papers using a paint scraper. Hold the tool at a shallow angle, and don't be too aggressive or you risk damaging the wall. If the paper won't budge, wet or steam it again.

2 You can simply wet the perforated surface to loosen the wallpaper. But using a rented steamer makes the job go much faster. The steamer plate directs steam into the wallpaper and breaks the glue bond. Don't hold the plate in one area for more than 15 minutes.

5 When all the wallpaper is off, clean the entire surface using a sponge soaked in phosphate-free trisodium and warm water. Be sure to wear rubber gloves, and rinse the sponge frequently. Let the walls dry for about a week before painting or installing new paper.

OTHER REMOVAL METHODS

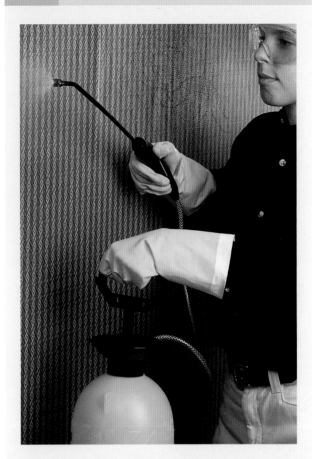

If you can't locate a steamer to rent, you can still wet-strip wallcovering by using a pail or garden sprayer. Here's how:

▌**With a pail:** Fill the pail with a mixture of hot tap water and wallcovering remover. (Follow the manufacturer's recommended proportions.) Cover the floor with a waterproof tarp sealed at the edges with tape. Protect your hands with latex gloves; then dip a rag or sponge into the pail; and rub the wallcovering with it. Be sure to soak the material well before scraping it off—the wetter, the better.

▌**With a garden sprayer:** First score the wallcovering as shown at left (Step 1). Then fill a sprayer (that has been thoroughly cleaned) with a mixture of hot tap water and wallcovering remover, following the manufacturer's instructions. Use the sprayer to saturate the wallcovering with the mixture. Then scrape off the wallcovering.

WALLCOVERING BASICS

Wallcovering includes a wide range of products, from traditional paper to treated fabrics and fabric-backed vinyl, paper-backed grass cloths, and even more exotic variations. For high-traffic areas such as kitchens and playrooms, look for a covering that withstands scuffs and cleans easily, such as solid vinyl.

Preparing for a Project

Most wallcoverings now come prepasted, but some types still must be pasted strip by strip as they go up. If you have a choice, choose the prepasted paper. Installation is easier, and there is less of a chance of problems developing. Both types must be applied to a clean, smooth surface. Cover unfinished drywall with a wallcovering primer/sealer. If your room's walls are already papered and the covering is still sound, you can probably scuff the surface with sandpaper to promote adhesion and apply a new wallcovering right over it. Check this with your wallcovering dealer before making a decision. It's frequently necessary to apply a wallcovering primer/sealer or to strip an old covering completely.

Planning the Job

Wallcovering is sold in rolls of various widths. Because patterned coverings must be matched side to side along the edges of the strips, there may be a fair amount of waste in trimming to keep the pattern repeating properly.

To estimate material needs, determine the number of square feet in the area to be covered (less openings like windows, doors, and any wall space taken up by cabinets), then divide by 30—a number derived by subtracting the likely wastage from the standard 36 square feet in a roll. Round up to the nearest whole number for ordering standard rolls. If you're buying other than standard 36-square-foot rolls, consult your dealer about how many you need.

The repeating pattern in wallcovering also requires careful planning of where the covering job should start and end. Theoretically, you can start the first strip anywhere as long as the pattern lines up as you apply each strip. But it is often best to begin in an inconspicuous corner, say behind a door. That way any mismatch that comes when you try to align the pattern from the last sheet with the one from the first strip will be less noticeable.

Cutting Wallcovering

Because wallcovering comes in rolls, it must always be cut to fit the height of the wall. Always use sharp cutting tools. To cut a piece of wallcovering to length, add about 2 inches to the wall height to allow for overlap at the top and bottom. This lets you adjust a sheet to match the pattern. You will trim to fit exactly once it is on the wall.

Long cuts on wallcovering should be marked at both ends, measuring from the edge that will meet the piece already on the wall. Measure at the top and bottom of the wall because corners are rarely plumb.

USING WALLPAPER PASTE

These days most wallcoverings come prepasted. To install them, just dip the pieces in a tub of water to activate the adhesive; then hang them on the wall. However, some papers need paste applied to the back. Paste comes in two forms: a ready-mixed liquid and a dry powder form that has to be mixed with water. The choice depends on personal preference. Experienced wallpaper hangers often pick the powered form so they can mix the paste to the consistency they like.

TOOLS & MATERIALS
- Pasting brush
- Clean, flat work table
- Wallpaper paste
- Wallpaper

1 Paste is available in premixed liquid form or in powder form that has to be mixed with water. If you mix your own, add the powder to the water, while stirring continuously, until the mix reaches a viscous consistency.

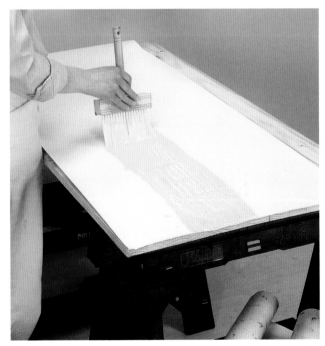

2 Roll the paper out onto a clean, flat worktable, and spread the paste on the back side using a pasting brush. Start at the middle, and work toward both sides. The best way to keep most of the paste off the table is to align two edges of the paper with the edges of the table.

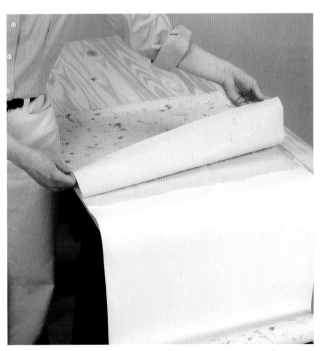

3 Fold the pasted section of the strip onto itself, a process that is called booking, and paste the remaining section of paper as shown in step 2. Take care when folding and moving the paper to avoid tearing it.

HANGING WALLPAPER

There are several common sense keys to successful wallpaper hanging. Work with a sharp utility knife; change the blade after just a couple of cuts. Keep your worktable clean and free of paste or adhesive. Make sure the outside of each strip of paper is cleaned with a damp sponge before you hang another piece in place. And handle the paper gently.

TOOLS & MATERIALS

- ▌4-ft. level ▌Tape measure
- ▌Utility knife with extra blades ▌Scissors
- ▌Long straightedge ▌6-in. taping knife
- ▌Smoothing brush ▌Sponge
- ▌Seam roller ▌Seam adhesive
- ▌Prepasted wallpaper
- ▌Wallpaper trough

1 To establish a starting line, take a sample piece of the new paper and hold it against the wall with one end folded ½ in. past the inside corner. Mark where the straight end of the paper falls on the wall.

RIGHT Vinyl wallcoverings make a good choice for kitchen walls. There are numerous colors and patterns from which to choose, and the paper itself is easy to keep clean. Consider a complementary border treatment.

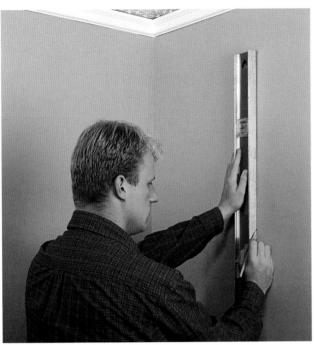

2 Use a 4-ft. level to mark a starting line on the wall. Draw the line from the floor to the ceiling, making sure that the line is exactly plumb along its entire length.

3 Cut a piece of prepasted paper to length; then roll it up loosely; and lower it into a tub of lukewarm water. Slowly pull the paper out of the tub, and spread it across a clean worktable. If you pull the paper out too quickly, the water may not have time to completely activate all the paste.

4 Fold the wet paper onto itself from both directions. This is called booking the paper and makes it easier to carry and install than trying to work with a long, unwieldy strip of wet paper.

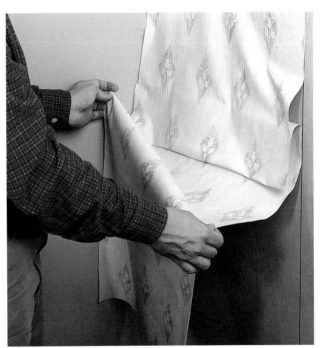

5 After the paper sets up according to the manufacturer's directions, carry it to the wall; peel away the top section; and press it against the wall. Make sure that one edge of the piece turns the corner slightly. Handle the paper carefully to avoid tearing it.

(continued on page 124)

(continued from page 123)

6 Align the strip with the plumb line that is drawn on the wall. Start the strip slightly away from the line, and gently push it over to the line. Leave excess paper at the top and bottom of the wall so that you can make the finished cuts.

7 Use a smoothing brush to remove any air bubbles from under the paper. Work from the center of the paper toward the edges in slow, firm strokes. But don't bear down so hard that you distort or tear the paper.

8 Trim the strip to length by first pressing a taping knife against the wall to create a crease. Then cut along the edge of the taping knife using a sharp utility knife. Use the same technique to cut the top of the paper against the ceiling.

9 Hang the next strip on the wall, and make sure any pattern lines up properly. Keep in mind that the paste doesn't set up immediately. You have time to manipulate the paper, either to push it against the first strip or adjust the seam.

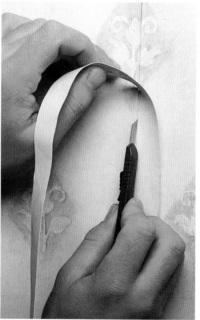

10 On pieces that overlap, use a sharp knife to cut through both strips at once. Discard the top piece; then lift the seam and pull out the other cut piece from underneath. Cutting both pieces like this creates a perfect seam.

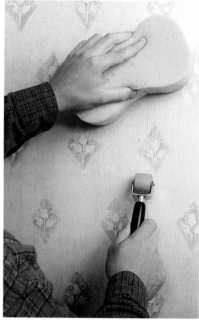

11 Roll the cut seams flat using a wallpaper roller. Use a damp sponge to wipe away any paste or adhesive from the surface. Also clean away any adhesive from the baseboard or the ceiling that may have rubbed off the paper.

PAPERING INSIDE CORNERS

project

Corners, both inside and outside, are easy to paper. The only real trick is always drawing a new plumb line on the second wall. By hanging the first sheet on this wall so that it's plumb, and cutting the other side of it to match the piece that's already installed, all the ensuing pieces on the second wall will fit correctly, even if the corner itself is out of plumb.

TOOLS & MATERIALS

▌ 4-ft. level ▌ Tape measure
▌ Long straightedge
▌ Utility knife with extra blades
▌ Scissors ▌ 6-in. taping knife
▌ Smoothing brush ▌ Sponge
▌ Seam roller ▌ Seam adhesive

smart tip

PAPERING OUTSIDE CORNERS

FOR WRAPPING OUTSIDE CORNERS, FOLLOW THE SAME PROCEDURE YOU USED FOR INSIDE CORNERS, BUT ADD ½ INCH TO THE MEASUREMENT. PLACE THE PAPER IN POSITION, BUT BEFORE WRAPPING IT AROUND THE CORNER, MAKE SMALL SLITS IN THE WASTE PORTIONS OF THE PAPER NEAR THE CEILING AND THE BASEBOARD. THE CUTS WILL ALLOW YOU TO TURN THE CORNER WITHOUT WRINKLING OR TEARING THE PAPER. HANG THE REMAINDER OF THE CUT SHEET SO THAT IT OVERLAPS THE FIRST PORTION. IF THE CORNER IS OUT OF PLUMB, DRAW A NEW PLUMB LINE ON THE SECOND WALL OF THE CORNER, AND ALIGN THE STRIP WITH THAT FIRST.

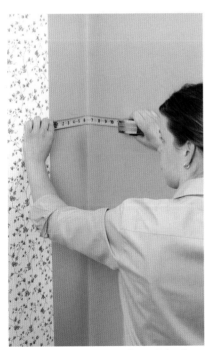

1 Measure to the edge of the last full sheet into the corner at the top, middle, and bottom of the wall. Cut the paper ⅛ in. wider than the widest measurement.

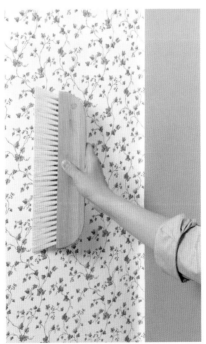

2 Hang the cut piece, and smooth it into place using a wallpaper brush. This piece should turn the corner slightly.

3 Draw a plumb line on the second wall that matches the width of the waste piece left when the first sheet was cut. Align this piece with the plumb line, and smooth it in place.

PLANNING THE LAYOUT FOR WALL TILES

project

Ceramic tile is a great wall finish for damp or wet areas like kitchens and bathrooms. And it's a frequent choice for laundry rooms and mudrooms. When properly installed, it's impervious to water and provides another design texture that livens up just about any room. Even though tiling a wall can be time consuming, it's not difficult work. One big reason: adhesives that are formulated to hold the tiles in place while the adhesives are still wet. This means the tiles can be installed without sagging or coming loose while the adhesive dries.

TOOLS & MATERIALS

- Layout board and marker
- Level
- Chalk line
- Tape measure

1 Prepare a layout board by marking lines on the face and edge that match the size of your tiles plus the grout joint. Then hold the board against the center of the wall, and transfer the layout marks to the wall.

4 Join the level marks at both ends of the wall using a chalk line. Drive a small nail in both marks; then hang one end of the chalk line to one nail. Wrap the other end around the second nail, and pull it tight. Then snap the string in the middle to leave a clear line.

5 Use your layout board to mark the tile increments on the chalk line. Then use a level to establish plumb marks at the top and bottom of the wall. The logical place to make this line is next to your layout marks.

2 When the layout reaches the ceiling, check the distance between the last mark and the ceiling to find out what size tile will fit in this space. A piece that's at least as big as half a tile will look best. If you wind up with a small piece, split the difference with the bottom row of tile at the floor.

3 Once you have established the final tile layout between the floor and ceiling, determine the layout from side to side. To do this, use a 4-ft. level to carry one of the layout lines to both ends of the wall. Do this in several steps, or just hold the level on top of a long straight board that spans the whole wall.

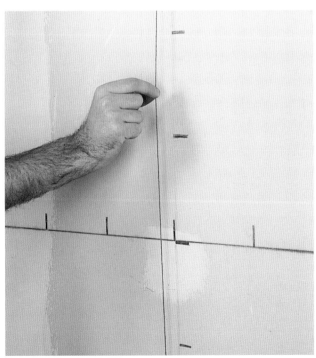

6 As you did with the horizontal guideline, drive nails through the plumb marks at the top and bottom of the wall. Then hang a chalk line on these nails and snap a clean line. Use the same process to establish other guidelines you may need for trim pieces.

7 Before starting to install the tile, mark the location on the floor of any important framing fixtures that are hidden behind the drywall. Examples are reinforcement blocks for grab bars, towel racks, or other specialized fixtures that you plan to hang on the finished wall.

INSTALLING WALL TILE

project

Installing tile is not difficult, but it can be time-consuming. Because of this, be sure to read the container label on your adhesive to find out what its "open time" is. This refers to how long the material can be exposed to the air before it starts to dry out and won't hold the tile. The best approach is to start by applying the adhesive to a small area—for example a 2 x 2-ft. square—and noting how long it takes you to get the tile in place. If you are well within the open time limitations, enlarge your working area for the next stage.

TOOLS & MATERIALS
■ Tape measure spirit ■ Level ■ Hammer
■ Nails ■ Tape ■ Putty knife ■ Notched trowel
■ Adhesive ■ Tiles ■ Spacers
■ Grout ■ Rubber float ■ Sponge

1 Establish a level baseline near the bottom of the wall using your layout lines as a guide. You can either snap a chalk line or use a 4-ft. level (as shown here) and mark a line from one end of the wall to the other.

4 Gently push each tile into the adhesive, twisting it slightly to ensure complete contact. Note how the first course rests on pairs of drywall nails.

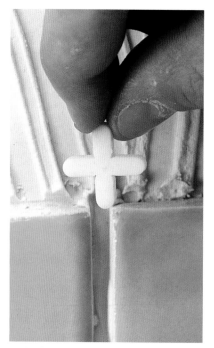

5 If your tiles have lugs on the sides that act as self-spacers, the proper grout joints are automatically formed. Otherwise, use small plastic spacers to keep the tiles aligned.

6 When you finish the rest of the wall, and the adhesive has started to dry, remove the support nails and install the bottom tiles. Tape them to the tiles above until the adhesive dries.

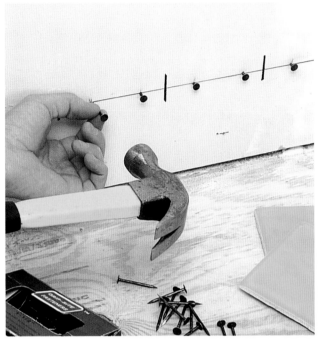

2 Adhesive is formulated to prevent tiles from sagging while it dries. But it's a good idea to support the bottom row of tiles anyway. You can screw a straight board to the wall and place the tiles on the top edge of the board. Or, you can drive two drywall nails for each tile in the wall, as we show here.

3 Use a notched trowel to apply the tile adhesive to the wall. The adhesive packaging will explain how deep the trowel notches should be. A typical recommendation is 3/16 in. Cover a wall area no bigger than what can be comfortably completed before the adhesive dries.

7 Once the wall is dry, mix up some tile grout and spread it on the wall with a rubber-faced float. Use firm, diagonal strokes to force the grout into the joints. Try to minimize the grout you leave on the face of the tile because it will be hard to remove later.

8 No matter how careful you are, the grouting process always leaves behind a haze on the tile. To remove this, use a large sponge that's frequently dipped in clean water. It can take several passes to clean the tile using water. Once the surface dries, buff it using a clean cloth to remove any leftover haze.

INSTALLING BRICK FACING

If you like the look of brick or stone and would like to use it inside your house, consider products called facing brick and facing stone. These materials are much thinner and lighter that the full-size versions so they can be installed just like ceramic tile, using either thinset mortar or mastic adhesive. No extra wall or floor support is required. These products are usually real brick and stone. But some manufacturers offer composite products that look like the real thing.

TOOLS & MATERIALS
- Notched trowel and mason's trowel
- Ceramic tile adhesive
- Brick facing
- Plywood strip and mason's string
- Grout bag ▪ Jointing tool

1 Carefully read the manufacturer's instructions to determine the proper way to lay out the wall. Make sure that the installation is centered on the wall, both vertically and horizontally, and that no perimeter tile is less than half a full-size tile. Spread adhesive on a small area with a notched trowel.

3 Before the adhesive sets, check all the joint spaces with a piece of ¼- or ⅜-in-thick plywood. Make any small adjustments by pushing the tile with your fingers. If a tile moves back after being adjusted, hold it in place with a few small plywood spacers.

4 Stop after installing three or four courses and check for straightness and level. Stretch a string from one end of the wall to the other; make sure it's level; then sight over the string to the top of each brick. Make sure the top of the brick is at the same height as the string.

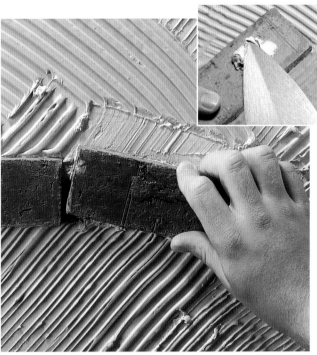

2 Place several dabs of adhesive on the back of a brick (inset). Then press it against the wall, and give it a slight twist to embed it in the adhesive. Continue installing tiles, maintaining the proper spacing between tiles as you go.

● STONE FACING

Most face stones are synthetic but made with irregular shapes that must be roughly aligned.

Stagger joints from one course to the next; string a line as a guide; and check every few courses with a level.

5 Let the adhesive set according to the manufacturer's instructions. Then remove all spacers and mix up a batch of grout. Fill a grout bag and use it to squeeze grout between the bricks. Work neatly to avoid spreading the grout on the face of the bricks.

6 Before the grout hardens, smooth the joints with a steel jointing tool or a wood dowel. Most people prefer a concave grout joint. But you can form a square recessed grout joint using a flat jointing tool.

MAKING BASIC SCARF JOINTS

The joint that is most often associated with interior trim work is the miter. This 45-degree joint is designed to bring together two boards that meet at a right (90-degree) angle. But the most common joint is actually the scarf joint. This is used wherever you want to join two boards in a straight line. When done properly, it can be almost invisible, especially if the boards end up being primed and painted. Because this joint is used so frequently, it's a good idea to master it, following the steps shown here, before you tackle any bigger trim jobs.

TOOLS & MATERIALS
- Miter saw ▌Base and shoe molding
- Glue and brush ▌Drill and bits
- Hammer ▌Nail set and finishing nails
- Wood filler ▌Sandpaper and block

1 Start a scarf joint by cutting a 45-deg. miter at one end of a board. You can use a power miter box, as shown here, or a hand-powered miter box. Keep in mind that the joint will be only as good as the cuts you make on the mating boards.

4 Drive the nails through the pilot holes and into the framing members behind. Set the nailheads below the surface with a nail set. Make the recesses at least $1/16$ in. deep.

5 If you are going to stain or apply a natural finish, then select a wood filler that is the same color as the wood. If the surface is going to be painted, any color filler will do. Force the filler into the nailholes and into any gaps in the joint. Rub the filler with your fingers to smooth it out.

2 Attach the cut board to the wall by driving 6d-finishing nails along the bottom edge into the wall plate. Nail the top of the board into the wall studs, usually spaced 16 in. apart. Spread yellow carpenters glue onto the miter cut with a small disposable brush.

3 Cut a matching miter joint on the end of the second board; then cut the board to length. Spread glue on this miter cut, too. Then push the board in place so the joint is flush. Drill pilot holes through the boards for finishing nails.

6 Once the filler is dry, sand it smooth with a sanding block covered with 120-grit sandpaper. Also sand the scarf joint so that both boards are flush. Brush off or vacuum up the sanding dust.

7 Once the baseboards are installed, they are usually covered with a shoe molding that is pressed tight to the floor. This second molding will cover any spaces between the baseboard and the floor. The shoe is installed with scarf joints just like the baseboards.

STILE AND RAIL WAINSCOTING

There are many different wainscotings. One of the most popular is made of beaded wainscot boards. This traditional approach was usually reserved for kitchens, bathrooms, and porches. For other interior rooms, a raised panel approach was considered preferable. While a traditional version can be expensive and time-consuming to install, an easier approach (shown here) yields the same basic results with less time and money. All that's required is to glue a ¼-in.-thick piece of birch plywood to the wall; then cover it with a framework of rails and stiles.

TOOLS & MATERIALS
- Combination square
- Lumber ∎ Wood glue
- Biscuit joiner and biscuits
- Mallet ∎ Tapping block ∎ Clamps

1 Begin by cutting ¼-in. birch plywood to size and gluing it to the wall using construction adhesive. Make sure the panel is flat and smooth. Then cut the rails and stiles that will form frames on the panel to size. Set the boards on a flat surface so they are square to each other, and mark a registration line across the joint.

2 Use a biscuit joiner to cut grooves in the edge of both boards. This half-moon-shaped groove is designed to receive a compressed wood joining biscuit that will hold the joints together. Wood dowels can do the same job if you don't have, and don't want to buy, a biscuit joiner.

3 Spread glue in the slots in both boards; push a biscuit into one groove; and slide the boards together. Line up the registration marks; check the joint for square; then apply clamps to pull the joint tight.

INSTALLING A CHAIR RAIL

project

Flat panel wainscotings, like the type shown on the facing page, are usually topped with a chair rail. Traditionally these boards were installed to protect walls from damage caused by chairs. These days, chair rails are considered decorative and don't always have to be built as part of a wainscoting job. They can also stand on their own. When they are installed this way, the wall below the chair rail is often painted a different color than the rest of the wall, or covered with a different color and pattern of wallpaper.

TOOLS & MATERIALS
- Chalk line ▮ Tape measure
- Lumber ▮ Miter saw ▮ Wood glue
- Nail gun and nails (optional)

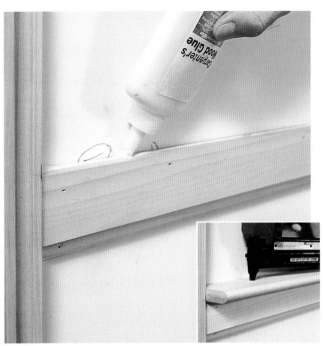

1 Snap a chalk line on the wall at the planned height; then nail a 1x2 or 1x4 to the wall underneath this line. Apply glue to the top of this rail board; then cut and nail the cap board to the top of the rail. Use either a hammer and finishing nails or a finishing nail gun if you have one (inset).

MAKING TIGHT MITERS

A properly adjusted miter box with a sharp blade should provide clean-edged cuts. But you can gain an advantage (and improve slightly inaccurate cuts) by undercutting the miter with a block plane. That way, the surfaces of the boards close first and close tightly.

Clamp the board, and shave the lower part of the edge with a block plane.

Leave the top edges of the boards intact so that they meet in a tight joint.

2 Finish off the chair rail installation by nailing a cove molding underneath the cap board. This molding is both decorative and structural; it helps support and strengthen the wider cap board.

INSTALLING WALL FRAMES

Preassembling wall frames, and attaching them to bare walls, is a great way to dress up any room. This is not a difficult job, but it does demand careful layout. The best approach is to create a design on graph paper before you cut any wood. This gives you a chance to experiment until you find just what you want. Keep in mind some general rules. Frames that are narrow and high tend to make the wall look shorter and the ceiling look higher. Wider and shorter frames, on the other hand, tend to make the wall look longer and the ceiling look lower.

TOOLS & MATERIALS
- Plywood ▮ Wall frame molding ▮ Drill-driver
- Screws ▮ Clamps ▮ Tape measure
- Wood glue and construction adhesive
- Spacer block ▮ Nail gun and nails ▮ Torpedo

1 Once you decide on the size of your wall frames, make an assembly jig by screwing together two pieces of plywood. The top piece defines the interior dimensions of the frame and the bottom piece supports the boards while they are being nailed together using a nail gun (inset).

ABOVE Install wall frames as independent units on a bare wall, or include them as decorative accents instead of solid wainscoting below chair rails and windowsills for a traditional look.

2 Snap level chalk lines around the room, and nail the chair rail boards to the walls. Then cut a scrap block to match the measurement between the bottom of the chair rail and the top of the frames. Slide this block along the chair rail while holding a pencil to the wall to draw a layout line.

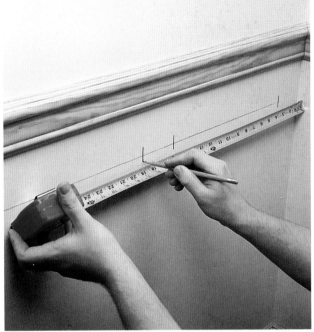

3 Using your graph paper layout, mark the location of all the frames on the surface of the wall. Once you have marked all these locations, go back and check the spacing between frames to make sure all of them are consistent.

4 Spread a thin coat of construction adhesive to the back of the frame. Then nail the top of the frame to the wall using the layout block as a support board. A nail gun is the preferred tool for this job.

5 Check one side of the frame for plumb with a torpedo level. Once the frame is plumb, nail it in place. Then move to the other side of the frame; check for plumb; and attach the frame to the wall.

6 Nail the bottom of the frame to the wall. Then fill all the nailholes with wood filler. Let the filler dry, and sand it flush to the surrounding surface using 120-grit sandpaper.

INSTALLING WINDOW TRIM

Although window trim is not difficult to install, it does take time because there are so many different pieces involved. For a traditional treatment, this means one stool, one apron, two rosettes, two leg casings, and one head casing for a typical total of seven boards. And, if your existing windows jambs don't extend to the outside surface of your wall, you'll have to add three extension jambs before you do anything else. This brings the board total to 10. Take your time with each one and you'll get good results.

TOOLS & MATERIALS

- Basic carpentry tools ▮ Router and bits
- Saber saw ▮ Power miter saw ▮ Table saw
- Nailing gun and nails (optional)
- ⁵⁄₄ sill stock ▮ Finishing nails ▮ Wood glue
- Casing and apron stock ▮ Rosette blocks

1 If you need extension jambs, nail these to the front edge of the window side and head jambs. Hold each casing board to its jamb, and mark its outside edge on the wall. Then make another mark ¾ in. away. This second mark establishes the end of the stool board.

ABOVE The horns of a window stool extend beyond the casing.

4 To establish the finished width of the stool, place a casing scrap on the stool with its back on the notch line. Mark the stool on the front edge of the casing board, and make a second mark ¾ in. from the first mark. Rip the stool along this second mark using a table saw or a circular saw with a rip guide.

2 Cut the stool to length, and hold it in place against the window. Use a square and sharp pencil to mark the inside dimension of the window jamb on both ends of the stool. Then use a combination square to measure the depth of the notches that must be cut in the stool so it can fit against the window (inset).

3 Mark the notches in both ends of the stool with a combination square and a pencil. Set the square to the depth of the notch; then slide it along the edge of the stool holding a pencil against the edge of the blade.

5 Once the stool is ripped to width, cut out the wall notch at both ends using a saber saw or a handsaw. Cut slowly to get a smooth, straight cut.

6 Some stools require more modifications before they can be installed. If this is the case with your window, hold the stool in place, and mark any required notches, like the one around the window stop above.

7 Some windows also require a rabbet along the edge of the stool where it meets the sill. This rabbet can be cut with a table saw or a router.

(continued on page 140)

139

(continued from page 139)

8 Once you've made all the necessary modifications to the stool, slide it into place, and check the clearance between the stool and the window sash. The gap should be about 1/32 in., which is the thickness of a piece of cardboard on the back of a writing tablet.

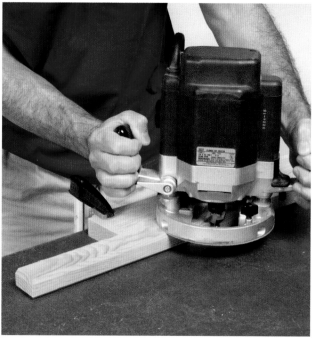

9 Shape the outside and end edges of the stool using a router. Usually this is done with a chamfering bit, like we show here. But a rounding-over bit or an ogee bit works too. Some people prefer a simple square edge that is rounded over slightly using 120-grit sandpaper wrapped around a wood sanding block.

13 Place a rosette on top of the casing board, and adjust it so it overhangs an equal amount on both sides of the casing. Its inside corner should be flush with the corner of the side and head jambs.

14 Install the leg casing and rosette on the other side of the window; then measure between the two rosettes; and cut the head casing to length. Nail it to the head jamb and to the wall framing.

15 Cut the apron board to length with a miter on both ends. Then cut a small mitered return for both ends of the apron and glue these in place. Hold the return with masking tape until the glue dries.

10 Use 8d finishing nails to attach the stool to the window jamb or sill. Before driving the nails, put a level on the stool to check for level and flatness. If necessary, shim the stool with cedar shingles.

11 Once the stool is level and nailed to the sill, drill pilot holes in both horns, and nail them to the wall framing using 8d or 10d finishing nails.

12 Hold a piece of leg casing on top of the stool and against the jamb. Mark a cut line at the top of the casing that is flush with the under side of the head jamb. Cut and nail the casing.

16 Hold the apron against the bottom of the stool and check it for fit. If there is a gap in the middle, use a sharp block plane to trim the top edge. Nail the apron in place using finishing nails or a nail gun.

WINDOW CASING ASSEMBLY

Head Casing

Rosette

Leg Casing

Stool (Sill)

DETAIL A

Stool

Horn

Apron

Apron

A

141

INSTALLING A COLONIAL DOOR CASING

Doors can be trimmed out with the same traditional components that are shown for windows on the previous four pages. Or they can be trimmed with simple colonial casing boards, which is the standard approach for most new houses. The biggest difference between the two is that this system features mitered joints where the leg and head casings meet. "Clamshell" moldings, sometimes called "ranch" moldings, are a common alternative to colonial trim boards. These boards are even plainer than colonial stock and are best for modern interiors.

TOOLS & MATERIALS
▌Hammer ▌Combination square
▌Power miter saw ▌Nail set
▌Clamshell or ranch casing
▌Finishing nails ▌Wood glue

1 Begin by marking a standard reveal on the edge of the head and side jambs. This reveal is usually ⅛ or 3/16 in. It doesn't matter which one, just be sure to use it consistently on all jambs. Tighten the blade of the square at the reveal dimension and use it and a pencil to mark the reveals.

4 Mark the length of the side casing board by running a pencil across the top edge of the head casing. Cut the board to length, and test fit the joint with the head casing. Modify the side casing cut, as necessary, to make a tight miter joint.

5 Spread a small amount of wood glue across the miter cuts on both casing boards. Smooth the glue using your finger or a small disposable brush. Then place the side casing against the jamb, and press it up against the head casing.

2 Cut a miter on one end of the head casing board. Then hold it in place and mark the other end where it intersects with the reveal mark on the side jamb. Use a sharp pencil to get the most accurate results.

3 Tack nail the head casing to the head jamb by driving a 4d finishing nail at both ends of the board. Leave these nail heads exposed so the nails can be pulled easily if necessary. Then cut a miter on one end of a side casing board, set the miter end on a piece of scrap casing (inset).

6 Nail the side and head casing boards securely to their jambs and the framing members inside the wall. Then drive a nail through the side casing board into the top casing to lock the miter together.

7 Drive all the nailheads about $\frac{1}{8}$ in. below the surface using a hammer and nail set. Fill these holes with wood filler. Then once the filler is dry, sand it flush to the surrounding surface.

smart tip

MARK ONCE

AS A GENERAL RULE, YOU ARE BETTER OFF DIRECTLY MARKING THE SIZE OF A TRIM PIECE RATHER THAN MEASURING ITS LENGTH. WHENEVER YOU MEASURE AND MARK A PIECE FOR LENGTH, THERE IS AN INEVITABLE DEGREE OF VARIATION IN THE WAY THE DIMENSION IS TRANSFERRED TO THE WORK PIECE. BY MARKING THE SIZE OF A PIECE DIRECTLY IN ITS ULTIMATE LOCATION, YOU REDUCE THE OPPORTUNITY FOR CARELESS ERRORS.

INSTALLING BASEBOARD TRIM

project

Designing a customized baseboard molding is a good way to express some of your own creativity. One simple design is shown here. It consists of three boards: a flat baseboard, topped with a stock cap molding, and a ³/₄-inch shoe molding. The height of the baseboard and the profile of the cap molding and shoe can be changed easily to something you like better. One great advantage to this approach is that the baseboard is installed with butted inside corner joints, so no coped joints are required.

TOOLS & MATERIALS
- ▌ Hammer ▌ Nail set
- ▌ Nail gun and nails (optional)
- ▌ Power miter saw ▌ Coping saw
- ▌ Baseboard molding ▌ Finishing nails
- ▌ Glue ▌ Shimming stock

smart tip

SCRIBING BASEBOARD

IF THE FLOOR IS DRAMATICALLY OUT OF LEVEL, YOU SHOULD SCRIBE THE BASEBOARD TO ABSORB THE DISCREPANCY. PLACE SHIMS BENEATH THE BASEBOARD TO BRING IT LEVEL; THEN USE A SCRIBER TO MARK THE BOTTOM FACE OF THE BOARD FOR THE REQUIRED ADJUSTMENT.

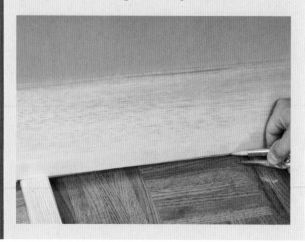

1 To install a three-board base assembly, first cut the baseboards to length, and test them for fit. If these boards don't sit flat on the floor, place them on shims; level them in place; then scribe the bottom edge to the floor, as shown below left. Here the shims represent the height of the finished flooring.

4 When a shoe molding ends next to a plinth block at the bottom of a door casing, hold the shoe next to the block. Then mark the end of the shoe molding to show how much of it is exposed beyond the front of the plinth block.

2 Nail the baseboards on the wall; then cut and nail the base cap boards in place. Form inside corners by nailing a square end base cap in place. Then cope the end of the other cap board and test fit the joint.

3 A finished outside corner shows how the boards are joined. The ends of the baseboards, the base caps, and the shoe moldings are all joined with miter joints. No coped joints are required.

5 Cut an open miter on the end of the shoe molding, so the scribed line is just visible. Then nail the shoe to the baseboard using 4d finishing nails. Make sure that you don't nail the shoe to the floor because it can split over time as the floor moves up and down.

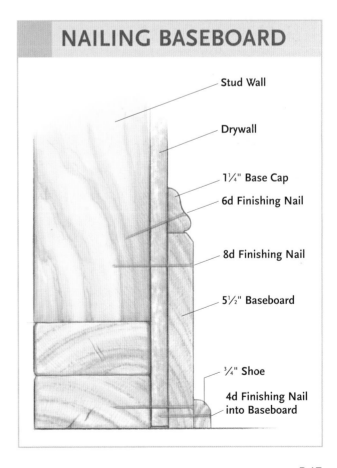

NAILING BASEBOARD

Stud Wall

Drywall

1¼" Base Cap

6d Finishing Nail

8d Finishing Nail

5½" Baseboard

¾" Shoe

4d Finishing Nail into Baseboard

148   FRAMING A CEILING OPENING

150   INSTALLING FRAMING FOR A SKYLIGHT

152   BUILDING A DEADMAN BRACE

154   INSTALLING A SUSPENDED CEILING

157   INSTALLING A WOOD-PANELED CEILING

158   INSTALLING A TIN CEILING

160   BUILDING A FALSE CEILING BEAM

162   INSTALLING A WOOD CORNICE

163   INSTALLING PLASTIC CORNICE

164   INSTALLING BUILT-UP CORNICE

167   INSTALLING A CEILING MEDALLION

6 ceilings

The ceiling may not be the first thing you look at when you enter a room, but this doesn't mean it should be ignored. From simple improvements, such as adding an ornamental medallion, to more complicated projects, such as installing solid-wood paneling, ceilings offer a blank slate that can be transformed with any number of different treatments. In most cases, the embellishments you add will be attached to the surface. But some, like a light shaft for a new skylight, require structural modifications. There's nothing particularly difficult about ceiling work, except for the strain caused by climbing up and down ladders and working over your head. In fact, in many ways, ceiling work is easier than dealing with floors and walls because there's nothing in the way.

FRAMING A CEILING OPENING

project

There are several common reasons for cutting a hole in a ceiling. One is to change the location of an attic access hole to a more convenient spot. Another is to install a folding attic stairway. And still another is to install a whole-house fan. Although this job can seem intimidating, it usually boils down to just cutting out a section of drywall and part of one joist. Headers are installed at both ends of the cut joist to support the weight. And the opening is framed in to fit the size required by what's being installed.

TOOLS & MATERIALS
- Tape measure ▍Safety glasses
- Dust mask ▍Circular saw ▍Handsaw
- Hammer ▍Framing lumber
- 12d common and drywall nails

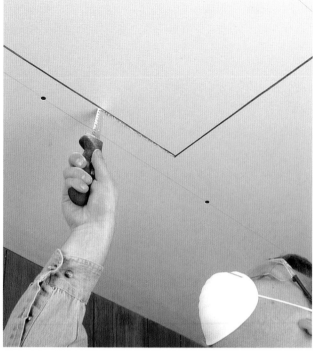

1 Establish the best place for the ceiling opening; then draw its outline on the surface of the drywall. Make sure the lines are parallel and square. Then cut through the drywall using a drywall saw or a keyhole saw.

2 Once the hole is cut in the drywall, mark cut lines on any joists that fall inside the opening. Then cut the joist using a handsaw or a reciprocating saw. You can make the cut from below, but it's easier to work from above. Just be sure to stand on a couple of scrap boards to distribute your weight over a wider area.

3 Install a header on both ends of the cut joist using the same size lumber. Nail the header into the end of the joist and the side of the adjacent joists. Screw the edges of the drywall to these headers from below; then install the stairway, fan, or other equipment in the opening.

● INSTALLING JOISTS

To connect solid-wood timbers, drive nails through perforated flanges to hold the joist to the hanger and the hanger to the adjacent header.

If you use engineered lumber, such as I-joists, you have to plan the job carefully and may have to order special framing connectors to fit.

Overlapping joists stagger the layout room to room but provide full bearing over the supporting wall.

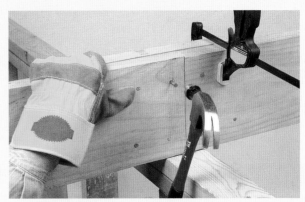

To align ceiling joists room to room, which is helpful when drywalling, add backup blocking.

● SUPPORTING A CEILING FAN

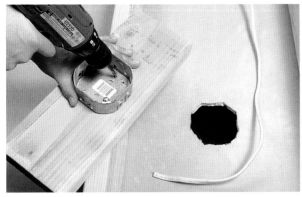

Cut an opening for the ceiling fan junction box, and screw the box to a nailer cut to fit between joists.

Run required electrical cable into the box; position the box over the hole; and fasten the nailer between joists.

149

INSTALLING FRAMING FOR A SKYLIGHT

project

Adding a skylight to your roof and building the light shaft below it is a difficult job. The most nerve-racking part, of course, is cutting the hole in your roof and getting the window installed before it starts to rain (or snow). For this reason, first assemble all the materials and tools you'll need. Then wait for a good weather report for the next few days. Concentrate on cutting the hole and installing the window in one day. If you don't make it, cover the hole with a tarp for the night; then do everything you can to make the roof weather tight the next day.

TOOLS & MATERIALS
- Tape measure ▮ Chalk line ▮ Hammer
- Circular saw and reciprocating saw
- Framing square ▮ 12d common nails
- Drywall nails ▮ Framing lumber ▮ Drywall

1 Lay out the light shaft hole on the ceiling, and drive a nail through the drywall at each corner. Then transfer the location of these nails to the roof rafters using a plumb line. Connect these marks with heavy lines drawn on the sheathing.

3 Cut away the roof shingles and sheathing, using the nails driven up through the sheathing as guides. Then mark the location of the support headers.

4 Cut out any rafters that fall within the opening, and install headers above and below to carry the load of the missing rafters.

5 Use 2x4s to frame the light shaft. Hold a straight one between the two openings to mark the location of both headers that support where the ceiling joists were removed.

2 Reinforce the rafters by nailing 2x4s across the rafters above and below the marked opening. Then establish the four corners of the opening by driving nails up from each corner so they poke through the top surface of the roof.

MAINTAINING ATTIC AIR FLOW

In attics, it's important not to block the ventilation necessary to moderate attic temperature and prevent condensation problems. Either install plywood stops near the overhang to keep vents clear or install venting baffles that channel air past the layers of insulation.

To add air baffles, first scrape away excess insulation in the roof overhang.

Staple a lightweight foam baffle to roof sheathing in bays between rafters.

6 Cut and nail headers to both ends of the ceiling opening to carry the weight of the missing joists. Once the headers are installed, cut out the drywall and screw the drywall to the perimeter of the opening using drywall screws.

7 Build a frame around the opening using 2x4s. Install the angled members first and then the short studs. Once the framing is done, install drywall on the inside surface and insulation behind the drywall.

151

BUILDING AND USING A DEADMAN BRACE

Installing drywall is usually a two-person job. To have help carrying and lifting the panels makes the work a lot easier. But help is not always around when you need it. Fortunately, you can work alone with the help of two common devices. The first is a rented drywall lift that costs about $50 a day. With this hand-powered tool you can install panels on ceilings and walls by yourself. The other option (shown here) is a deadman brace. Made of 2x4 scraps and a wall stud, this can securely hold a panel against the ceiling while you screw or nail it in place.

TOOLS & MATERIALS
- 2x4 lumber ▎Tape measure
- Circular saw and drill-driver
- Hammer and 12d common nails
- Drywall and drywall screws

1 A deadman brace is made of 2x4s. The top and bottom cross braces are 36 in. long. Nail these to the end on a stud so the whole assembly is 1 in. shorter than the distance from the floor to the ceiling.

● NAILS AND SCREWS

While most do-it-yourselfers fasten drywall with nails, pros generally use screws because they set uniformly with a small dimple that's easy to fill and provide more holding power, which means fewer nail pops to fix. But some pros use both. They start nails on some sheets before lifting them in place, and use a few nails to hold the sheet in place. Then they go back and drive screws in rows to finish the job.

Without a mechanical lifter or deadman, you need a helper on ceiling sheets.

2 Install 2x4 braces (at a 45-deg. angle) between the stud and the cross braces. Make sure the stud and cross braces are perpendicular. If they aren't, the deadman won't sit flat when it's wedged under a panel. To hold the other end of the panel, nail a cleat on the wall 1 in. below the ceiling (inset).

3 To install the panel, slide one end over the wall cleat; lift the other end up; and push it against the ceiling. Slide the deadman under the free end of the panel and straighten it up. The panel should stay in place while you get a ladder and some screws or nails.

STILTS VS SCAFFOLDS

Shoe stilts bring high walls and ceilings into reach, but you need to test them to get the feel of the stilts and use them safely.

A rolling scaffold is an ideal work platform for installing and finishing drywall on high walls and cathedral ceilings.

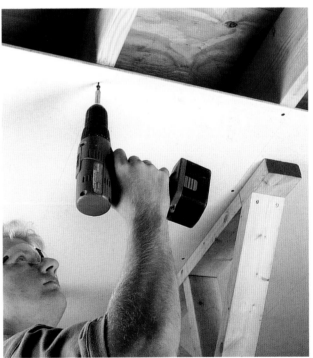

4 Nail or screw the edge of the panel to the ceiling joists. Then install fasteners, about every 6 to 8 in., across the width of each joist. If you have trouble hitting the joists with the fasteners, draw light reference lines on the panel to show where the joists are.

INSTALLING A SUSPENDED CEILING

Most suspended ceiling systems include four components. The first are the L-shaped metal edge strips that are installed on the perimeter of the room. The second are the T-shaped metal main runners that rest on the edge strips and are aligned perpendicular to the joists. The third are the metal crosspiece that are hooked between the main runners. And the fourth are the acoustical ceiling panels that are supported by the metal structure. A variety of designs are available for both the framework and the panels.

TOOLS & MATERIALS
▌Tape measure ▌4-ft. level ▌Chalk line
▌Drill-driver ▌Drywall screws ▌Nails
▌Framing square ▌Wire ▌Utility knife
▌Edge strips, runners, and crosspiece
▌Acoustical ceiling tiles

1 The best way to install the ceiling is on one level. To determine this height, find the highest point that will clear all the obstacles in the room. Then extend this mark around the entire room using a 4-ft. level. Work precisely so that the lines will meet when you get back to the starting point.

4 Support the main runners with wires that are hooked to the runner and wound around a nail driven into the sides of a joist. Install a wire every 3 or 4 ft. along the length of the runner. Check the bottom of the runner for level, and adjust the wires if necessary.

5 Once the runners are level, install the cross pieces by snapping their ends into the runner slots. Screw these crosspieces to the edge strips when they fall between a runner and the room walls.

2 Cut the L-shaped perimeter strips to length using tin snips. Then attach them to the wall by driving drywall screws through the strip and into the wall studs. If you have trouble driving the screws, bore pilot holes first.

3 Lay out the position of the main runners on the edge strips. These should be located so that the ceiling panels are centered in the room and the perimeter panels are at least half a panel wide. When satisfied with the layout, cut the runners to length, and place them on top of the edge strips.

6 Full tiles fit snugly into the track system. But perimeter tiles need to be cut. Use a framing square and a sharp utility knife to make the cuts. Don't try to save a few cents by pulling a dull blade through the cut. It can slip, tear the surface, and spoil the tile.

7 After each tile is cut, slide it over the metal grid and drop it in place. The beauty of this system is that the tiles are just as easy to remove as they are to install. This makes it simple to get access to plumbing pipes and electrical cables hidden by the ceiling.

WOOD PLANKING

In theory you can use any type of wood plank on a ceiling, including shiplap and other types that are normally used for exterior siding. But those materials generally are ³/₄ inch thick, which is not only unnecessary on a ceiling but also a disadvantage due to the weight.

Because there is no load on the planking (it just has to stay attached to the rafters or ceiling joists), you can use thinner material that is ¹/₂ inch thick or less. On ceilings, the standard installation has planks that interlock with a tongue and groove. This configuration is available in a wide variety of materials, including exotic hardwoods and plain pine. It's also available in different milling patterns—for example, with a small bead next to the seam or a more elaborate combination of shapes cut into the edges.

Several manufacturers offer packages of thin material in cedar or pine. The individual planks are extremely flexible

but firm up once you lock the joints together and add nails. Always check the manufacturer's installation instructions. On some thin material you may need to add a layer of strapping to provide more frequent support than standard rafters or ceiling joists set 16 inches on center.

On either a flat or sloped ceiling, start by ripping the grooved edge off the first board. A solid edge generally looks better unless you plan to cover the edge with wood trim. It's also important to make sure that the first board is straight, even if the wall against which it rests bows in and out. Because the boards interlock, you need to keep them straight in order to close the seams uniformly and tightly.

If the wall is straight, you can keep track of the boards by sighting down their lengths, stretching a string end to end, and measuring back to the starting edge every few courses. If the adjoining wall does bow, hold a full piece against the wall and scribe the first edge.

ABOVE Plank ceilings can be installed on nailer between rafters in cathedral ceilings, leaving some framing exposed.

INSTALLING A WOOD-PANELED CEILING

project

Installing lightweight boards to a ceiling is not difficult work. But it can be time-consuming for a couple of reasons. First, nothing goes quickly when you are working over your head. It's just an uncomfortable working position. And second, most boards are relatively narrow, only 3 or 4 inches wide, so it just takes a long time to cover a ceiling in such small increments. Because all the butt joints between boards must fall on a ceiling joist or rafter, it's a good idea to snap chalk lines that mark the location of these members before you start nailing boards in place.

TOOLS & MATERIALS
▮ Tape measure ▮ Power miter saw
▮ Chalk line ▮ Hammer ▮ Wood planking
▮ 6d finishing nails and nail set
▮ Drill-driver and 1/16-in. drill bit

1 Cut off the groove from the first board by ripping it using a circular saw. Run the saw along the backside of the board to get the cleanest cut line on the face of the board. Set the saw blade to a depth 1/2 in. deeper than the thickness of the board.

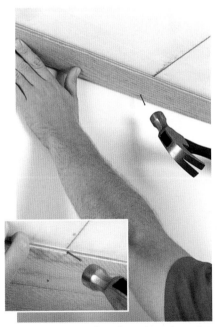

2 Push the first board against the wall; then pull it back about 1/8 in. to create a small expansion gap. Nail the back of the board through the surface. Nail the front of the board through the tongue (inset).

3 Periodically measure from the tongue edge of the last board back to the wall where you started. Do this in at least three places to make sure the boards are being installed in a straight line.

4 All the butt joints between the boards should fall on a joist or a rafter. Predrill the ends of the boards using a 1/16-in.-diameter drill bit to keep the boards from splitting when the nails are driven.

157

INSTALLING A TIN CEILING

Tin ceilings are making a comeback these days, about 100 years after their widespread popularity at the turn of the twentieth century. Many of the patterns available today are exact reproductions of original designs. These panels can be installed directly on the surface of a flat ceiling, if ³⁄₈-in.-thick plywood is installed first. But if the ceiling isn't flat, or if it's damaged, install furring strips and shim them until they are flat. Then attach the tiles to the furring.

TOOLS & MATERIALS
- Tape measure ▪ Gloves
- Circular saw ▪ Chalk line
- Tin snips ▪ Hammer
- 10d common nails ▪ Tin ceiling tiles
- 1x4 lumber and shims
- Recommended nails and molding

1 Begin by snapping a level chalk line on the walls that is low enough to clear any dips in the ceiling. Install the first furring strip next to the wall by nailing it into every ceiling joist using 16d nails. Use small scrap blocks or cedar shingles to shim down the strip until it meets the chalk line (inset).

ABOVE Tin ceilings can be installed over an uneven ceiling on nailer or directly to a layer of plywood on a flat ceiling.

4 Carefully measure and mark the location of any obstructions, such as ceiling fixture boxes. Then drill a starter hole in the middle of the cutout, and cut the line using tin snips.

2 Once the furring strips are installed around the perimeter of the room, use them to align the strips in the middle of the room. Hold a 4-ft. level on a perimeter strip; then measure how much an interior strip has to be shimmed. Slide the shimming shingles under the furring strip; then nail the strip in place.

3 Install crosspiece of furring between the main strips wherever the end of a ceiling panel falls. Toenail these short boards to the side of the longer boards.

5 Test fit the cut panel to make sure it will sit flat on the furring strips. Then attach it with nails. Make sure the power is off to the electric cable; then hang the fixture.

6 Join trim pieces at the corners by installing a full piece along one wall. Then make a miter cut using tin snips on the end of the mating piece. The process resembles making a coped cut on wood trim.

7 Gently push mating trim pieces together to check for fit. The first miter cut is rarely perfect. Usually it takes a few different cuts using the tin snips before the joint is tight.

INSTALLING A FALSE CEILING BEAM

False beams can be installed on a ceiling for a number of different reasons. You may simply like the way they look. You may want to hide something like a plumbing pipe that is hanging below the ceiling. And you may want to disguise a particularly poor ceiling, instead of tearing it down and starting over. The beam itself is easy to make. Just glue and nail three boards together. Installing it isn't much harder. Just attach a nailing board to the ceiling and hang the beam from this board.

TOOLS & MATERIALS
▮ Tape measure ▮ Table saw ▮ Drill-driver
▮ Clamps ▮ Hammer ▮ Wood glue
▮ Wood filler ▮ Router and beading bit
▮ 6d finishing nails and nail set
▮ Stain and brush ▮ 1x6 lumber

1 The three boards that form the beam are joined along their edges with glued miter joints. To make these joints, cut the boards to length; then cut a miter along the edges using a table saw. Adjust the blade height so it extends about $1/4$ in. above of the top of each board.

4 You can leave the metered edges on the beam just as they are. Or you can cut a decorative edge with a router. If you do rout an edge, make sure the cut isn't so deep that it hits the nails that were driven into the joint.

5 Sand the entire beam with 180-grit sandpaper and remove all the dust. Then finish the beam to match the rest of the room's decor. If you stain the beam, seal it with polyurethane after the stain is dry. If you want to paint the beam, prime and paint it before nailing it in place.

2 Push the board over the saw blade using the table fence as a guide. Keep your hands clear of the blade at all times. When the end of the board is within 6 in. of the blade, remove your hands and push the rest of the way with a block of wood bearing against the back end of the board.

3 Spread wood glue on all the metered edges; then clamp the two side boards against a scrap block, and nail the top board to the side boards. Use 4d finishing nails and keep them at least $3/8$ in. away from the edge. Set the nailhead and fill the holes with wood filler.

6 The best way to install a beam is to use a nailing board, like the one shown here. To make one, cut a board to width so it fits just inside the beam. Then screw this board to the ceiling joists so that it's located just where you want the beam, in this case over a plumbing pipe.

7 Lift the false beam up to the ceiling, and fit it over the nailing board. Push the beam tight against the drywall, and nail it to the board with finishing nails. Set the nailheads, and fill the holes with colored wood filler.

project

INSTALLING A WOOD CORNICE

Adding a cornice molding to the joint between walls and ceilings is a good way to add a touch of elegance to a room without spending a lot of money or time. There are a number of different stock design profiles available at your local lumberyard or home center. Chose one that matches (as much as possible) the rest of the trim in the house. Then nail support blocks on the wall and start installing the boards. Fitting the corner joints can take some time, but otherwise the job isn't very difficult.

TOOLS & MATERIALS
▌ Tape measure ▌ Chalk line
▌ Power miter saw ▌ Hammer and nail set
▌ 6d, 8d, and 10d finishing nails
▌ Coping saw and files
▌ Scrap lumber ▌ Crown molding

1 Snap a chalk line around the room to establish the bottom of the cornice molding. Then, cut triangular support blocks to fit behind the cornice board and nail them to the wall every 16 in. Cut the first cornice board to length, and nail it to the blocks (inset).

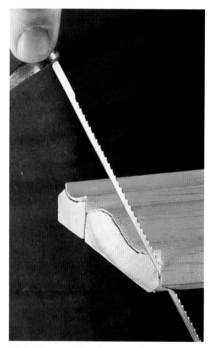

2 Use a miter box or chop saw to cut a miter on the end of the cornice board that abuts the first one. Cope the miter using a coping saw. Keep in mind that this saw works on the pull (not the push) stroke.

3 Use an oval file to clean up and refine the curved sections of the coping cut. Use a flat file for the straight sections.

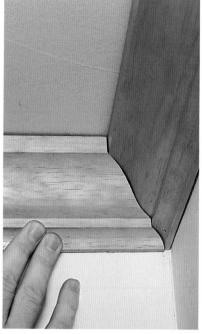

4 Test fit the coped board and make any necessary adjustments using wood files. Then nail the board to the wall; set the nail-heads; and fill the holes with wood filler.

INSTALLING A PLASTIC CORNICE

Plastic (usually polystyrene) molding is a material choice that appeals to many do-it-yourselfers. It comes in a variety of shapes that mimic traditional plaster molding. These "boards" are very light, so they are easy to transport and install. And they are typically available with matching corner and connecting blocks that eliminate the need for mitered and coped joints. If you want a more traditional look, keep in mind that any joint gaps can be easily filled with caulk and covered with paint.

TOOLS & MATERIALS
▌ Tape measure ▌ Chalk line
▌ Handsaw ▌ Hammer and nail set
▌ Caulk gun and construction adhesive
▌ 10d finishing nails ▌ Plastic cornice
▌ Latex caulk ▌ Paint and brush

1 Hold a section of molding in place, and mark guidelines along the top and bottom edges using a pencil. Make sure the bevels at the back of the molding sit flat against both the wall and the ceiling.

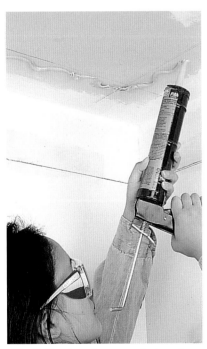

2 Following the manufacturer's directions, install a bead of construction adhesive just inside the guidelines on the ceiling and the walls.

3 Press the molding into the beads of adhesive, and attach it with finishing nails driven through the front of the molding into the wall studs behind.

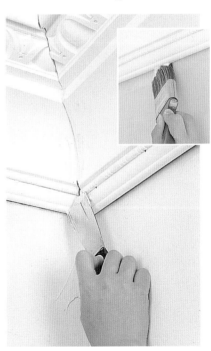

4 Where the molding sections meet, fill any gaps using latex caulk. Smooth the bead with a putty knife, and remove any excess caulk. Finish up by painting the trim boards (inset).

INSTALLING A BUILT-UP CORNICE

A built-up molding is a good way to create an elaborate ceiling molding without paying a small fortune for a custom made pieces. On this job, we started with a backer board that supports much of what comes later. We covered this with a soffit board and added a frieze under the soffit. Then a cornice was nailed between the frieze and soffit, and a fascia was nailed to the front of the soffit and backer. We finished up by installing a bed molding along the top edge and a cove molding along the bottom.

TOOLS & MATERIALS

- Power drill and bits ▌ Hammer ▌ Nail set
- Tape measure ▌ Miter saw ▌ Level ▌ Wood glue
- Nail gun and nails (optional) ▌ Screwdriver
- Cornice molding stock ▌ Backing stock
- Hollow-wall anchors ▌ Finishing nails

1 Hold a backer board in place against the ceiling, and drill screw pilot holes through the board and into the ceiling drywall. This will mark the location of each spiral anchor.

5 Nail a full-length cornice board to the backer and frieze boards. Then cut a miter on the end of a mating cornice board to form an inside corner. Cope this miter with a coping saw.

6 Cut outside miters on the cornice boards; test them for a tight fit; then nail them in place. A pneumatic gun drives nails better than a hammer and is worth renting if you have a lot of trim to install.

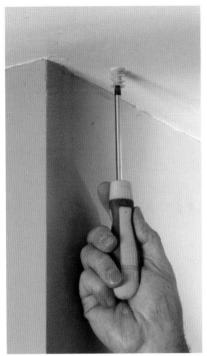

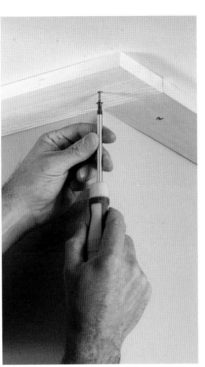

2 Install a spiral anchor wherever you can't locate a ceiling joist or other framing member to attach the backer boards.

3 Attach the backer board by driving screws through the pilot holes and into a ceiling joist or a spiral anchor.

4 Mark a level line to indicate the bottom edge of the frieze board. Then screw the frieze to the wall studs. Keep the screws in an area that will be covered by subsequent boards.

7 Install a fascia board over the front edge of the backer board and the soffit board that's under the backer. Keep the fascia 1/4 in. below the bottom of the soffit board.

8 Nail a bed molding over the fascia boards. Keep the bed tight against the ceiling so there are no visible gaps.

9 The finished cornice looks like one piece of molding, albeit an elaborate one. Instead, it's composed of seven separate boards.

CEILING DETAILS

If you want to dress up ceiling molding, you can use stock boards and other molding in combinations to present larger and more decorative profiles. There are also many molding that have detail built into the surface. Generally you get the least amount of detail with the least expensive molding that have embossed surface patterns, such as a row of leaves or a classic molding pattern called egg and dart. Because the pattern is pressed into the wood surface, the shapes are very shallow.

Knife-cut molding are carved from thicker stock in much greater relief. The extra depth, which is reflected in a higher price, creates the same kind of definition and

shadow lines that homeowners used to get with site-built plaster molding.

You can use any of these molding in a built-up assembly. There is no single, right way to combine profiles, although it pays to model your assembly after a reproduction of a full-size pattern.

Another option is to add a coffered ceiling to a room. These are recessed areas that are the result of intersecting beams. They are easier to create in new construction, but they are possible if you are replacing a ceiling.

You also can dress up ceilings with synthetic medallions. These lightweight, highly detailed pieces are easy to glue and nail in place, and you can paint them to match the ceiling color.

CEILING COFFER

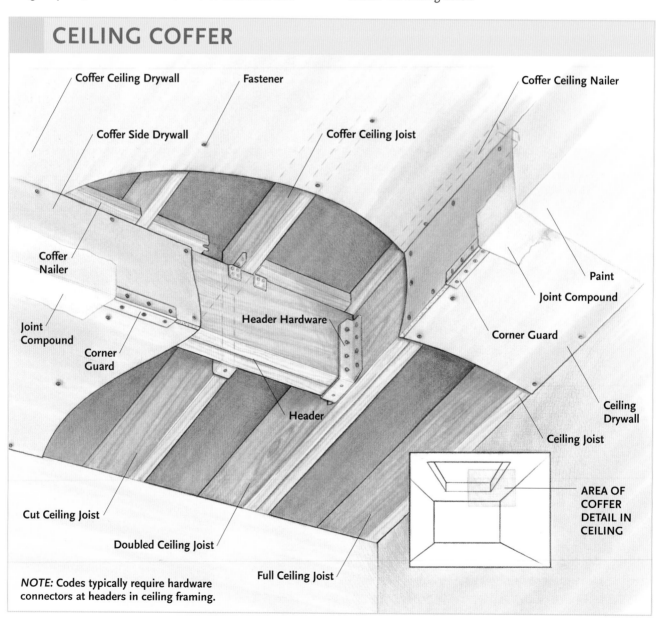

Coffer Ceiling Drywall · Fastener · Coffer Ceiling Nailer · Coffer Side Drywall · Coffer Ceiling Joist · Coffer Nailer · Header Hardware · Paint · Joint Compound · Corner Guard · Joint Compound · Corner Guard · Header · Ceiling Drywall · Ceiling Joist · Cut Ceiling Joist · Doubled Ceiling Joist · Full Ceiling Joist · AREA OF COFFER DETAIL IN CEILING

NOTE: Codes typically require hardware connectors at headers in ceiling framing.

INSTALLING A CEILING MEDALLION

Plastic ceiling medallions are lightweight, easy to install, and look exactly like traditional plaster medallions once they are painted. Medallions are available in different sizes and patterns. Some are even designed to allow a chandelier chain to fit through a center hole. The typical places to install a medallion are in the center of the living room ceiling or over the table in the dining room. But they can be used in other areas too, like hallways and near entry doors.

TOOLS & MATERIALS
- Tape measure
- Hammer and nail set
- Caulk gun and construction adhesive
- Medallion Paint and brush

1 Medallions are usually installed in the center of the room. Measure the same distance from parallel walls, and mark the ceiling to find the center point. Then hold the medallion on this point, and make a few light pencil marks around its circumference. Use these to accurately position the medallion during installation.

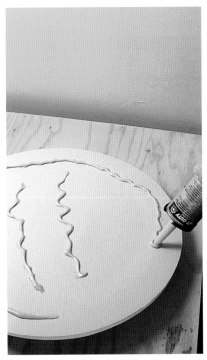

2 Apply adhesive to the back of the medallion. Follow the manufacturer's recommendations for the type and amount to use.

3 Carefully position the medallion over your alignment marks; then push it into place. Rotate it slightly to spread the adhesive.

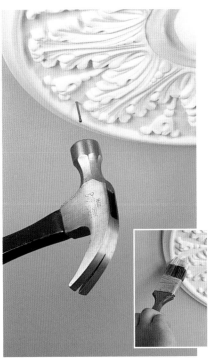

4 Locate a ceiling joist above the medallion, and drive a couple of finishing nails up into it. Set the heads; fill the holes with caulk; and paint the medallion (inset).

167

170   FLOORING LAYOUT

174   INSTALLING UNDERLAYMENT

176   INSTALLING VINYL TILES

178   INSTALLING VINYL SHEET FLOORING

180   INSTALLING CERAMIC FLOOR TILE

182   INSTALLING SLATE FLOORING

186   INSTALLING RADIANT-FLOOR HEATING

188   ROUTINE TILE CLEANING

190   INSTALLING A LAMINATE FLOOR

192   INSTALLING WOOD STRIP FLOORING

196   CARPETING

7 flooring

There's a wide range of finished flooring available today, from basic vinyl tiles up to high-end hardwood flooring. Most of it can be installed successfully by homeowners, and the information in this chapter shows you how. Remember that picking the right material is as important as installing it the right way. For example, a wet area, such as a bathroom, is a perfect place for vinyl sheet flooring but a terrible place for wall-to-wall carpeting. And an upstairs bedroom that doesn't get much use probably doesn't deserve an eye-catching (and expensive) hardwood floor. For help in making your material choices, talk to a flooring retailer. These people can give you a good idea of the pros and cons of each product. Factor in the part installation plays in your plans. Some products are easier to install than others.

FLOORING LAYOUT

Before planning a layout for new flooring, you will have to make sure that the floor is reasonably square.

Is the Room Square?

In small rooms, such as most bathrooms, you can check the squareness using a framing square positioned at each corner of the room, or by using the 3-4-5 triangle method: measure 3 feet along one wall, at floor level; then measure along the other wall 4 feet. If the distance between these two points is 5 feet, then the walls are square. For larger rooms, use a multiple of the 3-4-5 triangle.

If the walls are less than 1/4 inch out of square in 10 feet, it will probably not be noticeable. If they are more than 1/4 inch out of square, the condition will be visible along at least one wall, and you'll need to make angled cuts. Try to plan the layout so that the angled tiles are positioned along the least noticeable wall.

Making Working Lines

If you're installing any kind of tile flooring, plan the layout so that a narrow row of cut tiles does not end up in a visually conspicuous place, such as at a doorway. Often, the best plan is to adjust the centerline so that cut tiles at opposite sides of the room will be the same size. If you start by laying a full row of tiles along one wall or if you start laying tiles from the centerline, you can end up with a narrow row of partial tiles along one or both walls. To correct this, shift the original centerline, or working line, a sufficient distance to give you wider cut tiles at both walls.

Working Lines for a Square Layout. If the room is relatively square, snap a chalk line along the length of the area down the center of the room. Then snap a second chalk line across the width of the room so that each chalk line crosses in the center of the room. Check the cross with a framing square to make sure that the intersection forms a 90-degree angle.

Working Lines for a Diagonal Layout. When laying tiles diagonally, a second set of working lines is required. You'll need to snap a chalk line at exactly 45 degrees from your vertical and horizontal working lines; you can't just snap a line from the center point to the corner.

From the center point, measure out an equal distance along any two of the lines, and drive a nail at these points, marked A and B on the drawing at left. Hook the end of a measuring tape to each of the nails, and hold a pencil against the measuring tape at a distance equal to that between the nails and center point. Use the tape and pencil as a compass to scribe two arcs on the floor that will intersect at point C. Snap a chalk line between the center point and point C; then do the same thing on the other side of the room.

BASIC FLOOR LAYOUT

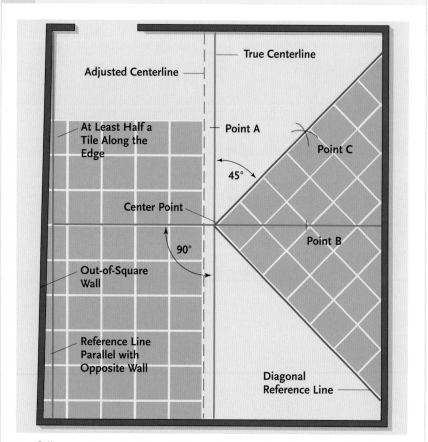

True Centerline

Adjusted Centerline

At Least Half a Tile Along the Edge

Point A

Point C

45°

Center Point

90°

Point B

Out-of-Square Wall

Reference Line Parallel with Opposite Wall

Diagonal Reference Line

Carefully snapping chalk layout lines before you begin to install the flooring will help you to make a balanced, symmetrical layout. The blue lines indicate the lines for a standard layout; the red lines for a diagonal layout.

CHECKING A ROOM FOR SQUARE

project

The biggest problem with an out-of-square room is not knowing about it. If you're in the dark, then you can't exercise any of the many strategies to hide the problem. One of the best is simply to identify the least visible wall and use that to absorb all the trouble. A good candidate is the bathroom wall that falls behind the toilet and the vanity. Another is along the tub. You can install the tub so it's square to the room and fur out the wall behind the tub.

TOOLS & MATERIALS
▮ Tape measure
▮ Chalk-line box
▮ 4-ft. level
▮ String ▮ Long 2x4
▮ 3 scrap blocks, all ¾ in. thick

1 The best way to check a room for square is to use a 3-4-5 right triangle. Measure from the corner along one wall to the 3-ft. point and mark the floor. Do the same with the other wall, but mark the floor at 4 ft. If the diagonal distance between these two marks is 5 ft., the room is square.

2 Level is another room characteristic you should check. Do this by placing a 4-ft. level on a long 2x4. If the floor is more than ½ in. out of level in 10 ft., it will be noticeable where the wall meets the floor. Because of this, it's a good idea to avoid using tile on the floor and the walls.

3 Also check the walls for straightness. Do this by running a string between same-sized blocks nailed to both ends of the wall. Then run a third block, of the same thickness, between the string and the wall, and mark where the wall isn't parallel with the string.

171

INSULATING CRAWL SPACES

Rooms located over crawl spaces or uninsulated basements often feel uncomfortable because the floor may be cold. Solve the problem by adding fiberglass batts between the floor joists or insulating the foundation walls.

Insulating the Floor

Cut sections of unfaced insulation to fit snugly between the floor joists. Keep them in place by stapling sheets of house wrap or polyethylene plastic to keep the material from falling down.

Protect pipes from freezing and ductwork from losing energy by wrapping them in insulation. Buy insulation designed for these jobs, and seal all joints with duct tape. If the ducts also serve the air conditioning system, the insulation will help save energy during the summer as well.

Insulating the Foundation

The most important part of this project is to keep moisture vapor generated in the ground from migrating into the house and the house framing. Spread a 6-mil sheet of polyethylene plastic over the exposed ground in the crawl space. Staple sheets of polyethylene to the sill plate, and let the plastic drape down the wall and overlap the sheet on the ground by about 12 inches. (See the drawing below.) Each sheet of plastic attached to the rim joists should overlap the one next to it by 12 inches.

Measure the distance from the top of the rim joist to the ground, and add 36 inches. Cut insulation to this length. Push the cut batts against the rim joist and between the floor joists. Staple the batts in place with the kraft paper covering facing into the crawl space. The batts should overlap the ground by about 36 inches. Hold them in place with 2x4s. Connect the batts together, creating a good seal, by stapling the seams together every 8 inches.

INSULATING CRAWL SPACES

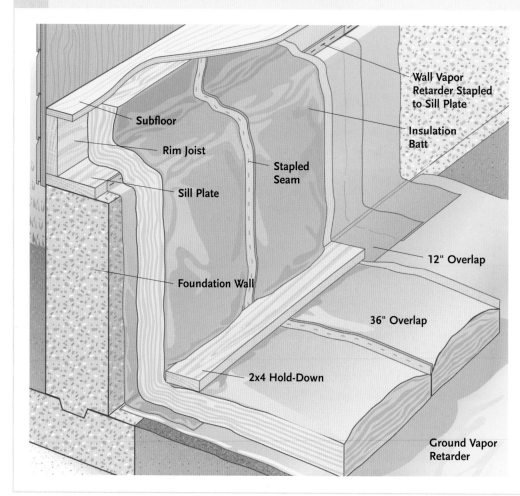

- Subfloor
- Rim Joist
- Sill Plate
- Stapled Seam
- Foundation Wall
- 2x4 Hold-Down
- Wall Vapor Retarder Stapled to Sill Plate
- Insulation Batt
- 12" Overlap
- 36" Overlap
- Ground Vapor Retarder

If your room sits above a crawl space, prevent cold feet by making sure there is enough insulation in either the floor or on the surrounding foundation. If you insulate the floor by installing fiberglass batts between the joists, be sure to wrap water pipes and ductwork in the crawl space with insulation. An alternative is to insulate the foundation walls and install a continuous vapor retarder as shown at left.

REINFORCING OLD FLOORS

project

You should never install a new floor over an old subfloor that squeaks or sags. These conditions will shorten the life of your new floor, in some cases dramatically. It's a better idea to take a few hours to make the old floor sound, as shown here, before proceeding. Start by thoroughly screwing the old plywood to the floor joists. Then reinforce any problem joists by gluing and screwing new ones next to them. Finish up by installing new plywood or backer board underlayment over the subfloor.

TOOLS & MATERIALS

▌ Power drill-driver and screwdriver bit
▌ Galvanized screws ▌ 4-ft. level
▌ Lumber to match existing joists
▌ Construction adhesive ▌ Caulking gun

1 If a floor squeaks when it's walked on, the joists may be weak. But a more likely cause is loose subflooring. Begin by pulling any loose nails; then drive new screws through the subfloor and into the joists. Use galvanized screws every 10 in. in the middle of a panel and every 6 in. around the perimeter.

2 Check for weak joists by seeing if any are sagging down. Hold a 4-ft. level on the bottom of the joists, and see if it rocks over any of these framing members. If any joist sags more than 1/2 in., it needs reinforcement.

3 Strengthen a weak joist using construction adhesive and screws to attach a new joist to one side of the old one. In severe cases (sagging more than 1 in.), the old joist should be jacked up and held while the new joist is being installed.

INSTALLING PLYWOOD UNDERLAYMENT

The correct underlayment will make your new flooring stay flat and resist water for many years. But it needs to be installed properly. First prepare the existing floor so that it provides a solid base. Then select an underlayment thickness that will make the new floor match the height of floors in adjoining rooms. Cut the panels to size, and place them on the floor so the joints are staggered. Then attach the panels with screws driven through the underlayment and subfloor, and into the floor joists.

TOOLS & MATERIALS

- Basic carpentry tools ▮ Wood filler
- 1-in. ring-shank nails or galvanized screws
- Circular saw with plywood blade
- Underlayment ▮ Power drill-driver

1 To cut plywood underlayment, place the panel on scrap boards; mark the length on both edges; and snap a chalk line between the two marks. Make the cut using a circular saw. Be sure to set the blade depth so the saw cuts through the panel but doesn't hit the floor.

2 Start the second course of underlayment with a sheet that's shorter than the first, so the joints in the underlayment will be staggered. Maintain a uniform $1/8$-in. expansion joint between sheets and along the room walls.

3 Underlayment panels should be attached to the floor joists, not just the flooring. Lay out where the joists fall, and snap chalk lines above each. Drive screws that are long enough to reach through all the layers of the flooring and at least 1 in. into the joists.

Types of Underlayment

Underlayment-grade plywood made from fir or pine is available in 4 x 8-foot sheets in thicknesses of $\frac{1}{4}$, $\frac{3}{8}$, $\frac{1}{2}$, $\frac{5}{8}$, and $\frac{3}{4}$ inch. Because it can expand when damp, plywood is not as good a choice for ceramic tiles as cement board.

Lauan plywood, a species of mahogany, is often used under resilient flooring. It is available in 4 x 8-foot sheets. The usual thickness for underlayment is $\frac{1}{4}$ inch.

Cement board is also called tile backer board. It is made of a sand-and-cement matrix reinforced with fiberglass mesh. It is usually available in 3 x 5-foot sheets in a thickness of $\frac{1}{2}$ inch. This is the preferred base for ceramic tile and stone floors in wet areas.

If the old flooring is not in good condition, remove it and smooth down the old underlayment before installing the new floor covering. If you can't remove the old floor covering, just apply the new underlayment over it.

UNDERLAYMENT OPTIONS

Floor Covering	Acceptable Underlayments
Resilient floor coverings	Old vinyl or linoleum flooring in sound condition Underlayment-grade plywood Lauan plywood
Wood parquet flooring	Old vinyl or linoleum floor in sound condition Underlayment-grade plywood Lauan plywood Hardboard
Laminate flooring	Any sound surface
Solid-wood flooring	Underlayment-grade plywood
Ceramic tile and stone	Old ceramic tiles, if sound Concrete slab Cement board Underlayment-grade plywood

VINYL FLOOR TILES

Installing vinyl or resilient floor tiles is fairly simple and requires only a few tools. For a professional effect, though, you'll need to plan the layout and prepare the substrate properly.

Most resilient floor tiles come in 12-inch squares. Trim strips in various accent colors are available in ¼- to 6-inch widths. When ordering, figure the areas in square feet to be covered (length times width) and add 5 to 10 percent for waste.

Start with the Right Base

When you pick out a resilient flooring material, check the manufacturer's instructions for acceptable substrates. This will guide you to the type of underlayment to use and its corresponding adhesive. Here are some commonly acceptable substrates for resilient tile and sheet flooring and what to watch out for:

Plywood that bears the stamp "Underlayment Grade" (as rated by the American Plywood Association) is the best underlayment for resilient flooring. Use only material of ¼-inch or greater thickness. Lauan, a tropical hardwood, is also used, but make sure you get Type 1, with exterior-grade glue. All plywood should be firmly attached, with surface cracks and holes filled and sanded smooth.

Wood strip flooring will serve as an underlayment only if it is completely smooth, dry, free of wax, and has all joints filled. Even then, the wood strips can shrink and swell, so a better bet is to put down an underlayment of ½-inch underlayment-grade plywood or ¼-inch lauan plywood.

Old resilient tile, sheet flooring, and linoleum should be clean, free of wax, and tightly adhered with no curled edges or bubbles.

Ceramic tile must be clean and free of wax. If the surface is porous, make sure it is completely dry. Joints should be grouted full and leveled.

Concrete must be smooth and dry. Fill cracks and dimples with a latex underlayment compound.

Preparing the Layout

Set tiles working from the middle of the floor outward. Begin by finding the middle of each wall and snapping a chalk line between opposite walls. Use a framing square to make sure the intersection of the lines is square.

project

INSTALLING VINYL FLOOR TILES

Vinyl floor tiles come in almost an endless array of colors, patterns, and finishes. But all of these can be categorized into just two basic types: tiles that are laid in adhesive, such as those shown here, and self-sticking tiles that come with protective paper on their sticky side. To lay self-sticking tiles, first thoroughly clean your existing floor; snap some layout chalk lines; then peel off the paper, and press the tile down onto the floor. While there's no question that self-sticking tiles are easier to install, the traditional type, with separate adhesive, is considered by most to yield the more durable installation.

TOOLS & MATERIALS
- Framing square
- Chalk line
- Tape measure
- Utility knife
- Rolling pin or floor roller
- Resilient tiles
- Adhesive
- Solvent
- Notched trowel (notch size as specified by adhesive manufacturer)

smart tip

ALWAYS CHECK WITH THE MANUFACTURER WHEN SELECTING AN UNDERLAYMENT MATERIAL. TWO THAT MOST MANUFACTURERS REJECT:
- *PARTICLEBOARD BECAUSE IT SWELLS GREATLY WHEN WET. IF YOU HAVE PARTICLEBOARD ON THE FLOOR NOW, REMOVE IT OR COVER IT WITH UNDERLAYMENT-GRADE PLYWOOD.*
- *HARDBOARD BECAUSE SOME TILE MANUFACTURERS DO NOT CONSIDER IT A SUITABLE UNDERLAYMENT FOR THEIR PRODUCTS.*

1 After marking work lines on the floor, lay out the tiles dry to make sure your installation plans will work. Place the tiles against the work lines in all four directions.

2 Check the adhesive container to find out how long the adhesive can be exposed before it starts to dry. Then plan to install an area that you can comfortably get done in this period. Spread the adhesive in this area using a notched trowel held at a 45-deg. angle.

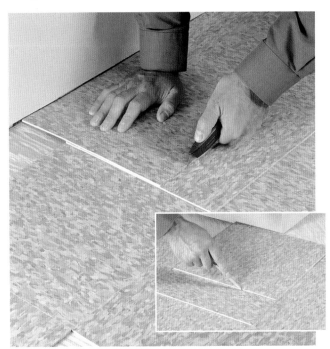

3 Carefully lower each tile into place to avoid smearing the adhesive. Press the tile down with your hands; then roll it smooth with a kitchen rolling pin or floor roller. If any adhesive squeezes up between tiles, wipe it up immediately with the solvent specified on the product container.

4 To cut a border tile, place a new full tile over the last full tile that has been installed. Then take another full tile and butt it against the wall. Cut along the edge of the top tile that's farthest away from the wall. To cut tiles for outside corners (inset), do the same thing, but on both sides of the corner.

INSTALLING VINYL SHEET FLOORING

Unlike laying vinyl tiles, installing vinyl sheet flooring requires some manipulation of large rolls of material. If you can find a big, open place to work, the job will be easier. Many people use the garage floor.

Before you begin the installation process, create a scale drawing of the room on a piece of graph paper showing the exact outline of the flooring. A day or two before you begin laying the floor, cut the roll to approximate size, and put the cut section in the room so it can acclimate to the room's temperature and humidity. Also, remove any shoe molding from around the baseboards. If you are careful removing it, you may be able to reuse it. Otherwise, plan on buying and installing new molding when the floor is done.

Some sheet-vinyl products require no adhesive, some call for adhesive just around the perimeter, while still others demand spreading adhesive over the whole floor. The last method is the one shown here.

TOOLS & MATERIALS
▌ Linoleum roller (rent one from your flooring supplier)
▌ 6- or 12-ft.-wide roll of resilient flooring
▌ Notched trowel ▌ Framing square
▌ Chalk line ▌ Tape measure
▌ Marker ▌ Utility knife
▌ Straightedge ▌ Seam roller
▌ Rolling pin ▌ Adhesive ▌ Solvent

Utility knife blades don't cost very much—about $1 for a package of 5. This means there's no excuse for not changing blades frequently when cutting vinyl flooring. If you try to force a dull blade, it can easily veer off and cut vinyl you don't want cut. Change blades after six cuts.

1 Begin installing sheet vinyl by rough cutting the roll to approximate size. Use a sharp utility knife and a metal straightedge to make the cut. If you can find a place to work where you can roll all of the sheet flat, all of your cuts will be easier.

5 To apply vinyl sheet adhesive, roll half of the flooring back to the center of the room. Then spread the adhesive on the bare section of floor; and roll the flooring back to its original place. Repeat the same procedure for the other half of the floor.

2 To cut around outside corners, slit the sheet margin down to the floor using a sharp utility knife. Be careful not to cut too far, or the cut mark will be visible on the finished floor.

3 To fit inside corners, cut diagonally through the sheet margin until you can get the vinyl to lie flat. Press the sheet gently down onto the floor on both sides of the cut.

4 To trim the vinyl along a wall, use a framing square to guide your cut. Leave a ⅛-in.-wide gap between the flooring and the wall.

6 To make a seam cut, apply adhesive up to 2 in. from the edge of the bottom sheet. Then overlap the second sheet on top of the first by 2 in. Cut through both pieces, and remove the waste. Install the second sheet in adhesive, making sure to keep the seam between sheets tight.

7 Use a rented floor roller to force out any air bubbles that might have formed while the flooring was being installed. Work out from the center of the room toward the edges.

LAYING CERAMIC FLOOR TILE

project

Ceramic floor tiles come in a wide variety of different shapes and colors. One of the primary differences is whether the tile is glazed or unglazed. The unglazed type shown here is a common choice for both bathrooms and kitchens. The reason is simple: most unglazed tiles provide better traction in wet conditions. To protect them from staining, a sealer is applied every year or two.

TOOLS & MATERIALS
▮ Rubber float ▮ Notched trowel ▮ Pail
▮ Sponge ▮ Soft cloths ▮ Hammer
▮ Tile cutter ▮ Tile nippers ▮ Small brush
▮ Jointing tool or toothbrush ▮ Roller and pan
▮ Tiles ▮ Grout ▮ Adhesive
▮ Solvent ▮ Sealant
▮ 12-in. piece of 2x4 wrapped with carpet

1 Begin by laying out the floor and snapping chalk lines to guide your work. Then spread only as much adhesive as you can cover with tile before it dries. The container will specify the open time of the adhesive inside. Use a notched trowel held at a 45-deg. angle.

4 After the tile adhesive has cured, clean out the grout joints between all the tiles using a soft broom or a shop vac. Then mix the grout, and spread it into the joints using a float tool. Make sure the grout fills all the joints.

5 To remove the excess grout, drag the rubber float across the joints at a 45-deg. angle. Do not press too hard because this can pull grout out of the joint and require you to apply a second coat.

2 Press individual tiles into the adhesive, giving each a slight twist to make sure the back of the tile is completely covered with adhesive. Keep tiles and grout lines aligned as you work.

3 Make sure all the tiles are embedded completely in the adhesive by tapping them with a padded board and a hammer. Use the block every couple of courses, and make sure the block spans several tiles every time you strike it.

6 Clean off any remaining grout with a sponge and clean water. Work in a circular motion, and clean the sponge frequently. Also change the water as soon as it becomes completely cloudy. When the tiles are as clean as you can make them, let the surface dry. Then buff the tiles using a clean, soft cloth.

7 Seal unglazed tiles and grout with a transparent sealer. Use a roller to apply it, according to the manufacturer's instructions printed on the product container. Diagonal strokes force the sealer into the grout joints better. If your tiles are glazed, apply sealer only to the grout with a brush.

PREPARING FOR A SLATE FLOOR

It's hard to beat slate for an entryway or foyer floor. It's attractive, durable, slip resistant and nearly waterproof when properly installed. Dirty shoes, boots, and sneakers don't stain the surface, and their mess can be cleaned quickly with a damp mop. In new construction, slate is sometimes set in a concrete base, which is the traditional way to install this material. But this method requires beefed-up floor framing, which is impractical for a remodeling project.

Slate manufacturers have made the process much easier by developing uniform ¼-inch-thick tiles that can de installed over plywood subfloors using heavy-duty mastic. These tiles come in a wide range of colors from grays and blues to reds and browns. And they're usually sold in packages that have a variety of precut sizes, from 6 x 6-inch units up to 12 x 24-inch pieces. The selection in each package is based on a standard pattern that is illustrated in the product literature.

TOOLS & MATERIALS
- Hammer
- 6-in.-wide putty knife
- ¼-in.-thick backer-board underlayment
- Patching compound
- Prybar
- Handsaw
- Sandpaper
- Backer-board nails
- Slate floor tiles

THE BEST WAY TO FIND LOOSE SPOTS IN THE SUBFLOOR IS TO SLOWLY WALK OVER THE ENTIRE AREA. LISTEN FOR SQUEAKS; MARK THEIR LOCATIONS; THEN NAIL OR SCREW THE SUBFLOOR TO THE FLOOR JOISTS.

1 Before you start to tear up the old floor, be sure to remove any shoe and baseboard moldings. Use a flat pry bar for the job, and work carefully to avoid damaging the walls so you can reinstall the boards later after the floor is done.

5 Cut ¼-in.-thick underlayment plywood to size and shape; then place it over the subfloor. Nail it in place with a 4- to 5-in. sq. pattern. Use underlayment nails, and set the heads below the surface using a large diameter nail set.

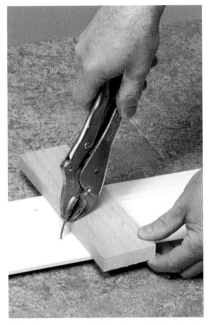

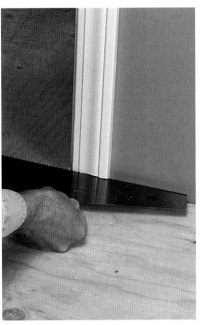

2 Once a molding board is pried from the wall, pull the nails out from the backside using locking pliers and a scrap block for leverage. This will prevent damaging the front of the board.

3 Usually, the bottom of each door casing has to be cut to provide clearance for the slate. To mark an accurate cut line, place a tile on the underlayment and scribe a line along the tile onto the casing.

4 Use a sharp, crosscut handsaw to cut the casing boards. Make the cut on the waste side of the line, and be sure to stop before cutting the door jamb board. Paint the cut edge with primer.

6 Once all the underlayment is nailed, cover the nailheads and any seams in the underlayment panels with floor patching compound. Once the compound is dry, sand it smooth using 100-grit sandpaper.

7 Place the tiles on the underlayment in the pattern shown on the manufacturer's package. Adjust the center of the pattern from side-to-side to minimize cutting waste around the perimeter.

INSTALLING A SLATE FLOOR

Once the slate is laid, as shown here, consider applying a sealer. While doing so is not necessary, coating the floor prevents the grout from staining over time. Apply the sealer with a paintbrush in thin, uniform coats. Most sealers dry in a couple of hours, and two coats should do the trick. Just stay off the floor for 24 hours after the each coat to avoid leaving footprints behind. To maintain the floor, clean it frequently with a solution of mild soap and water.

TOOLS & MATERIALS
- Circular saw with abrasive blade
- Wood or plastic grout spacers
- Paint brush ▍ Notched trowel
- Flat pointing trowel ▍ Mastic, grout sealer
- Sponge ▍ Burlap rag, sawdust

1 Slate is easy to cut using a standard circular saw with an abrasive or masonry blade. The job, however, is very loud and messy. Wear eye, ear, and breathing protection when cutting. Support the tile on the end of a sawhorse or worktable while making the cuts.

4 Let the mastic dry according to the manufacturer's specifications. Then mix your grout, and spread it into the spaces between the tiles with a trowel, pushing it into the bottom of each space. Smooth the joints with a flat pointing trowel.

5 Clean up the grout as you go, using a sponge and clean water. It's much easier to remove the grout now while it's still damp than it is later, after it's dried on the surface of the tile. Clean the sponge frequently to avoid spreading the grout around instead of picking it up.

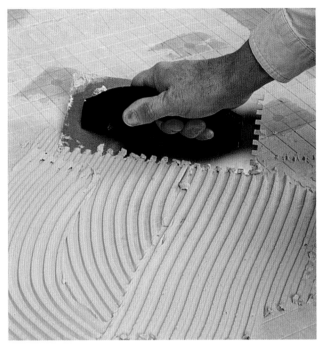

2 Begin spreading the mastic in the least accessible corner and work out, holding the notched trowel at a 45-deg. angle. Don't cover more area than you can reach over when placing the tile. Consult the product package to find out how long the adhesive can be uncovered before it starts to dry.

3 Place each tile in the mastic, and twist it back-and-forth to set it properly. Follow any visible layout lines, and use wood blocks or plastic spacers to keep the grout space consistent between tiles.

6 Once the grout is dry, clean and polish the slate by sprinkling the surface with sawdust and rubbing it with a burlap rag. Work from side-to-side and in a random circular pattern. Vacuum up the sawdust, and rinse the floor with a damp sponge.

7 Sealing the floor will keep the grout clean and the slate shiny. But you should wait about a month after the tile installation is complete. This gives the grout a chance to cure properly.

ELECTRIC RADIANT-FLOOR HEATING

Ceramic, slate, and tile floors are elegant and durable, although they often feel cold even at comfortable room temperatures. Radiant-floor heating systems are an effective and economical method of removing the chill from ceramic, marble, or stone-type floors. Installed between the subfloor and the finish flooring material, these cables will heat the floor to a comfortable warm temperature with a minimal use of electricity.

Heating Systems. There are a number of these products on the market, but in general they consist of an insulated, flexible resistance-type heating element with attached nonheating leads. The product shown here has the conductors contained in a fabric material. The fabric keeps the conductors spaced properly.

Where the final flooring is tile or stone, the system should have a heat density of 10 or 15 watts per square foot. The National Electrical Code requires that these systems be provided with ground-fault circuit-interrupter protection.

Floor Preparation. Heating cable may be installed over wood flooring. Drive protruding nails flush or below the flooring, and sand uneven edges where floorboards come together. Nail down any loose flooring. For concrete floor installation, remove all debris, and grind down sharp edges of small cracks. Some manufacturers recommend installing a thermal barrier or layer of insulation under the heating cables. Secure the thermal barrier to the floor with a high-temperature adhesive.

Testing Cables. Unpack the heating cable, and check the ohms, or resistance between the two conductor wires, to ensure that there is no break in the nonheating and resistance conductors. Each set of heating cables is marked with the proper ohms. Follow the manufacturer's testing procedures carefully. They are designed to keep you from tiling over a heating system that does not work.

Placing Cables. Plan the heating-cable layout. Remember that the nonheating conductors must be able to reach the control unit, which will be mounted on the wall. Don't overlap the heating cables, and do not allow the nonheating leads to overlap the heating area of the mat. The National Electrical Code requires nonheating conductors to be protected where they leave the floor by rigid metal conduit, rigid nonmetallic conduit, or by other approved means.

INSTALLING RADIANT-FLOOR HEATING

project

Radiant heat can be used in any room, especially if it is specified when the house is being built. But in the remodeling world, the most popular room for installing radiant heat is unquestionably the bathroom. There is nothing quite like stepping out of the shower onto a warm floor when it's about 10 degrees outside. In most cases, these systems are used under ceramic tile.

TOOLS & MATERIALS
- Radiant heating kit and controls
- Needle-nose pliers ▌ Notched trowel
- Ceramic tile or other suitable finished flooring ▌ Trowel ▌ Sponge
- Duct tape ▌ Multimeter
- Insulated screwdrivers ▌ Scissors
- Acrylic or latex thinset tile adhesive
- Mortar for tile grout ▌ Grouting float

3 Spread a layer of thinset adhesive over the heating pad, and start laying tiles. Don't cover the entire floor with adhesive. Spread only as much as you can comfortably cover with tile before the thinset dries. Consult the product container for drying times. When all the tiles are laid and dry, grout the joints.

1 Determine where you want radiant heat. There's no need to cover the entire floor, just the areas where you commonly walk or stand in bare feet. Cover this part of the floor with thinset mortar; let it dry; and install the fabric and cable over the thinset.

2 Locate the best spot for the temperature sensor by following the instructions that come with the radiant heating components. Use duct tape to hold the sensor cable in place on the heating pad. Make sure the cable falls between the heating elements.

4 Mount an outlet box on the side of a stud, and bring a power cable into the box. Bring the power wires from the heating mat, through rigid conduit, into the other side of the box. Join the like-colored wires using wire connectors.

5 Once the power hookups are done, install the temperature sensor cables to special terminals on the controller thermostat. Follow the product instructions for the specific unit you are installing.

ROUTINE TILE CLEANING

For day-to-day cleaning, simply wipe down tile with warm water and a sponge. On floors, regular sweeping or vacuuming should prevent dirt and grit from scratching the tile surface and grinding into grout joints.

There are many proprietary tile cleaners that can remove light buildups of dirt, grease, soap scum, and water spots. For stubborn stains, try a strong solution of soap-free, all-purpose cleaner or a commercial tile cleaner. Don't use acid-based cleaners; they can attack grout. Always rinse thoroughly with clean water. Unglazed tiles should be resealed after cleaning.

If you *really* need to scour the surface, use a woven-plastic pot scrubber rather than steel wool, which sheds flecks of metal that leave rust stains in grout joints. Avoid using soap-based detergents because they generally dull the tile surface. Remember not to mix different types of cleaners, and never mix ammonia with bleach or products that contain it. That combination can produce lethal fumes.

Removing Common Stains

Strong solutions of all-purpose cleaners or commercial tile cleaners will remove most stains. But in most households there are two common cleaning problems: mold on tile grout, and a buildup of soap scum that's sometimes combined with hard-water scale.

To clean grout joints, first rinse the area with water. Then use a toothbrush dipped in household bleach to remove stains. Stubborn stains may respond to a preliminary dose of straight bleach. If the grout is colored, test a spot to make sure the bleach will not cause discoloration. If it does, use a commercial tub-and-tile cleaner. Use household bleach with caution: wear rubber gloves and safety glasses.

Another option is to try a combination of household bleach and an abrasive cleanser (one that does not contain ammonia). Make a paste, scrub it on, and rinse. If some spots remain, cover them with a wet mound of the paste for several hours before scrubbing again. To tackle a stain that is deep in the grout, try a soupy poultice of baking soda and liquid detergent mounded up and left on the spot overnight to draw out the stain.

To remove mild soap deposits and hard-water spots, spray the surfaces with an all-purpose, nonabrasive cleaner, and let it soak in for a few minutes before rinsing.

STAIN REMOVAL CHART

Stain	Removal Agent
Grease & fats	Household cleaners
Tar, asphalt, oil, grease, oil paints, petroleum-based products	**Indoors:** Charcoal lighter fluid; then household cleaner, water rinse **Outdoors:** Concrete cleaner
Ink, mustard, blood, lipstick, merthiolate, coffee, tea, fruit juices, colored dyes	**Mild:** 3% hydrogen peroxide **Deep:** Household bleach
Nail polish	**Wet:** Charcoal lighter fluid **Dry:** Nail polish remover
Liquid medicines, shellac	Denatured alcohol
Rust	Rust remover; then household cleaner; rinse
Chewing gum	Chill with ice wrapped in cloth; scrape off surface

Caution: Some cleaning agents are toxic, caustic, or flammable. Use only as directed by the manufacturer and with adequate protective gear.

If some deposits remain, mist the area with vinegar, and let it sit for a few minutes before wiping. If all else fails, try a proprietary soap-scum remover.

Hard-Water Problems

If you are concerned mainly with mineral deposits in water that form white scale, check into the problem yourself with a water-hardness test kit, or try this simple home test. Add ten drops of liquid detergent to half a glass of tap water, cover, and shake. If the detergent forms high, foamy suds, you have soft water. If the detergent forms low, curdled suds, you have hard water and probably could benefit from a water-softening system.

CLEANING TILE FLOORS

project

Tile floors usually need lots of cleaning. They are installed in rooms that get a lot of wet traffic, such as kitchens, bathrooms, and mudrooms. Routine cleaning can be done with just a sponge mop and a bucket of clean, hot water. But serious stains and dirt need more, as explained on the facing page. Some people apply wax to the floor once it's clean to help ward off future dirt and stains. But wax is a mixed blessing. It does protect the floor, but it makes it slippery, which is not the best kind of surface for wet locations.

TOOLS & MATERIALS
▌Vacuum cleaner or broom
▌Cleanser ▌Bucket
▌Scrub brush and sponge
▌Roller and tile sealer
▌Rubber gloves

1 The first step in cleaning a tile floor is to vacuum up all the dirt and dust (inset) to avoid scratching the surface of the tile when it is washed. Then pour a standard floor cleaner into a bucket of water and mix thoroughly.

2 Use a scrub brush with soft bristles on stubborn stains. If this doesn't work, try using a small amount of bleach. If you do use bleach, be sure to wear gloves and safety goggles.

3 After cleaning the floor, rinse it thoroughly with a sponge and clean water. Once the surface dries, buff away any remaining glaze using a clean, dry cloth.

4 Finish up the job by applying a sealer to the floor to protect the tile and the grout joints. Use a paint roller and roller pan to apply the liquid sealer.

189

INSTALLING A LAMINATE FLOOR

A typical laminate floor is installed as a floating system. This means that the boards or tiles are glued to one another but not attached to the floor. This allows the flooring to "float" without buckling or cracking as it expands and contracts with changes in temperature and humidity. To create a barrier between the floating floor and the immobile subfloor, you install a foam pad that is about ¼ inch thick.

TOOLS & MATERIALS
▌Laminate flooring ▌Spacers
▌Foam underlayment padding ▌Glue
▌Hammer ▌Installation block
▌Plastic putty knife ▌Strap clamps
▌Circular saw or handsaw
▌Chalk line

1 Make sure the existing flooring is in sound condition; then roll out the foam padding starting at one corner. If you are covering a concrete slab, most manufacturers require you to lay a polyethylene vapor barrier underneath the foam.

2 Assemble the first two or three rows of boards by spreading glue along the tongues (inset) and pushing the boards together. Install plastic spacers between the boards and the edges of the floor. The gaps created by these spacers give the floor room to expand with increases in temperature and humidity without buckling.

3 If you can't push a board in place using only your hands, then gently drive the boards together using a soft wood block. Don't strike the block too hard because this might cause damage to the tongue on the board. Remove any excess glue using a plastic putty knife.

THE LAYERS OF LAMINATE

Laminate flooring has two things going for it: it is easy to install, and it can be made to look like anything, including wood, stone, ceramic tile, or any color of the rainbow. The inner fiberboard core provides dimensional stability and water resistance that make these products suitable for installation in a kitchen; the wear layers protect a decorative image. You can install laminate flooring over any substrate except carpeting. Simply make sure that the original flooring is clean and level. Most manufacturers require foam padding under the floor. A glue-type installation is shown opposite, but some manufacturers also offer a glueless version where the individual components snap together.

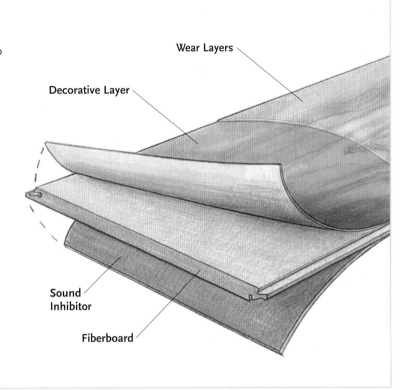

Wear Layers

Decorative Layer

Sound Inhibitor

Fiberboard

4 After you've installed three or four rows of boards, hold them with strap clamps, and let the glue set up for about an hour before continuing. As you progress across the floor, just lengthen the clamp straps.

5 To measure the perimeter boards that need cutting, first lay a full plank over the last installed board. Use a third board, pushed against the wall, to scribe the board that needs cutting. Make the cut using a circular saw and a fine-tooth blade.

INSTALLING WOOD STRIP FLOORING

These days, many different wood species are used for flooring, generally as veneers glued over plywood panels. But traditionally, solid maple and oak were used for floors because the wood was so hard and the trees were so plentiful. Solid wood floors may be difficult and time-consuming to install, but they look wonderful and are very durable, often outliving the houses where they were installed.

TOOLS & MATERIALS
▌15-lb. felt building paper ▌Backsaw
▌Chalk line ▌Basic carpentry tools
▌Electric drill with assorted bits
▌Flooring and finishing nails ▌Wood flooring
▌Nail set ▌Rented nailing machine
▌Pry bar ▌Dust mask
▌Circular saw or handsaw

1 Start the job by removing the moldings along the floor. If you want to reuse these boards, then carefully pry them from the wall, and pull the nails out from the back side using locking pliers. Also be sure to label them on the back so you'll know where each came from.

5 Drive each board into the last row until the joint is tight. Then use a rented floor nailer to edge-nail the board. Place the tool over the tongue, and strike the plunger with a mallet. Nail the flooring at the frequency recommended by the manufacturer.

6 Some boards are warped and won't fit easily into the previous row. If these boards are very distorted, set them aside and cut shorter boards out of them later. But for modest problems, you can drive the board into place by tapping a wedge between the board and a block that's screwed to the floor.

2 Use a piece of scrap flooring as a guide to undercut doorway casing boards. Then lay 15-lb. felt paper across the entire floor, and staple it in place.

3 Snap a chalk line for the first board; then push the board against the perimeter spacer blocks. Drill pilot holes along the back edge, and face-nail the board.

4 Test fit several rows of boards. This allows you to plan for staggered joints as well as matching variations in the color between the boards.

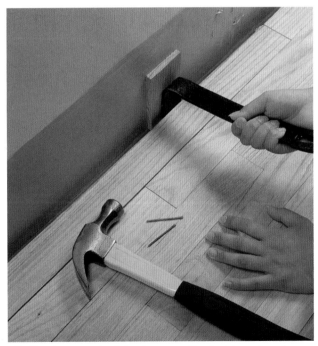

7 To fit boards that finish a row, hold the board up to the gap, and put a spacer at the end next to the wall. Mark the board, and cut it to length using a miter saw or a circular saw.

8 To close up the joint between the last board and the wall, use a pry bar against a wood block to protect the wall. Hold the joint tight, using the pry bar if necessary, and drive nails along the back edge of the board. Cover the gap with baseboard and shoe moldings.

REFINISHING A WOOD FLOOR

Solid hardwood floors are one of the most attractive building materials available. So it makes good sense to repair ones that are damaged instead of replacing them. Probably the most common repair is refinishing the surface. At the end of this job, you're bound to love the results. But getting there can cause an incredible amount of dust. For this reason, make sure to seal any doorways and heat registers using heavy polyethylene plastic and duct tape.

You also have to protect yourself. There is no substitute for wearing a respirator equipped with dust-filtering canisters. A simple paper mask just isn't enough. The respirator is also required, this time with vapor canisters, for when you are applying the finish on the floor.

TOOLS & MATERIALS
▍ Hammer (and nail puller if necessary)
▍ Sharp wood chisel
▍ Drum sander ▍ Edge sander
▍ Hand-held sander
▍ Medium-grit sanding belt and pad
▍ Fine-grit sanding belt and pad
▍ Hand-held floor scraper
▍ Vacuum ▍ Rotary buffer
▍ Lamb's wool applicators
▍ Tack cloth ▍ Polyurethane

To revive a polyurethane finish over an undamaged floor, go over the floor with a sanding screen attached to a rotating floor polisher. The screen removes the old finish without cutting into the floor as traditional sanding with a drum sander does. Do not screen floors with wax top coats.

1 Check the surface of the floor for any raised nail-heads and lifted board edges. Either pull out the raised nails or set their heads below the surface and fill the holes. Use a sharp chisel to shave down any lifted edges.

5 Sand the entire floor at least twice, finishing up with a fine-grit abrasive. Completely remove all the sanding dust from the floor and room using a shop vac. Then stain the floor or start applying the first coat of polyurethane finish using a lamb's wool applicator.

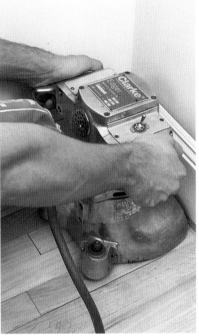

2 Install a medium-grit belt on a rented drum sander, and go over the floor in the direction of the wood strips. Keep the tool moving to avoid damaging the floor.

3 Switch to a rented edge sander to remove the finish close to the walls. Be careful: this sander uses rotating disks that can create circular scratches on the boards.

4 Use a hand scraper to remove the finish from areas that the edge sander couldn't reach. The scraper is also a good tool for removing any scratches left from the edge sander.

6 Allow the first coat of finish to dry; then buff it using a rotary buffer with a steel wool pad attached. Keep the buffer moving at all times, and work in the direction of the strips, not across the strips.

7 After buffing, clean all the dust and steel-wool particles off the floor using a floor vacuum. Then use a slightly damp cloth or a tack cloth to remove anything that's left behind by the vac. Apply at least one more coat of polyurethane, followed by buffing and vacuuming.

195

WALL-TO-WALL CARPETING

Wall-to-wall carpeting is the most popular floor covering in the United States. It's quiet, warm, and comfortable when you walk or sit on it; isn't slippery; doesn't hurt as much if you fall; and comes in styles and colors to suit any decor. Best of all, it can cover a plywood subfloor at less cost than that of any other floor covering. While some home-owners see wall-to-wall carpeting as a tem-porary solution while saving up for wood or tile, others invest in top-quality products and plan to enjoy them for many years.

When shopping for carpeting, know your fibers. Each one has its strengths and weaknesses. Acrylics, for example, are usu-ally the most expensive because they look like wool and resist staining, crushing, and fading. They do not hold up to heavy traf-fic, however, making them more suitable for bedrooms and other private areas in the home. Nylon, the first synthetic fiber for carpeting, remains the favorite among homeowners due to its durability and steadfast colors. Its resilient fibers stand up well to furniture and traffic but can be damaged if exposed to sunlight for long periods.

Polyesters are less durable and resilient than nylon but less costly, too. They are available in a wide range of deep vivid colors that resist fading and staining. Olefin (poly-propylene) is commonly used in commercial and indoor-outdoor applications due to its low cost and superior stain resistance.

OPPOSITE Elegant, restrained patterns distinguish today's wall-to-wall carpeting.

ABOVE RIGHT Choose a compact loop pile and moisture-proof padding for a child's room.

RIGHT Shag carpeting is back, but new thicker pile gives it a plushier feel and makes it less likely to flatten.

RIGHT Wall-to-wall synthetic carpeting, although affected by higher oil prices, remains one of the least-expensive flooring solutions. At the same time, it's one of the most comfortable and versatile for both formal and casual settings.

CARPET TEXTURES

Carpet texture is based largely on whether the pile (yarn surface) is cut or not. With cut pile, the loops of a woven or tufted carpet are trimmed to create a smooth, brush-like pile. Velvet, plush, and saxony are examples of smooth cut-pile carpeting and are well-suited for use in formal areas. The same method is used to produce textured, shag, and frieze carpeting.

Loop-pile carpets, on the other hand, leave the yarn loops uncut. Berber, cable, and multilevel-loop styles are all loop-pile carpets. They hold up well to traffic, are easy to clean, and hide footprints and furniture depressions extremely well.

Plush or Velvet

Saxony

Frieze or Twist

Loop Pile

Cut and Loop

Textured

TUFTED VERSUS WOVEN CARPETS

For centuries, rugs and carpets were woven. In the beginning of the twentieth century, tufted rugs were pioneered in Dalton, Georgia. Today, tufted products are the most prevalent in the wall-to-wall category due to cost, but they cannot match the beauty or durability of woven carpet. Tufted carpet technology, however, continues to improve and can now be used to create intricate patterns not possible in the past.

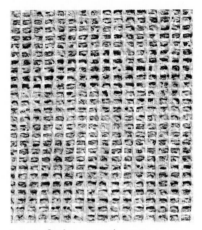

In a tufted carpet, the yarn is inserted through a mesh backing (visible at left) and held in place with adhesive. Once the tufting is complete, a second mesh backing (above) is adhered to the first for stability.

Woven carpets are made with various types of weaving processes, each with a distinct character. In general, strong warp (vertical) yarns are interwoven with softer weft (horizontal) yarns. With a woven carpet, you can often see the surface design (shown right) on the back (above).

● FIBER FACTS

Berber-style carpets, originally inspired by coarse-textured carpets that were handcrafted in northern Africa, are now available in myriad styles.

Tufted carpet manufacturers create interesting "sculpted" patterns by combining short loops and cut pile.

One of several specialty weaves, Axminster produces patterns with beautiful clarity.

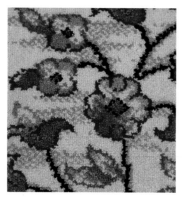

Although the majority of wall-to-wall carpeting is of the tufted variety, it is also available in woven styles, such as this Wilton weave.

ABOVE Carpeting is the perfect surface for families that spend as much time lounging on the floor as they do on couches and chairs. To make the floor really inviting, you can install a radiant-floor heating system under the carpet, but choose your padding carefully. Slab-rubber or synthetic-fiber carpet cushions are best at allowing heat to penetrate the room.

OPPOSITE TOP Today's "jute" paddings are made from synthetic fibers. They are available in many different weights to handle low, medium, and high-traffic situations. Install padding that is waterproof to preserve your wood floors underneath the carpet.

OPPOSITE BOTTOM Carpet tiles have a light adhesive backing and come in dozens of textures and colors. Create area rugs or wall-to-wall carpets of any size. A big advantage to carpet tiles: you can replace stained or damaged tiles quickly and easily.

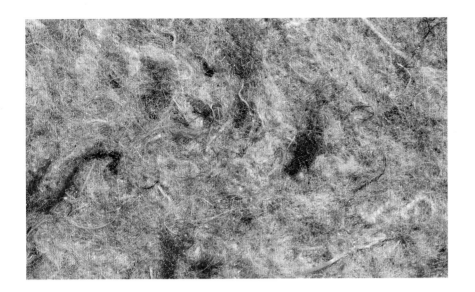

smart tip

UPGRADE

CARPET DEALERS OFTEN THROW IN THE PADDING WITH YOUR CARPET PURCHASE, IF YOU HAVE THEM DO THE INSTALLATION. BUT IN THE LONG RUN IT MAKES MORE SENSE TO UPGRADE TO A BETTER PADDING, LIKE SLAB RUBBER OR FROTHED FOAM, EVEN IF YOU HAVE TO PAY FOR IT. BETTER PADS WILL IMPROVE THE CARPET PERFORMANCE BY MAKING IT MORE COMFORTABLE, DURABLE, AND RESILIENT. AND IN THE PROCESS, BETTER PADDING CAN PREVENT SPILLS FROM LEAKING THROUGH TO THE FLOOR BELOW.

DUAL PURPOSE

Padding is generally recommended for use under carpeting. Available in various thicknesses, from $\frac{1}{4}$ to $\frac{7}{16}$ inch, it serves two purposes: first, it makes carpeting more resilient and consequently more comfortable for walking; second, it helps to preserve the carpet by preventing fibers from being crushed. From good to best, padding types include rebond (a high density foam), slab rubber, jute or fiber (made from jute or synthetic fiber), and frothed foam (high-density polyurethane).

201

204   PATCHING DRYWALL HOLES

206   REPAIRING CORNER BEADS

207   PATCHING PLASTER

208   REPAIRING SOLID-WOOD PANELING

209   REPAIRING PLYWOOD PANELING

210   REFINISHING WOOD TRIM

212   REPLACING A BROKEN TILE

214   REINFORCING JOISTS

216   INSTALLING ATTIC STAIRS

218   FIXING A LEAKING SKYLIGHT

8 repairs

Making repairs in floors, walls, and ceilings can be tough because so many different skills are involved. Fortunately, you don't have to be an expert in any of them. Repairing sagging floors makes use of basic carpentry skills only, as does installing an attic stairway and repairing wood paneling. Your refinishing skills certainly won't be overtaxed by stripping paint from some woodwork. And your tiling abilities won't be embarrassed if you just have to replace some broken tiles. For better or worse, the bulk of your work will be devoted to fixing drywall, which is easy to do thanks to joint compound. This material can fill small holes, scratches, and gouges by itself. And when used with pieces of drywall, joint compound can make short work out of large holes, too.

PATCHING LARGE HOLES IN DRYWALL

Minor blemishes to drywall surfaces are easy to repair by just filling the spots with joint compound, letting it dry, and sanding it smooth. But larger holes require more effort. You can use one of the kits described in the box on the opposite page. Or you can use scrap lumber, construction adhesive, and a drywall scrap that's large enough to cover the hole. While it's not necessary to square up the hole before you make the patch, it's a good idea because it makes every following step in the process easier.

TOOLS & MATERIALS
- Drill-driver and 1¼ in. drywall screws
- 1x3 scraps and drywall
- Caulk gun and construction adhesive
- 4- and 10-in. taping knives and drywall tape
- Joint compound and sanding block

1 Enlarge the hole so it's a square or a rectangle; then cut two lengths of scrap 1x3 so they extend 2 in. past the opening on the top and bottom. Spread adhesive along one edge; hold the board against the back of the drywall; and attach it using screws driven through the front of the wall.

2 Install the other board on the other side of the opening. Once both 1x3s are in place, spread some construction adhesive on the exposed parts of the boards. Smooth the adhesive using a putty knife.

3 Measure the wall opening, and cut a piece of scrap drywall to match. Make sure the patch you cut is the same thickness as the drywall that's in place. Attach the patch to the 1x3s using drywall screws.

REPAIRING SMALL HOLES IN DRYWALL

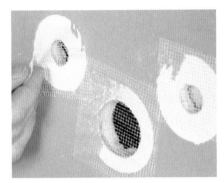

Repair kits for small holes include self-stick mesh patches that hold and reinforce the repair compound.

The mesh prevents compound from falling into the wall cavity, so you can smooth out the surface.

Quickly patch larger holes with clip kits. Set a clip on each side, and fasten it using a drywall screw.

Set a piece of drywall in place, and fasten it through each clip. Then you can snap off the exposed clip strips.

4 Using a 4-in. taping knife, spread a coat of joint compound over the seams. Cover this with paper tape, followed by another coat of compound. Let the compound dry; sand it smooth; and use a 10-in. taping knife to apply another coat of compound.

5 Once the joint compound is dry, sand the whole patch with a medium-grit sanding block or a piece of 120-grit sandpaper wrapped around a wood block. Vacuum up the sanding dust; prime the patch; and finish up with a topcoat of paint.

REPAIRING CORNER BEADS

project

Corner beads are the angled metal strips that are applied to the outside corners of drywall walls. Once they are covered with joint compound during the wall finishing process, they blend in and look like the rest of the drywall. They are used to protect outside corners from the damage that is inevitable when a corner juts out into the room. They work most of the time, but they aren't indestructible. If they are struck hard enough, the bead will bend, the joint compound will crack and fall out, and you'll be confronted with a repair that is more involved than you might expect. To fix one, follow these steps.

TOOLS & MATERIALS
▌Utility knife ▌Tin snips
▌Drill-driver and 1¼-in. drywall screws
▌4-in. taping knife ▌Joint compound
▌Hacksaw ▌Corner bead

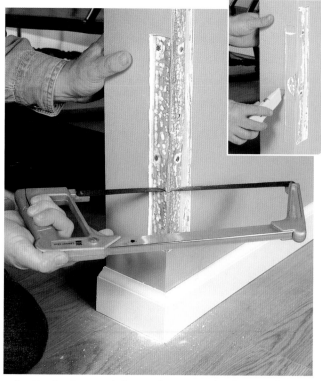

1 Begin the repair by cutting away the damaged joint compound with a sharp utility knife (inset). Then use a hacksaw to cut through the distorted corner bead. Pull out any nails that are holding this section to the corner, and remove the damaged bead.

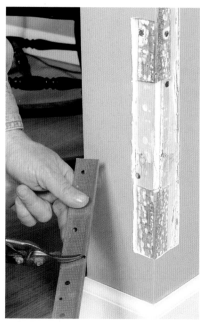

2 Measure the length of the bead that was removed, and cut a new piece to match using tin snips. Test fit the new bead, and trim it if needed.

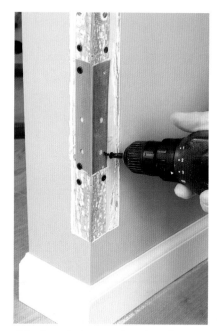

3 Attach the new bead to the corner using drywall screws. Your goal is to create a smooth seam between the existing beads and the patch. The smoother these transitions are, the better the repair will be.

4 Use a 4-in. taping knife to spread joint compound over the corner bead. Run the knife against the drywall on one side and the edge of the corner bead on the other.

PATCHING PLASTER

Repairing plaster damage is usually more involved than fixing drywall problems. Small cracks and gouges in plaster can all be repaired with a thin coat of drywall joint compound. But deeper and wider cracks, and damage that breaks out large pieces of plaster, require a different approach. The damaged area first has to be cleaned so it's free of dust and plaster debris. Then the hole must be filled to just below the surrounding surface with patching plaster. Once this base coat is dry, the repair can be completed with a smooth coat of joint compound.

TOOLS & MATERIALS
▮ Patching plaster or joint compound
▮ Spray bottle filled with clean water
▮ Paint roller and roller tray
▮ 6- and 10-in. taping knife

1 Use patching plaster to fill most of the repair hole. Mix it according to the package directions, and spread it using a 6-in. taping knife. Once the plaster is almost dry, mark a crosshatch pattern in the surface to create better bonding for the joint compound. Before applying the joint compound, spray the surface with water.

2 Finish the repair by covering the patching plaster with a coat of drywall joint compound. Use a 10- or 12-in.-wide taping knife to get the smoothest surface. Rest one corner of the blade on the wall, and pull the knife over the patch.

3 Once the joint compound is dry, sand it flush to the surrounding surface using 100-grit sandpaper. Remove the sanding dust, and cover the patch with primer. When the primer is dry, cover the repair with paint. You may have to paint the whole wall to hide the patch.

REPAIRING SOLID-WOOD PANELING

Solid-wood paneling is a beautiful addition to any room, and it makes sense to repair it if it ever gets damaged. For surface scratches and scars, rub a small amount of stain that matches the color of the wall into the damaged fibers. Then once the stain is dry, cover the repair with a few coats of paste wax. For deeper damage, use wood filler. Buy one that has a color close to the wall color, and use it according to the directions on the product container. Once the filler is dry, sand it with 120-grit sandpaper, and if the color isn't quite right, apply some stain. Cover it with a matching finish.

TOOLS & MATERIALS
- ▌ Circular saw ▌ Pry bar and small block
- ▌ Tongue-and-groove board
- ▌ Hammer ▌ Nail set ▌ 6d finishing nails

1 Serious damage, like the deeply scarred board shown here, requires removing the board and installing a new one. First, find a board that matches the damaged one. Then cut the damaged one into two parts using a circular saw.

2 To remove the board, use a flat pry bar. Drive it into the saw kerf, and gently lift up one piece of the cut board. Use a scrap block behind the pry bar for extra leverage. When one half of the board is out, pry out the other half.

3 Test fit the replacement board to make sure it fits into the opening. Then cut off the backside of the groove joint, and press the tongue of the board into the groove of the adjacent board. Push the board into the opening until it's flat. Then nail it in place.

REPAIRING PLYWOOD PANELING

project

Plywood paneling has been a do-it-yourself favorite for a long time. It looks good and can make short work of finishing any room, especially extra space that's been reclaimed from an attic or basement. Minor surface repairs can be accomplished with a little stain or some colored wood filler. But larger holes, like the one shown here, need to be patched. The biggest challenge in this job is finding a replacement panel that can be used for the repair. If you can't find one, the best approach is to simply screw a board in place to cover the hole and apply a finish to match the wall paneling.

TOOLS & MATERIALS
▪ Paneling patch ▪ Utility knife
▪ Caulk gun and construction adhesive
▪ Scrap 1x3 stock ▪ Hammer
▪ Nail set ▪ 4d finishing nails

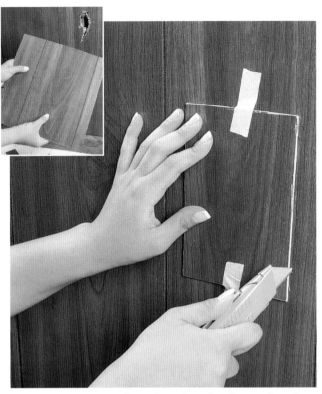

1 Select a piece of paneling that closely matches the color, grain, and groove pattern of the damaged area. Then cut a patch from this panel that will cover the damaged area and tape it on the wall. Score the perimeter of the patch using a sharp utility knife.

2 Remove the patch, and carefully cut along the score lines using the utility knife. Don't try to make the cuts in a single pass. Instead, make repeated light passes until the blade breaks through the panel.

3 Glue and clamp 1x3 backing boards to the sides of the panel opening. Once the glue is dry, apply adhesive to the boards, and spread it smooth using a putty knife.

4 Push the patch into the opening, and nail it to the backing boards using finishing nails. Set the nailheads just below the surface, and cover the heads with colored wood filler that matches the paneling.

REFINISHING WOOD TRIM

Elaborate wood trim, especially in older houses, is a real asset because it looks great and performs the critical function of blending rooms together into a cohesive interior design. Unfortunately, it's difficult and expensive to replace, so most people refinish it instead. This usually involves removing old paint to expose the wood underneath, and then, applying a new finish. This job requires more elbow grease than carpentry skills. In fact, perseverance is probably the most important trait that you can bring to the job.

TOOLS & MATERIALS
▌ Scraper and putty knife ▌ Crevice tool
▌ Heat gun (or chemical stripper)
▌ Sandpaper and block ▌ Brush and finish

1 The easiest and quickest way to remove paint from flat wood trim surfaces is to use a paint scraper. Be sure to keep the blade sharp, and use the tool on the pull stroke, not the push stroke. This tool won't work on curved surfaces.

3 Crevice tools, like this one with a triangular blade, are good for cleaning paint from deep joints. Use it carefully because you want to remove only the paint, not scrape away any of the wood. For the tool to work well, it must be sharpened frequently with a file.

4 Once the paint is removed, sand the trim with 120-grit sandpaper. Remove the paper from the block, and fold it in half to sand deep crevices. You can also use a random-orbit power sander on flat surfaces.

2 Using a heat gun to remove paint doesn't require as much effort as a paint scraper, but it usually takes longer. Keep the tip of the gun as close to the paint as possible without burning the wood, and use a putty knife to scrape away the soft paint.

5 Remove all the sanding dust from the trim; then brush on a shellac-based sanding sealer. Once this is dry, lightly sand it smooth; remove the dust; and apply at least two coats of polyurethane finish.

FLOATING TRIM

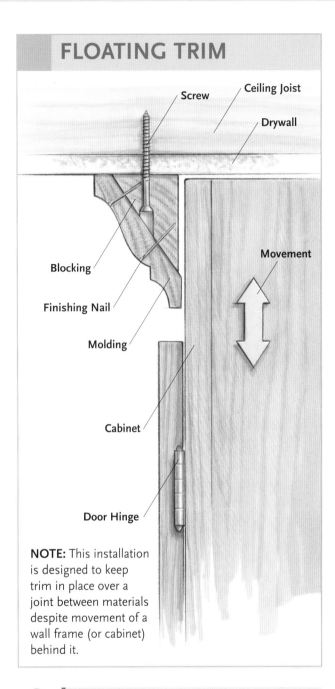

Screw
Ceiling Joist
Drywall
Blocking
Finishing Nail
Molding
Movement
Cabinet
Door Hinge

NOTE: This installation is designed to keep trim in place over a joint between materials despite movement of a wall frame (or cabinet) behind it.

smart tip

PAINT SCRAPERS ARE GREAT TOOLS FOR REMOVING PAINT, BUT THEY CAN BE TIRING TO USE IF YOU ARE STRIPPING A LOT OF PAINT. MAKE THE JOB EASIER BY KEEPING THE SCRAPER BLADE SHARP. EITHER REPLACE IT FREQUENTLY, OR SHARPEN IT WITH A FILE AS SOON AS YOU FEEL IT STARTING TO DULL.

REPLACING A BROKEN TILE

The most important part of a tile repair job (especially in a shower) is to do it quickly, just as soon as you find the loose or broken tile. If not, a lot of water can get behind the tile and degrade the drywall behind. Which, of course, would make for an even bigger repair job in a very short time. You can temporarily fix a loose or broken tile by filling the grout gaps and cracks with silicone caulk. But this will only buy you a week or two. The better approach is to remove the tile.

TOOLS & MATERIALS
▌Drill with masonry bit
▌Utility knife or grout saw
▌Chisel
▌Notched trowel and tile adhesive
▌Replacement tile

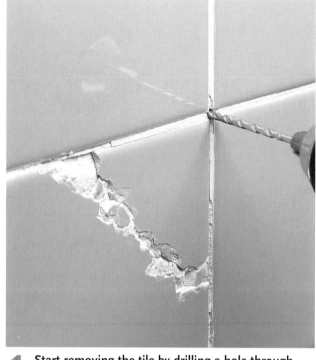

1 Start removing the tile by drilling a hole through the grout at all four corners using a masonry bit in a power drill. Your goal is to focus just on the problem tile. Don't do anything that will damage the surrounding tile and grout.

2 Remove the grout around the tile using either a small grout saw, such as the one shown here, or a sharp utility knife. Remove the grout in repeated slow cuts. Don't try to do it all at once.

3 Once the grout is removed, work an old chisel under the tile, and twist it to break the tile free from the adhesive. If the tile isn't cracked, strike it with a hammer to break it.

● WALLCOVERING SPOT REPAIRS

To re-cover a damaged area, align a patch piece of wallcovering with the underlying pattern; tape it to the wall; and cut through both layers for a perfect fit.

Remove the patch piece and damaged section below it. Scrape or sand the wall as needed. Then activate the adhesive on the patch, and set it into the tailor-made cutout.

You can slice open bubbles in wallcovering with a razor knife and peel back the edges. Then add fresh adhesive; reset the wallcovering; and roll it smooth.

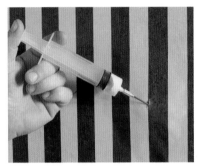

Some wallcovering pros favor this special syringe for fixing air bubbles. You simply puncture the bubble; inject some adhesive; and smooth the raised section.

4 Using a dull chisel, scrape away the old adhesive until the surface behind the tile is flat and smooth. When all the adhesive is gone, brush away any dust and vacuum around the entire opening.

5 Apply adhesive to the wall using a notched trowel. Make sure the whole section is covered with adhesive. Then press the tile into the opening. If the tiles have alignment ears, then the new tile should just slip in. If it doesn't, use plastic spacers to align the tile.

REINFORCING FLOOR JOISTS

There are several ways to beef up attic floor joists so the space above can be used for a bedroom, home office, or a second family room. Usually the best approach is to double-up the existing joists. This means gluing and screwing a board of the same size to the side of the joists that are already in place. Make sure that each new joist is installed with its crown pointing up, and that it's long enough to reach from the top plate of the outside house wall to the top plate of a bearing wall in the middle of the house.

TOOLS & MATERIALS

- Tape measure ▌ Framing lumber
- Caulk gun and construction adhesive
- Drill-driver ▌ 2½-in. drywall screws

1 If any of the attic floor joists is sagging more than ¾ in., it should be jacked up so it's straight. To do this, wedge a 2x4 post (that is just a couple inches longer than the room is high) under the bottom edge of the joist, and push it up until the joist is flat.

2 Spread a thick bead of construction adhesive along the side of an existing joist using a caulk gun. Apply a winding bead so both the top and bottom of each joist will be glued to the new joist.

3 Screw the doubled-up joists together with 2½-in.-long drywall screws. Drive three screws in a vertical line every 16 in. along the length of the joist. Then go up to the floor above, and screw the floor plywood to the top of the new joists.

REINFORCING CEILING JOISTS

Sometimes ceiling joists, particularly in upstairs bedrooms in old houses, are undersized. As a result they can sag and cause cracks in the ceiling plaster or drywall. One good way to stiffen up these ceiling joists is to install a framing member called a strongback. This is constructed of two boards; one is a 2x4 that is screwed to the top of the joists. The other is a 2x6 that is glued and screwed to the edge of the 2x4. Once the strongback is installed, the joists can't sag without bending the 2x4-and-2x6 assembly.

TOOLS & MATERIALS
- Tape measure ▮ Chalk line
- Framing lumber
- Caulk gun and construction adhesive
- Drill-driver
- 3-in. drywall screws

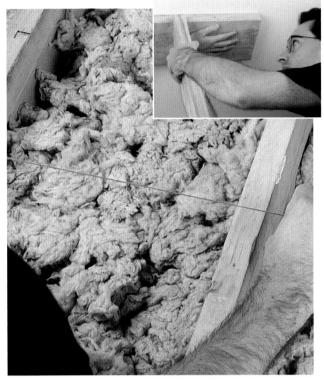

1 Lift a sagging ceiling joist by pushing a 2x4 wedge under the joist. Use a scrap block of wood to protect the drywall or plaster (inset). Then go into the attic, and snap a chalk line down the center of the joists to establish the location of the strongback.

2 Fasten a 2x4 to the top of the joists by driving two 3-in. screws into the top of each joist. Don't remove the brace underneath until the 2x4 is screwed to all the joists.

3 Spread construction adhesive along the side of the 2x4 using a caulk gun. Smooth the adhesive using a putty knife to make sure the entire surface is covered.

4 Place the 2x6 on top of the joists and next to the 2x4. Then screw the 2x6 to the 2x4 every 8 in. Finish up by driving screws down through the 2x6 into the joists.

215

INSTALLING ATTIC STAIRS

If you want to add living space to your attic and don't have a full set of stairs going up there, you should hire a professional to make and install a staircase for you. But if you just want a better way into an attic that currently has only a small access hole, then consider installing a fold-down stairway. This job is within reach for most homeowners and can make getting up and down much easier. The starting point is buying the staircase unit at a lumberyard or home center.

TOOLS & MATERIALS
▮ Tape measure ▮ Framing square
▮ Circular saw, handsaw, and clamps
▮ Framing lumber and shims
▮ Drill-driver and 3-in. drywall screws
▮ Socket wrench and lag screws
▮ Fold-down attic stairs

1 Begin by marking the rough opening dimensions on the surface of the ceiling. Then cut away the drywall to gain access to the attic. Stand on a ladder, and cut any ceiling joists that are in the way. Install double headers at each end of the cut joist (or joists) to support the weight that was carried by the cut joist.

2 Double up the joist that runs alongside the stairway opening, too. Cut stock to length; then screw it in place using 2½-in.-long drywall screws.

3 Frame the other side of the opening with a joist installed in joist hangers. Layout the headers and nail the hangers in place first. Then cut the filler joist to length, and nail it to the hangers.

4 To support the staircase while it's being installed, screw scrap boards in place that extend into both sides of the opening. This creates a stable ledge that will prevent the staircase from falling.

LEFT Large gable-end windows can be combined with dormers and skylights to flood light into a remodeled attic bedroom.

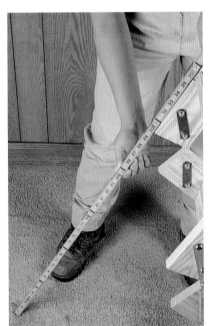

5 Lift the staircase into the opening, and rest it on the support ledges. Attach it to the ceiling framing with lag screws. Shim between the staircase frame and the opening with cedar shingles.

6 Fold down stairs must be cut to length after the unit is installed. To do this, first unfold the stairs and take a measurement (using a ruler as shown) from the top and bottom of the middle stringer to the floor.

7 Transfer the two measurements to the bottom section of the stringer; mark a line between them; and make a cut. Do the same thing to the other stair stringer. Sand the cuts smooth and test the stairway.

217

FIXING A LEAKING SKYLIGHT

A skylight is a great addition to just about any room, especially one that is starved for natural light. But one of these units can also be the source of water leaks that cause internal rot and ceiling stains. Typically the first sign of trouble is a faint brown-edged ring on the ceiling. You can be sure that this indicates a roof leak, instead of just water condensation inside the attic, because the dark edge is caused by traces of asphalt from roofing shingles or roofing cement. A leak must be repaired.

TOOLS & MATERIALS
- Gloves
- Hammer and roofing nails
- Pry bar
- Roofing cement
- Small trowel

1 The first step in repairing a leak around a skylight is to remove the roofing shingle underneath the bottom flashing and set it aside. If this shingle isn't set in roofing cement, this is probably the source of the leak.

3 Gently lift up the flashing where the nails were driven and bend it back slightly so you can apply plastic roof cement under the flashing.

4 Spread a thick coat of roofing cement under the flashing. Use a trowel to make sure the cement is smooth; then press the flashing down into the cement until is sits flat on the roof.

2 Next, look for any nails driven through the side flashing into the roof sheathing below. If you find nails, be sure to pull them. These nails are another likely source of leaks.

● REFLASHING A VENT PIPE

To reseal an old vent pipe, start by scraping away layers of surface tar. Then peel back surrounding shingles and tar paper to inspect the roof for damage, and make repairs as needed.

Install modern flashing with a rubber ring to seal the pipe and a flange to weave into the shingles. The high side goes under the shingles; the low side rides on top.

5 Cover the top of the nail hole and the surrounding flashing with roofing cement, smoothing it in place with a trowel. Be sure to cover the edge of the flashing where it meets the roof.

6 Lift up the flashing at the bottom of the unit, and spread roofing cement underneath its entire width. Then slide a roof shingle that's cut to size and shape under the flashing and on top of the cement.

7 Once the bottom shingle is in place, fold down the side shingles, and press them into roof cement. Do not use any nails to attach shingles within 6 in. of the flashing.

222   LIGHTING OPTIONS

223   FIXTURE TYPES

226   LIGHTBULBS

226   INSTALLING A CEILING FIXTURE

228   RECESSED LIGHTS

228   INSTALLING A RECESSED LIGHT FIXTURE

230   INSTALLING TRACK LIGHTS

232   CHANDELIERS

233   INSTALLING A CHANDELIER

234   INDOOR LIGHTING DESIGN

9 lighting

A quick walk through any home center will give you some idea of just how important lighting is. The lighting area is usually bigger than appliances and almost as big as all the paint aisles put together. What's going on? Are consumers specifying every light fixture in all the new houses that are being built? Well, not exactly—though many homeowners do. The real popularity of light fixtures is based on the variety of light fixture styles and designs, how easy they are to install, and how much they can change the look of a room. Keep in mind that lighting is more than fixtures and bulbs. Good lighting can create a whole personality and ambience for a room, just like paint, paper, and furniture. All it takes is a little planning and some basic know-how.

LIGHTING OPTIONS

Good lighting plays a key role in efficient design—and goes a long way toward defining the personality of the room. With the proper fixtures in the proper places, lighting can help you avoid working in shadows or relaxing in dimly lit rooms. Install several different lighting circuits, controlled by different switches, and you can change your room's atmosphere easily. Start designing a lighting plan by determining the type of lighting you need within a given room.

For living rooms, dining rooms, and family rooms, consider ceiling-mounted fixtures or recessed lighting to provide general illumination throughout the space. But you may want to also include table lamps or some type of focused lighting, called task lighting, to make the space cozy and comfortable to promote conversation or provide illumination for activities.

For an effective lighting scheme, plan a mix of light levels within a room. (See "Recommended Ranges of Light Levels," page 225.) Bear in mind, though, that several factors affect how much general and task lighting a given room needs. Dark surfaces absorb more light than lighter ones. Glossy surfaces reflect more light (and glare) than matte finishes. And different fixture types do different lighting jobs.

ABOVE A good lighting plan includes general illumination, task lighting over work areas, and accent lighting.

● FIXTURE TYPES

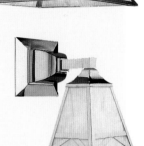

Suspended   Globes, chandeliers, and other suspended fixtures can light a room or a table. Hang them 12 to 20 inches below an 8-foot ceiling or 30 to 36 inches above table height.

Surface-Mount   Attached directly to the ceiling, it distributes very even, shadowless general lighting. To minimize glare, surface-mount fixtures should be shielded. Fixtures with sockets for several smaller bulbs distribute more even lighting than those with just one or two large bulbs.

Recessed   Recessed fixtures, which mount flush with the ceiling or soffit, include fixed and aimable downlights, shielded fluorescent tubes, and totally luminous ceilings. Recessed fixtures require more wattage—up to twice as much as surface-mount and suspended types.

Track   Use a track system for general, task, or accent lighting—or any combination of the three. You can select from a broad array of modular fixtures, clip them anywhere along a track, and revise your lighting scheme any time you like. Locate tracks 12 to 24 inches out from the wall to minimize shadows.

Under-Cabinet   Fluorescent or incandescent fixtures (with showcase bulbs) mounted to the undersides of wall cabinets bathe counters with efficient, inexpensive task lighting. Shield under-cabinet lights with valances, and illuminate at least two-thirds of the counter's length.

Cove   Cove lights reflect upward to the ceiling, creating smooth, even general lighting or dramatic architectural effects. Consider locating custom cove lights on top of ornamental soffits or trim.

Types of Bulbs

Most homes include a combination of warm and cool tones, so selecting bulbs—called lamps by professionals—that provide balanced lighting close to what appears normal to the eye is usually the most attractive choice. Experiment with balancing various combinations of bulbs to create the desired effect. To help you achieve the balance you want, here is a brief description of the different bulbs.

Incandescent. Like sunlight, incandescent bulbs emit continuous-spectrum light, or light that contains every color. Illumination from these bulbs, in fact, is even warmer than sunlight, making its effect very appealing. It makes skin tones look good and enhances the feeling of well-being. Also, these bulbs come in a variety of shapes, sizes, and applications. One type even features a waterproof lens cover that makes it suitable for use near a sink

or above the cooktop where steam can gather. Incandescent bulbs may be clear, frosted, tinted, or colored, and they may have a reflective coating inside. The drawback is that incandescents use a lot of electricity and produce a lot of heat. Therefore, they cost more to run than other types.

Fluorescent. These energy-efficient bulbs cast a diffused, shadowless light that makes them great for general illumination. They are economical, but the old standard fluorescents produce an unflattering light, making everything and everyone appear bluish and bland. Newer fluorescent bulbs, called triphosphor fluorescent lamps, are warmer and render color that more closely resembles sunlight. Fluorescents are available both in the familiar tube versions and in newer, compact styles. Mixing these bulbs with incandescent lamps, plus adding as much natural light to the room plan as possible, can make fluorescents more appealing. Be aware, though, that in some parts of the country local codes require fluo-rescent lights be the first type turned on when entering a room to conform to energy-conservation mandates.

Halogen. This is actually a type of incandescent lamp that produces a brighter, whiter light at a lower wattage, with greater energy efficiency. The disadvantages are a higher price tag and higher heat output that requires special shielding. Although halogens cost more up front, they last longer than conventional incandescent lights. A popular subcategory of halogen is the low-voltage ver-sion. It produces an intense bright light, but is more en-ergy efficient than standard halogen. Compact in size, low-voltage halogens are typically used for creative accent lighting.

Fiber Optics. One of countless innovations gradually finding their way into the home, a fiber-optic system con-sists of one extremely bright lamp to transport light to one or more destinations through fiber-optic conduits. Used to accent spaces, fiber-optic lighting has the advan-tage of not generating excessive heat. This makes it ideal as an alternative to decorative neon lights, which get very hot and consume a great deal of energy.

ABOVE AND BELOW Hanging fixtures, above, usually provide general illumination. The tops of the wall cabi-nets, below, glow from low-voltage accent lights.

ABOVE When used correctly, lighting becomes an important design element in any room, especially a kitchen.

RECOMMENDED RANGES OF LIGHT LEVELS

Activity	Easy or Short Duration	Critical or Prolonged
Dining	Low	Low
Entertaining	Low to high	Low to high
Grooming	Moderate	High
Craftwork *	Moderate	High
Kitchen/laundry chores	Low to moderate	High
Reading	Low to moderate	High
Studying	Moderate	High
TV viewing	Low to moderate	Low to moderate
Computer work	Moderate	High
Workbench *	Moderate	High
Tabletop games	Low to moderate	Moderate to high
Writing	Low to moderate	High

* Benefits from supplementary directional light.

LIGHTBULBS

Lightbulbs are rated by lumens, which measure the amount of light that the bulb produces, and watts, which measure the rate at which electrical energy is used. Watts don't measure brightness; though a 100-watt incandescent bulb is brighter than a 40-watt one, a 13-watt fluorescent may be brighter than the 40-watt incandescent.

Types of Bulbs

Compared with an energy-guzzling 100-watt incandescent, compact fluorescents use 75 percent less electricity and last longer. But the harsh, bluish light of a fluorescent is also not necessarily what you want over the bathroom mirror. If you are stuck with fluorescent fixtures, a lighting expert can help by choosing warmer bulbs or cooler tubes to suit the situation. Halogen bulbs have a kind of clear-white quality, and are about 25 percent brighter than standard incandescent bulbs of the same wattage, but they require special fixtures. They are also extremely hot and should be treated with caution. High-intensity-discharge (HID) bulbs, such as halide and high-pressure sodium, are also bright and efficacious but require special fixtures.

project

INSTALLING A CEILING FIXTURE

First cut a hole in the ceiling; then fish a power cable into this hole; and install a retrofit ceiling box. Once both are in place, strip the sheathing and wire insulation from the cable, and screw a hanging strap to the box. Join the wires from the fixture and the box; then tighten the fixture in place. Install the proper lightbulb (or bulbs), and screw on the fixture globe.

TOOLS & MATERIALS
▌Insulated screwdriver
▌Electrical box ▌Cable ripper
▌Needle-nose pliers ▌Wire stripper
▌Cable clamps ▌Wire connectors
▌Light fixture ▌Threaded nipple
▌Mounting strap

 ## LIGHTING CAPACITY

Before deciding on a fixture, be sure to have enough lighting capacity. Determine how much you need by matching the power consumption in watts to the floor area to be lighted: for fluorescent lighting, 1.2 to 1.6 watts per square foot; for incandescent lighting, 3.5 to 4 watts per square foot.

Unfortunately, there is no simple rule of thumb for task lighting. Because task lighting must focus on a specific target to be effective, the location of the lamp is as important as the amount of light it yields.

To light a mirror with incandescent lamps, figure on at least three bulbs of 15- to 25-watt capacity at each side or a series of strip lights (pictured at right) around the sides and top of the mirror. Strip-lighting fixtures are generally available in 18- 24-, 36-, and 48-inch lengths.

An enclosed tub or shower also requires lighting. Choose a recessed vapor-proof fixture with a 60- or 75-watt bulb. For safety, position the switch so that it is out of reach from inside the compartment.

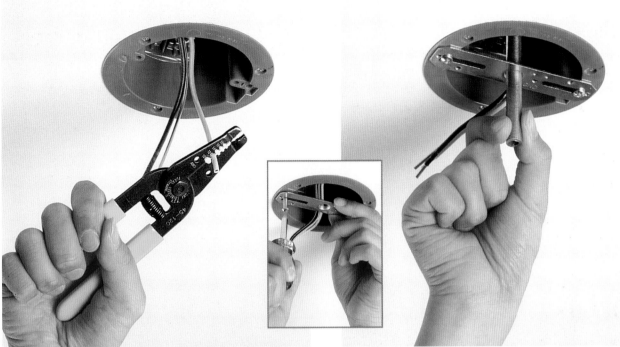

1 Begin by cutting a box hole in the ceiling and installing a retrofit ceiling box and cable in this hole. Remove the cable sheathing, and strip the ends of the wires using wire strippers.

2 Screw a metal hanging strap to the bottom of the ceiling box (inset). Then turn a threaded nipple into the strap collar. This nipple will hold the light fixture in place.

3 Join the fixture wires to the box wires by combining like-color wires with wire connectors. Add a short pigtail wire to the ground wires, and tighten it under the grounding screw.

4 Slide the fixture over the box, and turn the retaining nut onto the threaded nipple. Tighten the nut until the fixture is against the ceiling. Add the recommended bulbs, and install the globe that came with the fixture.

RECESSED LIGHTS

Some recessed systems must be installed before the ceiling is closed. If that is not possible, be sure to buy a system that you can install from below in a finished ceiling. Also check to make sure that the housing you are considering is compatible with the clearances you have for both depth and proximity to insulation. Low-profile downlights and rectangular fluorescent fixtures called "troffers" can be used in spaces as shallow as 4 inches.

Recessed lighting fixtures for damp areas such as bathrooms must be clearly marked "Suitable for Wet Locations" or at least "Suitable for Damp Locations." These fixtures must be installed so that water cannot enter the wiring compartments. Recessed lights that are designed for wet locations can even be used inside a shower or over a tub or whirlpool. Make sure you use shatter-resistant white acrylic lenses that eliminate the danger of glass breakage are best. Always put the switch out of reach of those in the tub or shower to reduce the risk of electrocution.

Unless the fixture is rated safe for insulation contact, insulation batts should be cut back so that they are at least 3 inches away from the fixture's housing. If the ceiling has loose-fill insulation, you'll need to install baffles to keep the insulation away from the fixture.

RECESSED FIXTURES

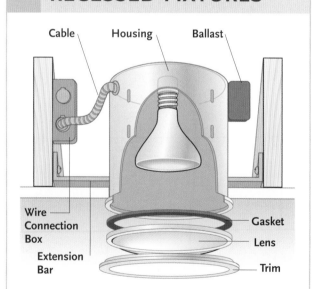

Cable   Housing   Ballast

Wire Connection Box
Extension Bar
Gasket
Lens
Trim

A recessed lighting fixture in a bathroom should be clearly marked as suitable for wet or damp locations. It must have a watertight cover with a gasket.

INSTALLING A RECESSED LIGHT FIXTURE

project

Recessed lights come in different configurations. But generally, the unit features a light housing mounted on sliding brackets with a separate electrical box for making the wiring connections. Start the job by installing the unit between ceiling joists. Then open up the electrical box; install the switch cable; and replace the box cover. Install a bulb, lens, gasket, and trim ring.

TOOLS & MATERIALS
■ Insulated screwdrivers
■ Nails or screws
■ Hammer (if necessary)
■ Power drill-driver ■ Cable ripper
■ Needle-nose pliers ■ Cable clamps
■ Multipurpose tool ■ Wire connectors
■ Recessed lamp housing

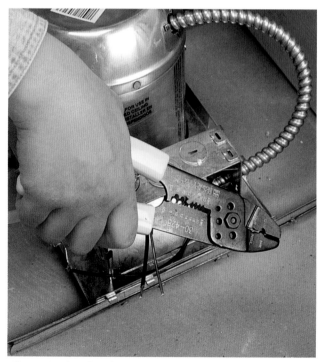

3 Strip the sheathing from the switch cable; then remove approximately ½ in. of insulation from the end of each wire.

1 Begin by establishing the location of the light unit, and cut a hole in the ceiling drywall. Then take the fixture into the attic; pull back the insulation; and adjust the extension bars until the fixture is centered over the hole. Screw the brackets to the sides of the joists.

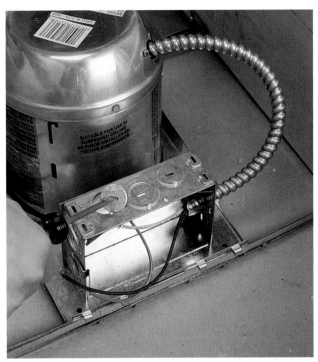

2 Take off the side cover to the box and, using a flat-bladed screwdriver, remove one of the box knock-outs. Install a cable connector in this hole; then slide the switch cable through the connector and tighten it in place.

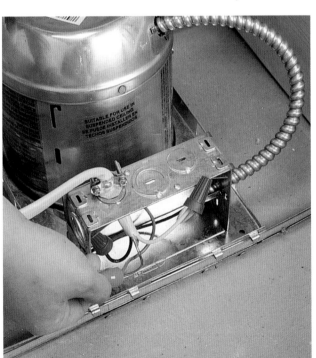

4 Join the like-color wires from the switch cable and the fixture cable with wire connectors. Hand tighten each connector. Make sure to install the proper size connector. In this case, the connector must be rated for at least two 14-gauge wires.

5 Carefully tuck all the wire connections into the box, and replace the side cover. Then go back to the room and install the gasket, lens, and trim ring.

project

INSTALLING TRACK LIGHTS

If you'd like to try some track lighting to change the look of your room or to direct more task lighting where you need it, then you're in luck. Installing one of these systems is not difficult, especially if you already have a switch-operated ceiling fixture where you want the track to go. All you have to do is shut off the power to the fixture, remove it, and start installing the tracks. Once they are attached to the ceiling, install the light heads and turn on the power.

TOOLS & MATERIALS
▌Track lighting kit ▌Insulated screwdrivers
▌Basic electrical tools
▌Drywall nails or screws
▌Straightedge ▌Power drill-driver

1 Turn off the power at the service panel, and remove the old ceiling fixture. Mark the ceiling for the location of the tracks according to the manufacturer's instructions in the track lighting kit.

2 Start installing the tracks by threading the wires from the power connector through its mounting plate holes. Then connect like-color wires from the connector to those in the ceiling box. Make the wire splices using the right size wire connectors.

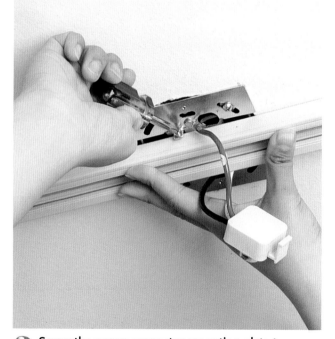

3 Screw the power connector mounting plate to the electrical box. Make sure the plate is tight and doesn't pinch any of the cable or fixture wires. Then lift up a section of track; slide it between the connector wires; and attach it temporarily to the mounting plate.

ABOVE Track fixtures can be used for general lighting or to provide task lighting to specific areas.

4 Temporarily install all the tracks and the connectors. When you are satisfied with the layout, mark all the track-mounting holes on the ceiling; then take down the tracks. Where the track passes under a ceiling joist, you can use drywall screws to attach it. In the spaces between joists, use toggle bolts.

5 Permanently install the tracks and any T- or L-connectors, and make sure they are all tight against the ceiling. Slide the light fixtures onto the track, and lock them in place. Turn on the lights, and adjust the direction of the lamps if necessary. Then touch up the ceiling paint to cover any installation marks.

CHANDELIERS

Hanging a chandelier differs from installing a ceiling-mounted light fixture because of the added weight of the fixture. This requires modifying the ceiling box to accommodate the extra weight. Special chandelier-hanging hardware is used for this purpose, including a threaded stud and nipple, a hickey, and lock-nuts. If you can't work from an attic space above the ceiling, you will have to cut a hole in the ceiling drywall to gain access to the ceiling joists. Cut a 16 x 16-inch hole, from one ceiling joist to the next, and install wood blocking to support the chandelier. Then attach a box; fish a power cable into the box; and install new drywall.

RIGHT The added weight of a hanging fixture must be supported by the ceiling box.

● BRINGING CABLE INTO A METAL BOX

To bring cable into a metal box, you must first remove one of the knockouts on the box. Some boxes have a pryout built into them that can easily be removed using a flat-blade screwdriver. Others have a circular knockout that must be punched out using a hammer and a screwdriver or knockout punch. Once the knockout hole is open, a cable clamp can be inserted into the opening. The clamp secures the cable in place and protects it from chafing against the sharp metal edges of the box opening.

Some metal boxes have pryouts that can be removed using the flat blade of a screwdriver.

Pryout

Knockout

Other boxes have knockouts that must be punched out using a hammer and screwdriver, or using a special tool called a knockout punch.

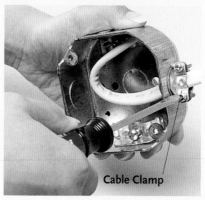

A cable clamp screws into the pryout or knockout opening to secure the cable entering the box and protect it from chafing against the sharp edges of the opening.

Cable Clamp

INSTALLING A CHANDELIER

project

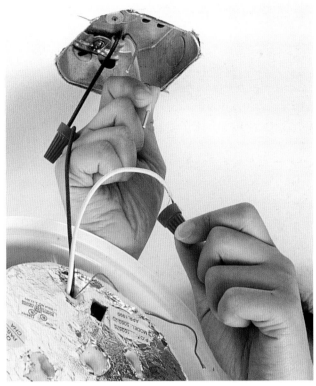

Many chandeliers, especially heavy ones, come with instructions that explain the support the fixture needs. If your fixture doesn't call for special support, then you can probably replace your existing fixture with a chandelier as we show here. If, on the other hand, extra support is called for, then you have two options. One is to cut a hole in the ceiling and nail wooden support blocks in place. The other is to install an electrical box support brace that has the proper weight-limit specification.

TOOLS & MATERIALS
▮ Chandelier ▮ Collar nut ▮ Threaded nipple
▮ Stud ▮ Insulated screwdrivers
▮ Adjustable wrench ▮ Wire connectors
▮ Escutcheon plate ▮ Hickey
▮ Locknuts ▮ Neon circuit tester
▮ Needle-nose pliers ▮ Multipurpose tool

1 Turn off the circuit power to the existing light fixture at the service panel. Then remove the screws that hold the fixture in place, and unthread the wire connectors that join the circuit and fixture wires.

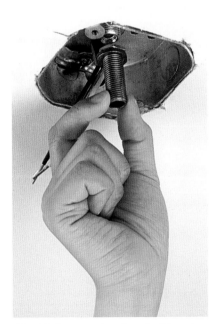

2 Make sure the electrical box is securely mounted to the ceiling framing. Then remove the center knockout plate; install a stud in the knockout hole; thread a hickey into the stud, and a nipple into the hickey.

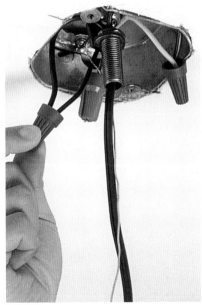

3 Have someone hold the chandelier or support it on a step-ladder while you work. Thread the chandelier wires through the threaded nipple. Then connect the fixture wires to the box wires.

4 Once the wires are joined, slide the chandelier escutcheon plate up against the ceiling box. Hold it in place as you screw the collar nut onto the threaded nipple in the middle of the box.

233

INDOOR LIGHTING DESIGN

Use lighting the way an artist uses a brush, to downplay or highlight elements in a room. Lighting focused on an object will draw the eye to that object in contrast to its background. For example, lighting the corners in a room makes it seem larger, as the eye takes in its entirety. In comparison, a soft pool of light created around a sofa will focus attention on the piece of furniture. The remainder of the room recedes into shadow, making it seem smaller.

Not everyone reacts to light in the same way. Some people are more photosensitive than others, preferring a lower field of general lighting. To others, the toned-down lighting suitable to photosensitive people may be depressing. Consider the personal preferences of all family members when you design your lighting system.

The functions of lighting divide into three basic categories: to provide general or ambient lighting, task lighting, and accent or decorative lighting.

General Lighting. General or ambient lighting provides overall brightness for an area. Furnishing background illumination, it can vary with day and night, winter and summer, or different moods and activities.

Task Lighting. Task lighting makes it easier to see what you are doing. Individual fixtures concentrate light in specific areas for chores such as preparing food, reading, or doing crafts.

Accent Lighting. Accent or decorative lighting highlights an area or object, emphasizing that aspect of a room's character. These mood-makers of lighting, to be effective, must contrast with their background of ambient lighting.

ABOVE Widely dispersed, recessed lights present one way to create aesthetically pleasing ambient lighting.

LEFT Ceiling fixtures wash an entire wall in light or focus on a single item. Unusual lamps provide decorative accents.

LEFT This living space effectively uses recessed ceiling lights to create ambient lighting and wall washers to accent the fireplace and entry-way. A freestanding fixture provides both task and decorative lighting.

BOTTOM LEFT An elegant chandelier on a dimmer switch provides both ambient mood and task lighting.

BOTTOM RIGHT Wall sconces provide task lighting as well as a decorative flourish to this bathroom.

238 VENTILATION BASICS

239 ROOF VENTS

240 INSTALLING A VENTILATING FAN

242 WIRING A VENTILATING FAN

244 WIRING A CEILING FAN

246 INSTALLING A WHOLE-HOUSE FAN

10 ventilation

If no one lived in your house, ventilation wouldn't be a big deal. No one would be polluting the air and no one would be suffering the ill effects of bad air. But if people do live in your house, ventilation reduces their exposure to such diverse pollutants as dust mites, carbon monoxide, formaldehyde, and even radon. Good ventilation also reduces high levels of water vapor that can cause structural problems or create mold that can cause serious respiratory troubles. Good ventilation also serves to cool your house, from the simple range hood that takes heat from the kitchen to the much bigger whole-house fan that can rid your entire house of hot air in just a couple of hours. Generally, all that's needed to improve ventilation is to install a couple of different types of ventilating systems.

VENTILATION BASICS

When it's a comfortable, air-conditioned 70 degrees F in the house despite a heat wave outside, the unconditioned attic may be baking at 125 degrees or more. You don't live under the eaves, so you don't feel the heat directly. But overheated attics drive up cooling costs, shorten the life span of conditioning equipment, and can contribute to mold, rot, and other problems.

Before you increase ventilation to reduce the baking effect, the first step is to provide an insulating barrier between the attic and the living areas below. To satisfy modern energy codes, you may need to blow in loose fill, spread loose insulation from bags, or lay another layer of batts across the tops of the joists.

Vent Inlets and Outlets

There are many types of attic vents and many good places to install them. But one type in one place can't handle the job of keeping attic air close to the temperature of the air outside. You need a combination with about the same square footage of air inlet and air outlet.

On the roof, you can install turbine vents that spin as hot air escapes and encourage the flow of more air. Another option is a roof vent with a hood that keeps out rain. The most effective roof installation is a continuous ridge vent. The plywood roof deck is built (or cut back on retrofits) short of the roof peak so that air can sweep up under the attic roof and out the vent.

One of the most common outlet options is a gable-end vent. This louvered vent nestles under the roof ridge on the end wall of the attic. If you have two exposed gable walls, a louver (screened on the back to keep out insects) on each one encourages cross ventilation.

There are four basic ways to bring air into the attic along the roof overhang. Plug vents are small screened and louvered circles made of metal. You simply cut a hole in the soffit between each pair of rafters and snap in a vent. Increase the vent area with the same approach by cutting large openings between bays and installing rectangular vents about the size of floor registers. A better option is to install a continuous strip-grille vent. It is only a few inches wide but extends the full length of the overhang to provide a larger vent area and eliminate unvented dead spots. If your wood soffit is badly deteriorated, consider replacing it with perforated aluminum panels.

● TYPES OF SOFFIT VENTS

Set a plug vent by drilling a hole in the soffit between rafters and pressing the vent in place.

Perforated vents are typically made of vinyl panels that supply ventilation through the entire soffit.

Register vents are installed like plug vents, but you need to drill a starter hole and use a saber saw to cut the larger opening for the vent.

Attach surface-mounted strip vents over slots in the soffit using $1/2$-in. screws about a foot apart.

VENTING THROUGH THE ROOF

Roof Vents. Several types of vents can be installed in the roof surface. But these require a hole in the roof, which increases the chance of leaks. You can use slightly commercial looking turbine vents or hooded vents designed to shed water on a sloping roof. Vents generally come as waterproof units attached to wraparound flanges designed to fit into the water-shedding overlaps of the shingles.

Trim back shingles, and cut the roof deck using a reciprocating saw.

Slip the upper flange underneath shingles, and seal the nails.

Gable Vents. These vents are commonly installed in low-slope and steeply pitched roofs. Many sizes are available, including large units that can handle the air movement of a whole-house fan. Sometimes, large automated louvers are wired to the fan motor so that the panels open when the fan runs. If the gable-end vents you use are not backed with screening, add a layer to keep insects out of the attic.

Frame a rough opening, and install headers between studs.

Caulk under the edges of the vent, and nail it to the gable-end frame.

Ridge Vents. This is the most effective roof-mounted vent because it allows ventilation along the entire attic, and rarely leaks if installed properly. It's also easy to install during construction and has become a standard fixture on most new homes. But you can easily retrofit an older home by removing (and possibly saving) the old cap shingles. That allows you to strip away tar paper and cut back roofing and sheathing on both sides of the ridge.

Nail the vent over the open ridge where roofing has been removed.

Most vents can be concealed with a row of standard cap shingles.

INSTALLING A VENTILATING FAN

An exhaust fan is a welcome addition to any bathroom because it takes away harmful water vapor. To install one, first locate the best position, and cut a hole in the ceiling. Attach the fan housing to a framing member, and install the duct work. Then complete the job by cutting a vent hole through the roof and installing a vent hood.

TOOLS & MATERIALS
- Ventilating fan ▌ Power drill-driver
- Reciprocating, keyhole, or saber saw
- Hammer ▌ Duct tape ▌ Screwdriver
- Flexible aluminum duct and vent cap kit
- 10-in.-long rigid aluminum duct
- Silicone caulk and caulking gun
- 8d common nails ▌ Drywall screws
- Roofing cement ▌ Screw clamp

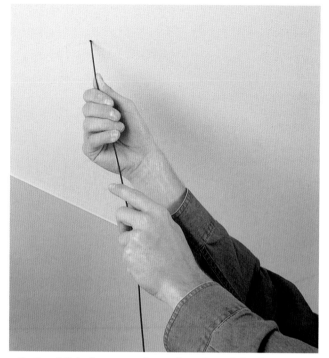

1 Establish the approximate location of the fan on the ceiling. Then drill a small hole, and feed a coat hanger wire up through the ceiling and the insulation above if any is present.

● VENTILATING FAN CAPACITY

To remove moist air and odors effectively from a bathroom, you need to match the fan capacity to the room's volume. Ventilating fans are sized by the number of cubic feet of air they move each minute (cfm). A fan should change all of the room's air at least eight times each hour. For 8-foot ceilings, the following formula can help determine what you need:

**Fan capacity (cfm) =
Room Width (feet) x Room Length (feet) x 1.1**

Fans are also rated in "sones" for the amount of noise they produce, from 1 to 4 sones. A fan rated at 1 sone, the quietest, is about as loud as a refrigerator.

4 Place the fan housing over the ceiling hole, and screw it to a framing member. Then choose the best path for the vent duct, and attach it to the end of the fan housing using a screw clamp.

2 Pull back any insulation to find the reference wire. Then establish the fan location. It should be installed against a framing member to provide adequate support. Drill small holes through the ceiling at the corners of the fan.

3 Press the fan housing against the ceiling so its corners fall within the four holes you drilled from above. Trace around the housing to mark the ceiling, and cut the drywall using a keyhole or saber saw (inset).

5 Extend the vent duct up to the point where it goes through the roof. Then attach an aluminum vent collar to the end of the duct using duct tape.

6 Cut a vent hole through the roof using a saber saw. If you don't have one, use a reciprocating saw or a keyhole saw.

7 Once the hole is cut, pull up the vent duct, and attach it to the vent hood. Seal the adjacent shingles using roof cement.

WIRING A VENTILATING FAN

project

There are a couple of code-approved ways to provide power to a fan housing. Usually the easiest approach is to bring a power cable to the fan, and then run a switch-leg cable down to the wall switch. In this configuration, the wire connections are made as follows: join the white wires from the fan to the power source; connect the black wire from the power source to the switch cable; and join the black wire from the power source to the white wire (wrapped with black tape) on the switch cable. All these connections are made with wire connectors.

At the switch box, there is just a single cable. Code the white wire with black tape; then connect the black wire to one switch terminal and the white-with-black tape wire to the other.

Another approach is to run power to the switch box, and then run a switch leg up to the fan. In this option, the white wires from the fan and the power cable are joined, and the black wires from the fan and the power source are joined.

Once all the wiring connections are done, install the fan motor in the housing, and plug it in to the power receptacle that is provided. Finish up by attaching the grille to the bottom of the fan housing.

TOOLS & MATERIALS
▌ Cable ripper
▌ Multipurpose tool
▌ Insulated screwdriver
▌ 14/2 cable with ground
▌ Switch
▌ Pigtails
▌ Switch box
▌ Wire connectors

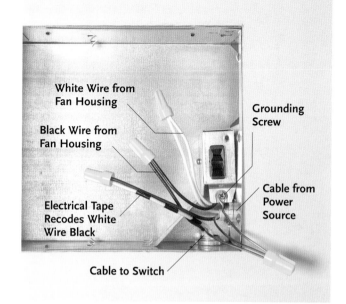

White Wire from Fan Housing

Black Wire from Fan Housing

Grounding Screw

Electrical Tape Recodes White Wire Black

Cable from Power Source

Cable to Switch

1 Every electrical outlet has to be supplied with power either directly from a branch circuit or from a controlling switch. In the photo above, the power comes directly from a circuit and then is directed down to a controlling switch.

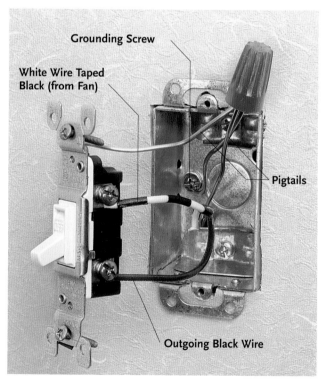

Grounding Screw

White Wire Taped Black (from Fan)

Pigtails

Outgoing Black Wire

2 When power goes to the fan first and only a single cable goes to the switch below, the wiring connections are simple. The black wire goes to one terminal. The white wire (that should be wrapped in black tape) goes to the other terminal.

caution

BECAUSE VENTING AN EXHAUST FAN CAN BE DIFFICULT, IT'S TEMPTING TO OMIT THE DUCT ALTOGETHER AND JUST VENT THE EXHAUST FAN INTO THE ATTIC SPACE. NO BUILDING CODES PERMIT THIS AND THEIR MOTIVATION ISN'T BASED ON AN EXCESS OF CAUTION. BY DUMPING LARGE AMOUNTS OF WATER VAPOR INTO THE ATTIC, YOU VIRTUALLY ASSURE THAT WATER WILL CONDENSE OUT OF THE VAPOR AND COAT THE FRAMING MEMBERS. THIS GREATLY INCREASES THE LIKELIHOOD OF SERIOUS DAMAGE CAUSE BY ROT.

DUCT LOCATIONS

Vent

Vent Collar

Rafter

Optional Route for Ductwork

Flexible Duct

Fan Housing

Joist

Boxed Soffit

Vent

Running the vent from a bathroom exhaust fan to the outside can take some creativity. The most direct route is usually straight up through the roof. But the one that is most protected from the weather is running the duct between ceiling joists and out through the soffit.

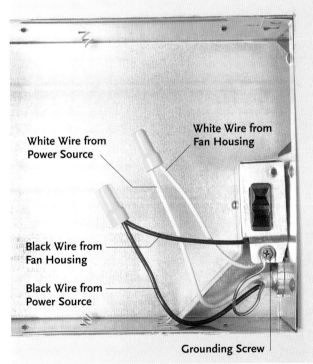

White Wire from Power Source

White Wire from Fan Housing

Black Wire from Fan Housing

Black Wire from Power Source

Grounding Screw

3 When the power goes to the switch first and only a single cable goes to the fan, connect the fan by joining like-color wires with wire connectors.

4 After installing the fan housing, put the fan into the housing, and plug its pigtail extension cord into the receptacle provided in the housing. Cover the whole assembly with the fan grille.

INSTALLING CEILING FANS

When it comes to installing ceiling (paddle) fans, homeowners commonly assume that a fan can be suspended from an existing ceiling box. This is often not the case. A ceiling-suspended fan weighing up to 35 pounds, for example, requires an electrical box that is approved for the weight of the fixture. If it does not have this approval, an existing box must be replaced with one that does. The electrical box must be firmly secured to the structural framing. If the box is not completely rigid, the fan will wobble.

CEILING FAN SUPPORT

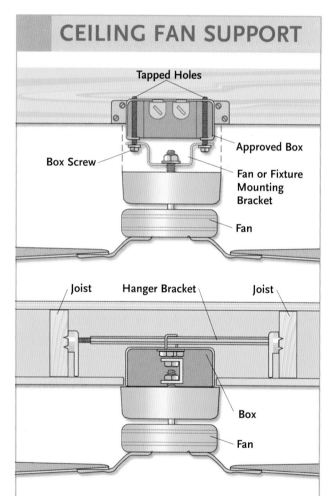

The NEC requires that a ceiling-suspended fan be supported by one of two methods, depending upon the weight of the fixture. If the fixture weighs up to 35 lbs., it can be supported by an electrical box listed for that purpose. If it weighs over 35 lbs., the fixture must be supported independently of the electrical box.

WIRING A CEILING FAN

project

Installing a standard ceiling fan is one of the easier electrical installation projects. Just cut in a single switch box and a round fan box in the ceiling. But if you want to add a light kit to the bottom of the fan, you have to add a second switch in the wall box to control the light.

TOOLS & MATERIALS
- Ceiling fan/light ▪ 12 or 14/2G cable
- Cable ripper ▪ Multipurpose tool
- Wire connectors
- Hanger Bracket (for box fans over 35 lbs.)
- Insulated screwdrivers
- Fan switch ▪ Needle-nose pliers
- Cable clamps (if boxes are metal)
- Approved ceiling-fixture box
- Square light-switch box ▪ Light switch

● BOXES & CONTROLS

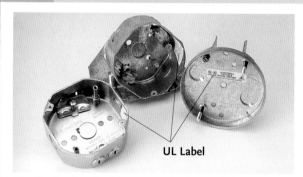

UL Label

The fan's electrical box must be labeled (by Underwriters Laboratories) to carry the weight of the fixture.

You can install wall switches to control the fan and light independently for your ceiling fan.

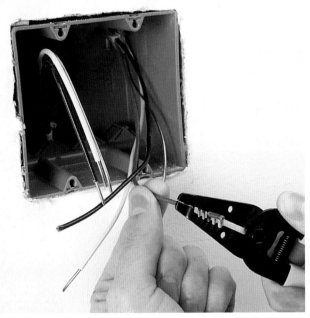

1 Start this job by installing a double-wide cut-in box in the wall. Trace around the box on the wall; cut out the drywall; and fish a power cable into the box. Also fish a 3-wire cable from the switch box up to the ceiling fan box. Strip the sheathing from the cables and the insulation from all the wires.

2 Cut a hole for a round fan box in the ceiling, and pull the 3-wire cable from the switch box into this hole. Slide the cable into the box, and install the box in the ceiling hole. Strip the sheathing from the cable and the insulation from the wires.

3 Join the fixture wires to the cable wires using wire connectors. The blacks go together; the whites go together; and the red wire from the switch goes with the third fixture wire color, in this case blue. Join both cable ground wires to a pigtail, and connect this pigtail to the fixture grounding screw.

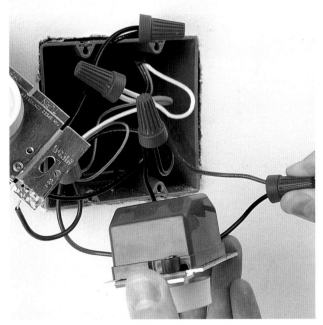

4 In the switch box, join both white wires using a wire connector; join all the ground wires under another wire connector; and hook the dimmer switch and the fan speed control switch together.

245

INSTALLING A WHOLE-HOUSE FAN

A whole-house fan is a great way to keep things cooler in the summer without installing central air conditioning. The wiring on this job isn't difficult, but installing the fan can be. Just make sure, if you tackle the job, to install a fan that's the right size. Discuss the square footage of your attic with your fan dealer.

TOOLS & MATERIALS

- Whole-house fan ▮ Stepladder ▮ Work gloves
- Tape measure ▮ Circular saw ▮ Dust mask
- Joist lumber ▮ ½-in. plywood panels
- 1½-in. rigid foam board ▮ Multipurpose tool
- 12/2G and 12/3G cable ▮ Safety glasses
- Speed-control fan switch ▮ Wire connectors
- Screened louver vents ▮ Keyhole saw ▮ Nails
- Carpenter's hammer ▮ Bracing lumber
- Insulated screwdrivers ▮ Needle-nose pliers
- Junction box ▮ Switch box ▮ Wire staples

1 Establish a good location for the fan in the ceiling just below the attic. In a two-story house, just above the top of the stairs is a good choice. Mark an opening on the ceiling according to the fan manufacturer's instructions; then cut out the drywall using a drywall or keyhole saw.

4 Install the fan louver underneath the fan assembly by screwing its frame to the rough opening lumber. Make sure the louvers move freely and weren't distorted during shipping or installation.

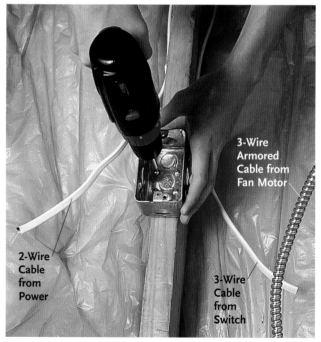

3-Wire Armored Cable from Fan Motor

2-Wire Cable from Power

3-Wire Cable from Switch

5 Install a junction box next to the fan's plywood box by screwing it to the top of a ceiling joist. The box will hold the 2-wire power cable, the 3-wire switch cable, and the 3-wire armored cable that comes from the fan.

2 Cut away any ceiling joist segments that fall in the fan opening. Install headers on both sides of the opening to support the cut joists and to frame a rough opening to support the fan. Use the same size lumber that was used for the ceiling joists.

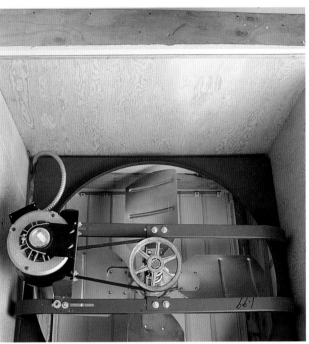

3 Install the fan in the opening; then build an insulated plywood box above it. Also build an insulated cover for this box for use in the winter months when the fan isn't in use. The box sides should extend about 12 in. above the top of the fan.

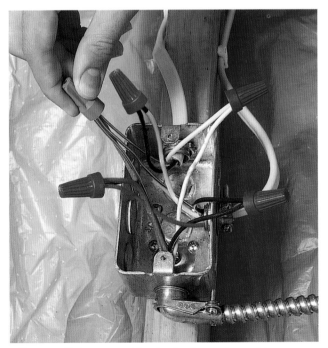

6 Install the two cables in the box using cable connectors and the armored cable using an armored cable connector. Strip the sheathing from the cables and the insulation from the wires. Then join the wires using wire connectors as shown above.

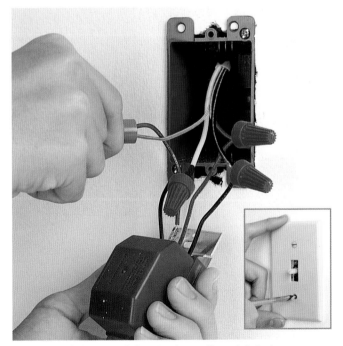

7 Install the switch box in the wall, and fish the 3-wire cable from the fan junction box in the attic into this switch box. Strip off the cable sheathing and wire insulation, and attach the switch leads to the cable leads. Push the switch into the box, and add a cover plate (inset).

This list of manufacturers and associations is meant to be a general guide to additional industry and product-related sources. It is not intended as a listing of products and manufacturers represented by the photographs in this book.

Alcoa
201 Isabella St.
Pittsburg, PA 15212
888-252-6212
www.alcoa.com
Manufactures aluminum products

American Olean Tile Co.
1000 Cannon Ave.
Lansdale, PA 19446-0271
215-855-1111
www.americanolean.com
Manufactures ceramic tile

Andersen Corporation
100 Fourth Ave. North
Bayport, MN 55003-1096
888-888-7020
www.andersencorp.com
Manufactures windows

Armstrong World Industries
Attn: Customer Response Center
P.O. Box 3001
Lancaster, PA 17604
800-233-3823
www.armstrong.com
Manufactures cabinets, flooring, and ceiling materials

Balmer Architectural Mouldings
271 Yorkland Blvd.
Toronto, Ontario M2J 1S5
Canada
800-665-3454
www.balmer.com
Manufactures polyurethane moldings, medallions, door surrounds, mantels

Celotex, a div. of CertainTeed
750 E. Swedesford Rd.
Valley Forge, PA 19482
800-233-8990
www.certainteed.com
Manufactures building products

Corian
Chestnut Run Plaza
721 Maple Run
P.O. Box 80721
Wilmington, DE 19880
800-426-7426
www.corian.com
Manufactures solid-surfacing material for home and commercial kitchens

CraftMaster Door Designs
1 South Wacker Dr., Ste. 3600
Chicago, IL 60606
800-405-2233
www.craftmasterdoordesigns.com
Manufactures interior molded door facings

Dura-Stilts
800-225-2440
www.durastilt.com
Manufactures professional stilts

Elmwood Reclaimed Timber
P.O. Box 10750
Kansas City, MO 64188-0750
816-532-0300
800-705-0705
www.elmwoodreclaimedtimber.com
Provides reclaimed timber and stone products

Expanko, Inc.
3135 Lower Valley Rd.
Parkesburg, PA 19365
800-345-6202
www.expanko.com
Manufactures cork and rubber flooring

Forbo Linoleum Inc.
Humboldt Industrial Park
P.O. Box 667
Hazleton, PA 18201
570-459-0771
www.forbolinoleumna.com
Manufactures linoleum flooring

Georgia-Pacific
133 Peachtree St., NE
Atlanta, GA 30303
404-652-4000
www.gp.com
Manufactures building products and related chemicals

Hartco Hardwood Floors, a div. of Armstrong
P.O. Box 4009
Oneida, TN 37841
800-769-8528
www.hartcoflooring.com
Manufactures engineered hardwood and solid wood flooring

Helios, a div. of Mohawk Industries
500 Town Park Lane, Suite 400
Kennesaw, GA 30144
800-843-5138
www.helioscarpet.com
Manufactures wool carpets and area rugs

InterfaceFLOR
116 North York Rd., Suite 300
Elmhurst, IL 60126
866-281-3567
www.interfaceflor.com
Manufactures carpet tiles

Lindal Cedar Homes
P.O. Box 24426
Seattle, WA 98124
800-426-0536
www.lindal.com
Manufactures custom cedar homes

Mannington Mills, Inc.
75 Mannington Mills Rd.
Salem, NJ 08079
856-935-3000
www.mannington.com
Manufactures flooring

Marvin Windows & Doors
P.O. Box 100
Warroad, MN 56763
888-537-7828
www.marvin.com
Manufactures windows and doors

Mohawk Industries, Inc.
160 South Industrial Blvd.
Calhoun, GA 30701
1-800-266-4295
www.mohawkflooring.com
Manufactures flooring

Pella
Customer Service Department
102 Main Street

Pella, Iowa 50219
800-374-4758
www.pella.com
Manufactures windows and doors

Rejuvenation
Sales and Service
2550 NW Nicolai St.
Portland, OR 97210
888-401-1900
www.rejuvenation.com
Manufactures lighting fixtures

Shaw Industries, Inc.
616 East Walnut Ave.
Dalton, GA 30722-2128
800-441-7429
www.shawinc.com
Manufactures flooring

Tasso Wallcovering
www.tassoglas.se

Teragren
12715 Miller Rd. NE, Suite 301
Bainbridge Island, WA 98110
800-929-6333
206-842-9477
www.teragren.com
Manufactures bamboo flooring, panels, and veneers

Therma-Tru
1687 Woodlands Dr.
Maumee, OH 43537
800-537-8827
www.thermatru.com
Manufactures doors

Thibaut Wallcovering
480 Frelinghuysen Ave.
Newark, NJ 07114
Phone: 800-223-0704
www.thibautdesign.com
Manufactures wallpaper and fabrics

Unique Carpets, Ltd.
7360 Jurupa Ave.
Riverside, CA 92504
951-352-8125
www.uniquecarpetsltd.com
Manufactures wool, sisal, and synthetic carpets.

Velux-America, Inc.
450 Old Brickyard Rd.
P.O. Box 5001
Greenwood, SC 29648
800-888-3589
www.velux.com
Manufactures skylights, roof windows, and solar energy systems

York Wallcoverings, Inc.
750 Linden Ave.
York, PA 17404
800-375-9675
www.yorkwall.com
Manufactures wallpapers and borders

Acclimatization   Storing flooring on site to adjust to local humidity levels, which helps prevent future shrinking, swelling, or buckling; especially important with wood floors.

Anaglypta   A textured wallpaper invented in 1887 as a lightweight alternative to deeply embossed Lincrusta.

Asbestos   Mineral fiber harmful to the lungs commonly used in older construction materials, including floor tiles and flooring adhesive; removing or abrading these materials can release fibers into the air and should be avoided.

Baseboard molding   Decorative molding made of wood, resin, or MDF (medium density fiberboard); finishes and protects walls where they meet the floor and conceals floor expansion joints.

Battens   Narrow wood strips that typically cover vertical joints between siding boards.

Beam   A steel or wood framing member installed horizontally to support a structural load.

Bearing wall   A wall that provides structural support for framing above. Joists typically run at right angles to a bearing wall and rest on its top plate above a stud.

Border   A stripe or more elaborate design that runs around the perimeter of a floor; serves as a frame or accent. Available ready-made in many materials, including wood, ceramic, vinyl, and linoleum.

Building code   Municipal rules regulating building practices and procedures. Local building permits are almost always required for new construction or major renovations.

Casing   The exposed trim boards around the surfaces of windows and doors.

Caulk   A flexible material designed to seal cracks and joints against water, air, and noise. Usually sold in tubes, it is applied with a hand-squeeze gun.

Cement backer board   Cement and fiberglass mesh sheets used to cover wood subfloors before laying ceramic or stone tile.

Ceramic tile   Tiles made of natural clay and baked in a kiln; more porous than porcelain tiles.

Chalk line   The mark left by a chalked line stretched taut between two points on a flat surface, pulled up in the center, and allowed to snap back. The snap deposits chalk in a straight line.

Coped joint   A curving profile cut on a piece of trim that makes the reverse image of the piece against which it must butt; made with a coping saw.

Corner bead   Metal molding used at exterior corners of plastered and drywall-paneled walls.

Cornice   The trim where the exterior wall of a building meets the roof.

Cove molding   A molding with a concave face used as trim and to finish interior corners.

Crown molding   A molding that is usually convex and ornate installed where the wall meets the ceiling.

Dormer   A projection above the main roof designed to increase headroom and admit light, often used to turn attic areas into living spaces.

Drywall   Panels made of gypsum sandwiched between treated paper that are installed with nails or screws. Seams are taped and coated with compound to make a smooth wall surface that can be painted or papered.

Engineered wood   Flooring made up of thin plies of wood and topped with a hardwood veneer.

Epoxy   Bonding substance made of thermosetting resins that is water- and chemical-resistant, and durable; typically used as a skid-resistant floor coating over concrete or as an adhesive and grout for tiles.

Feather   To create a smooth transition from one surface level to another by means of a filler, such as patching compound; useful when preparing for installation of a new floor over an old floor or slab.

Fiberboard   Wood or vegetable fibers bonded together and compressed into sheets or used as the core for various types of flooring; comes in various densities.

Fiberglass insulation   The most common insulating material used to prevent the passage of heat, available in batts, rolls, and loose fill.

Foam board   Dense insulation formed into panels, generally with a high R-value per inch of material.

Furring   Wood strips fastened to a wall or other surface to form an even base for the application of other finish materials, such as wallboard or siding.

Grout   The fine-particle cement filler in the seams between ceramic tiles. It is available either ready-mixed or as dry powder that is mixed with water, and comes in a wide range of colors.

Header The thick horizontal structural member that runs above rough openings, such as doors and windows, in a building frame.

Jamb The typically one-by boards that surround window and door openings to provide a finished transition from the rough framing.

Joint compound A premixed gypsum-based paste used to fill the seams between drywall panels, cover nails and screws, and patch imperfections.

Joint tape Paper or synthetic mesh tape about 3 inches wide that reinforces seams between drywall panels.

Joist One in a series of parallel framing members that support a floor or ceiling load.

Kerf The narrow slot a saw blade cuts in a piece of lumber, usually about $1/8$-inch thick.

Lincrusta A type of thick, embossed wallcovering invented during the Victorian Era.

Knee wall A short wall, typically in attics, that is about 4 feet high, extending from the floor to a slanted ceiling.

Laminate flooring A tongue-and-groove interlocking system of flooring that floats above the subfloor; consists of a decorative resin surface coated with aluminum oxide over a wood composite core.

Lath Wood strips or metal mesh used as a foundation for plaster or stucco.

Miter A joint in which two boards are joined at angles, typically 45 degrees, to form a corner.

Molding A decorative wood strip installed along edges of walls, floors, ceilings, doors, and windows.

Nail set A blunt-pointed metal tool used to sink nailheads below the surface of wood. The pointed end is held on the nailhead as the other end is struck with a hammer.

On center The distance between the centers of regularly spaced structural members, such as studs. An on-center layout allows the edges of adjoining materials, such as drywall panels, to fall on one framing member.

Overlayment Typically refers to the application of a polymer reinforced cement layer to level, repair, or decorate an existing floor.

Partition wall An interior wall that does not carry structural loads from above and simply divides up floor space. Also called a nonload-bearing wall.

Plumb and level The two key planes along which almost all construction, except sloping roofs, is built. Plumb is exactly vertical, and level is exactly horizontal.

Prehung door A door delivered from the supplier already hinged in its jamb framework. Prehung doors may come with locksets already installed.

Rafter Dimensional lumber that forms the roof frame and supports plywood sheathing.

R-value The standard measure of insulation effectiveness, printed on all insulation. The rating is provided per inch thickness of material; the higher the number, the greater the insulating value.

Shellac A thin varnish made by dissolving this substance in denatured alcohol, used to finish wood.

Shim A narrow wedge of wood driven between a fixed surface and a movable member to alter the position of the movable member.

Soffit The underside of a structural member; the board that runs the length of a wall on the underside of the rafters, covering the space between the wall and the fascia.

Stud A vertical member in a frame wall, usually placed every 16 inches to facilitate covering with standard 48-inch-wide panels.

Tongue-and-groove Reciprocal profiles milled on wood or laminate strips and planks that fit together and produce strong joints.

Underlayment Material installed over a subfloor and under a finished floor; may be used to prevent transmission of moisture or sound or to smooth a rough subsurface.

Vapor barrier A material (paper, plastic, metal, or paint) used to prevent the passage of moisture, such as from a concrete slab to the flooring above.

VOCs (volatile organic compounds): Chemicals containing carbon at a molecular level that easily form vapors at room temperature; some flooring and flooring adhesives emit VOCs, which can be potentially harmful to people and the environment.

Water jet A method of cutting stone or tile using water and abrasive shot through small nozzles at high pressure.

Wet Saw A saw, available at rental outlets, used to cut ceramic and stone tiles.

index

A

Accent lighting, 234
Acoustical ceiling tiles, 40
Acrylics, 197
Adhesives, thinset, 40
Air baffles, 151
Air flow, maintaining attic, 151
Ambient lighting, 234, 235
Area rugs, 200
Asbestos insulation, 12
Attic access hole, changing location
   of, 148
Attic air flow, maintaining, 151
Attic stairs
   folding, 148
   installing, 216–17
Awning windows, 66

B

Backer board, 175
   installing, 90
Backsaw, 20
Baffles
   air, 151
   lightweight foam, 151
Bamboo, 50
Baseboard
   installing trim, 144–45
   nailing, 145
   scribing, 144
Bay windows, 69
Bench power tools, 24
Berber-style carpets, 200
Boards, edging and joining, 22
Brick, 44
Brick facing, installing, 130–31
Brush-like pile, 198
Built-up cornice, installing, 164–65
Built-up trim, 45
Bypass doors, adjusting, 79

C

Cables
   bringing into metal box, 232
   placing, 186
Carbon monoxide, 236
Carpenter's ruler, 14
Carpets
   berber-style, 200
   shag, 197
   textures of, 198
   tufted, 199, 200
   upgrading padding, 201
   wall-to-wall, 197–201
   woven, 199
Carpet tiles, 200
Casement windows, 66
Ceiling(s), 146–67
   coffered, 166
   details for, 166
   framing opening, 148
   installing false beam, 160–61
   installing light fixture, 226–27
   installing suspended, 154–55

   installing tin, 158–59
   installing wood-paneled, 157
   plank, 156
   reinforcing joists, 215
Ceiling fan
   installing, 244–45
   supporting, 149
   wiring, 244–45
Ceiling medallions, 45, 166
   installing, 167
Ceiling tile, 40
Cement-board, 90, 175
Cementitious backer unit (CBU), 40
Ceramic floor tile
   laying, 180–81
   routine cleaning, 188–89
Ceramic tiles, 40, 48, 176
   shapes and patterns, 40
   trim options, 41
Chair-rail, 45
   installing, 135
   making tight miters, 135
Chandeliers, 232, 235
   installing, 233
Circular saws, 22, 24, 157
Classic curved-claw hammer, 18
Cleanup, doing preliminary, 110
Coffered ceiling, 166
Combination square, 14
Combing, 117
Concrete, 176
Continuous ridge vent, 238
Continuous strip-grille vent, 238
Coping saw, 20
Cork floors, 51
Corner beads, repairing, 206
Cornice
   built-up, 164–65
   plastic, 163
   wood, 162
Cornice moldings, 45
Cove lights, 223
Cracks
   filling deep, 110
   filling surface, 110
Crawl spaces, insulation, 172
Crevice tools, 210
Crosscut saw, 10, 20
Cutouts, making, for electrical boxes,
   86–87

D

Deadman brace, 152
   building and using, 152–53
Decorative lighting, 234
Decorative paint techniques, 117
Demolition tools, 12–13
Diagonal layout, working lines for, 170
Dimmer switch, 235
Door(s)
   adjusting bypass, 79
   construction of, 81
   energy-efficient, 64
   installing, 78–79
   metal-clad, 80

   strengthening, 80
   types of, 68
   vinyl-clad, 80
Door casing, installing colonial, 142–43
Double glazing, 64
Double-hung windows, 66, 67
Drills, 24
Drop-forging, 18
Drywall, 36, 84, 86–97
   construction of, 87
   curves and, 97
   estimating quantities for, 91
   fastening systems for, 86
   finishing seams, 94–96
   handling, 86
   inside corners, 97
   installing, 88–89
   installing backerboard, 90
   making cutouts for electrical boxes,
      86–87
   options for, 37
   outside corners, 97
   patching large holes in, 204
   preventing joint cracks, 96
   repairing small holes in, 205
   resurfacing wall, 92–93
   setting screws, 89
   types of, 36
Drywall compound, 26
Drywall finishing tools, 26–27
Drywall hammer, 37
Drywall lift, 152
Drywall screwguns, 89
Duct locations, 243
Dust mites, 236
Dutch doors, 69

E

East light, 67
Egg and dart, 166
Electrical boxes
   extenders, 93
   making cutouts for, 86–87
Electric radiant-floor heating, 186
Engineered lumber, 149
Exhaust fan, venting, 243
Extension bar on folding ruler, 14

F

Face-nailing, 57
False ceiling beam, installing, 160–61
False header, making, 83
Fans
   ceiling, 244–45
   ventilating, 240–43
   whole-house, 246–47
Fasteners, concealing, 39
Fastening systems for drywall, 86
Fiber facts, 200
Fiber-optic lighting, 224
Fire code panels, 36
Fixed windows, 66
Flat-panel wainscoting, 104–7
Floating trim, 211
Floor covering, 46–51

Floors, 168–201
 installing slate, 184–85
 installing vinyl sheet, 178
 insulating, 172
 laminate, 190–91
 layout of, 170
 refinishing wood, 194–95
 reinforcing joists, 214
 reinforcing old, 173
 slate installing, 184–85
 preparing, 182–83
 wood strip, 176, 192–93
Floor tiles
 ceramic, 180–81
 vinyl, 176
Fluorescent, 223–24
Flush doors, 68
Focused lighting, 222
Formaldehyde, 236
Foundation, insulating, 172
Frames, strengthening, 80
Framing
 ceiling opening, 148
 installing, for skylight, 150–51
Framing square, 170
Freestanding fixture, 235
French doors, 69
Furring strips, paneling over, 100–102

G
Gable-end windows, 217
Gable vents, 238, 239
General lighting, 234
Glass-block wall, building, 76–77
Greenhouses, window, 69
Grout, 48

H
Halogen lighting, 110, 224, 226
Hammer, drywall, 37
Handsaws, 20–21
Hand tools, 18–19
Hardboard, 176
Hard-surface flooring, 47–49
Hard-water problems, 188
Hardwoods, 50
Headers, 148
 making false, 83
Heat gun, 211
Heavy-duty fiberglass, 44
High-intensity-discharge (HID) bulbs, 226
Holes
 patching large, in drywall, 204
 repairing small, in drywall, 205

I
Incandescent lighting, 223
Indoor lighting design, 234–35
Insulating crawl spaces, 172

J
Joint compound, 89
Joists
 ceiling, 149, 215
 floor, 214

K
Keyhole saw, 10
Keyless chuck, 24
Knife-cut molding, 166
Knockouts, 232

L
Laminate floor, 48, 49
 installing, 190–91
Lauan plywood, 175
Layout lines, 14
Layout stick, 16
Layout tools, 14–17
Layout triangle, 14
Lead-based paint, 12
Levels, 16–17
Lighting, 220–35
 accent, 234
 ambient, 234, 235
 bringing cable into metal box, 232
 chandeliers, 232, 233
 decorative, 234
 fiber-optic, 224
 fixture types, 223
 focused, 222
 functions of, 234
 general, 234
 halogen, 110, 224, 226
 high-intensity-discharge, 226
 indoor design, 234–35
 installing ceiling fixture, 226–27
 installing track lights, 230–31
 light bulbs, 226
 lighting capacity, 226
 options for, 222
 recessed lights, 228
 recommended ranges of levels, 225
 task, 222, 226, 234, 235
 types of bulbs, 223–24, 226
Lightweight foam baffle, 151
Line level, 16
Linoleum, 176
Loop-pile carpets, 198
Low-profile downlights, 228

M
Masonry veneers, 44
Mastic, 184
Measuring, 14
Measuring tape, 14
Medallion, ceiling, 167
Metal box, bringing cable into, 232
Metal-clad doors, 80
Metal corner guard, 97
Mildew, killing, 110
Mirror walls, 44
Miters, making tight, 135
Molding, knife-cut, 166
Multilevel-loop styles, 198

N
Nail guns, 22
Nailing techniques, 57
Nails, 152

National Electric Code, 186
Nippers, 30
North light, 67
Nylon, 197

O
Old resilient tile, 176
Olefin, 197

P
Padding, upgrading, 201
Paint, 42
 washing dirty, 110
Paint brushes, 28
 checklist for, 29
Painting
 decorative techniques, 117
 preparing plaster for, 112
 preparing woodwork for, 113
 tools for, 28–29
 of wall, 114–16
Paint scrappers, 211
Paint spinners, 28
Panel doors, 68
Paneling, 84
 repairing plywood, 209
 repairing solid-wood, 208
 sheet, 98–101
 solid-wood, 84, 102–3
Panel-look doors, 68
Parquet flooring, 50
Particleboard, 176
Partitions
 building, 56
 removing old, 54
Patches, priming, 110
Perforated vents, 238
Picture-rail, 45
Pipes, protecting, from freezing, 172
Plank ceilings, 156
Planking, wood, 156
Planks, with square edges, 39
Plaster
 patching, 207
 for preparing painting, 112
Plastic cornice, installing, 163
Plug vent, 238
Plumb bob, 16
Plywood, 84
Plywood paneling, repairing, 209
Plywood subfloor, 197
Plywood underlayment, installing, 174–75
Pneumatic nail gun, 106
Pocket doors, 81
Polyesters, 197
Power painters, 28
Power saw, 20
Power screwdriver, 37
Power tools, 22–25
Prefabricated sunrooms, 69
Prefinished real-wood veneers, 98
Priming, 42
Pry bar, 54

index

R

Radiant-floor heating
electric system, 186
placing cables, 186
preparation, 186
testing cables, 186
Radon, 236
Ragging, 117
Recessed lights, 223, 228, 235
installing, 228–29
Reciprocating saw, 54
Rectangular fluorescent fixtures, 228
Refinishing wood floor, 194–95
Register vents, 238
Repairs, 202–19
fixing leaking skylight, 218–19
floating trim, 211
installing attic stairs, 216–17
patching large holes in drywall, 204
patching plaster, 207
refinishing wood trim, 210–11
reflashing vent pipe, 219
reinforcing ceiling joists, 215
reinforcing floor joists, 214
repairing corner beads, 206
repairing plywood paneling, 209
repairing solid-wood paneling, 208
replacing broken tile, 212
wallcovering spot, 213
Replacement windows, 67–68
Resilient flooring, 175
Resilient vinyl tile and sheet flooring,
46–47
Resurfacing walls and ceilings, 92–93
Ridge vents, 239
Ripping-claw hammer, 18
Rip saws, 20
Rollers, 28
checklist for, 29
Rolling scaffold, 153
Roof, venting through, 239
Roof vents, 238, 239
Room, checking, for square, 171

S

Safety
clamping stile to worktable, 105
in stripping walls, 12–13
Safety equipment, 32
Saws
circular, 22, 24, 157
crosscut, 10
keyhole, 10
reciprocating, 54
utility, 10
wet, 31
Scarf joints, making basic, 132–33
Screwdriver, power, 37
Screws, 152
setting, 89
Scribing baseboard, 144
Seams, finishing drywall, 94–96
Setup, completing, 110
Shag carpeting, 197

Sheet flooring, 176
Sheet-mounted tiles, 41
Sheet paneling, 98–101
concealing fasteners in, 39
over furring strips, 100–102
over studs, 99
scribing to uneven surface, 101
Shoe stilts, 153
Skylights, 68, 217
fixing leaking, 218–19
installing framing for, 150–51
Slate floor, 48
installing, 184–85
preparing for, 182–83
Sliders, 68–69
Sliding windows, 66
Snap cutter, 30
Soffit vents, types of, 238
Softwoods, 50
Solid paneling, 84, 102–3
concealing fasteners in, 39
installing, 103
installing flat-panel wainscoting, 104–7
plank grades and appearance, 102
repairing, 208
Sound-deadening, 63
Soundproof wall, building, 62–63
South light, 67
Spattering, 117
Specialty tools, 32–33
Sponging, 117
Sprayers, 28
checklist, 29
Square
check for, 14
checking room for, 171
Square edges, planks with, 39
Square layout, working lines for, 170
Stains
covering deep, 110
removal chart for, 188
Stairs, attic, 148, 216–17
Steam removal, methods for
wallcovering, 119
Steel studs, 60
Step-ahead layout, 14–15
Stile
clamping, 105
rail wainscoting and, 134
Stippling, 117
Stone, 48
Stone facing, 131
Stone veneers, 44
Strongback, 215
Studs
framing with steel, 60
paneling over, 99
sizes of, 59
Sunrooms, prefabricated, 69
Surface-mounted strip vents, 238
Surface-mount lights, 223
Surface-prep materials, 42
Suspended ceiling, installing, 154–55
Suspended lights, 223

T

Task lighting, 222, 226, 234, 235
Thinset adhesives, 40
3-4-5 triangle method, 170
Tile pavers, 48
Tiles
carpet, 200
ceiling, 40
ceramic, 40
replacing broken, 212
Tile tools, 30
Tin ceiling, installing, 158–59
Tin panels, 44
Tongue-and-groove boards, 39
Tools
demolition, 12–13
drywall finishing, 26–27
hand, 18–19
layout, 14–17
painting and papering, 28–29
power, 22–25
specialty, 32–33
tile, 30
Track lights, 223
installing, 230–31
Triangulation, 14
Trim, 45
built-up, 45
Trim saw, 20
Triphosphor fluorescent lamps, 223
Troffers, 228
Tufted carpet, 199, 200
Turbine vents, 238

U

Under-cabinet lights, 223
Underlayment, types of, 175
Utility knife blades, 178
Utility saw, 10

V

Veneers
masonry, 44
prefinished real-wood, 98
stone, 44
Ventilating fan
capacity of, 240
installing, 240–41
wiring, 242–43
Ventilation, 236–47
boxes and controls, 244
duct locations, 243
installing ceiling fans, 244–45
installing ventilating fan, 240–41
installing whole-house fan, 246–47
types of soffit vents, 238
ventilating fan capacity, 240
venting through roof, 239
vent inlets and outlets, 238
wiring ventilating fan, 242–43
Vent inlets and outlets, 238
Vent pipe, reflashing, 219
Vents, keeping clear, 151
Vinyl-clad doors, 80

Vinyl floor tiles, 176–77
  installing, 176
  preparing layout, 176
  start with right base, 176
Vinyl sheet flooring, installing, 178–79

W

Wall(s)
  basic repair, 26
  building glass-block, 76–77
  building soundproof, 62–63
  building temporary support, 55
  mirror, 44
  painting, 114–16
  stripping safely, 12–13
Wallcovering, 43
  adhesive versus prepaste, 43
  alternatives for, 44
  cutting, 120
  hanging, 122–24
  papering inside corners, 125
  papering outside corners, 125
  planning job, 120
  preparing for project, 120
  spot repairs for, 213
  steam removal methods, 119
  tools, 28–29
  using wallpaper paste, 121
  wet-stripping, 118–19
Wall finishes, 108–45
  brick facing, 130–31
  decorative paint techniques, 117

hanging wallpaper, 122–24
installing baseboard trim, 144–45
installing chair rail, 135
installing colonial door casing, 142–43
installing wall frames, 136–37
installing window trim, 138–41
making basic scarf joints, 132–33
painting, 114–16
prep, 110–11
preparing plaster for painting, 112
preparing woodwork for painting, 113
stile and rail wainscoting, 134
stone facing, 131
wallcovering, 120–25
wall tiles, 126–29
wet-stripping wallcovering, 118–19
Wall frames, installing, 136–37
Wall framing basics, 57
Wall niche, installing, 82
Wall paneling, 38
  types of, 38
Wall sconces, 235
Wall tiles
  installing, 128–29
  planning layout for, 126–27
Wall-to-wall carpeting, 197–201
Water-resistant panels, 36
West light, 67
Wet saw, 31
Wet-stripping wallcovering, 118–19
Whole-house fan, installing, 246–47
Window greenhouses, 69

Windows
  awning, 66
  bay, 69
  casement, 66
  casing assembly for, 141
  double-hung, 66, 67
  downsizing, 67
  energy-efficient, 64
  fixed, 66
  framing opening, 58
  installing new, 72–73
  replacement, 67–68
  replacing, 74–75
  sliding, 66
  types of, 64–66
Window sash, installing new, 70–71
Window trim, installing, 138–41
Wiring ventilating fan, 242–43
Wood cornice, installing, 162
Wood floors, 50
  refinishing, 194–95
Wood furring, installing, 61
Wood-paneled ceiling, installing, 157
Wood planking, 156
Wood strip flooring, 176
  installing, 192–93
Wood trim, refinishing, 210–11
Woodwork, preparing, for painting, 113
Working lines, 170
  for diagonal layout, 170
  for square layout, 170
Woven carpet, 199

photo credits

Project sequences by John Parsekian/CH except where noted.

page 14: bottom left and right Brian C. Nieves/CH page 28 both Brian C. Nieves/CH page 32 Brian C. Nieves/CH page 40 top courtesy of Celotex page 42 bottom left and right Brian C. Nieves/CH page 44 both left Robert Anderson/CH top right courtesy of Corian middle right courtesy of Tasso Wallcovering bottom right Jessie Walker page 45 top left courtesy of Georgia Pacific middle left courtesy of Balmer Studios bottom left Thibaut Wallcovering both right Brian C. Nieves/CH page 46 both courtesy of Armstrong Floors page 47 top courtesy of Forbo bottom courtesy of Armstrong Floors pages 48-49 left courtesy of American Olean middle Brian Vanden Brink, architect: Van Dam & Renner top right courtesy of Mannington page 50 left courtesy of Teragren right courtesy of Hartco/Armstrong page 51 all top courtesy of Expanko bottom courtesy of Elmwood Reclaimed Timber page 62 all Brian C. Nieves/CH page 63 top left and right Brian C. Nieves/CH pages 64-65 both Tony Giammarino/Giammarino & Dworkin, architect: Susan Kipp Construction page 66 Phillip Ennis Photography, architect: Lim Chang page 68 top Mark Lohman bottom Mark Samu, designer: Jim DeLuca, A.I.A. page 69 Mark Samu, courtesy of Hearst Specials pages 70-71 all Freeze Frame Studio/CH page 75 middle right courtesy of Pella bottom middle courtesy of Andersen Windows bot-

tom right courtesy of Marvin Windows & Doors page 76 top Freeze Frame Studio/CH bottom www.davidduncanlivingston.com page 77 all Freeze Frame Studio/CH page 79 Brian C. Nieves/CH page 80 both courtesy of Therma-Tru page 81 courtesy of Craftmaster/Colonist Door Design pages 90-91 all Freeze Frame Studio/CH page 98 courtesy of Georgia Pacific page 100 both left Brian C. Nieves/CH page 101 both top Brian C. Nieves/CH page 102 top Bob Greenspan pages 104-107 Neal Barrett/CH page 110 Gary David Gold/CH pages 112-113 all Freeze Frame Studio/CH pages 118-119 all Freeze Frame Studio/CH page 120 York Wallcoverings page 121 Freeze Frame Studio/CH page 122 bottom Grey Crawford page 125 all Freeze Frame Studio/CH pages 138-145 all Neal Barrett/CH pages 150-151 all except top right Velux America page 153 small top David Houser/CH small bottom David Baer/Smith-Baer Studios/CH page 156 Jesse Walker page 158 bottom left Jesse Walker pages 164-165 all Neal Barrett/CH page 169 courtesy of Mannington page 171 all Freeze Frame Studio/CH page 174 all Freeze Frame Studio/CH page 175 courtesy of Shaw page 177 all Freeze Frame Studio/CH pages 178-181 all Freeze Frame Studio/CH pages 182-185 all Neal Barrett/CH pages 190-191 all Freeze Frame Studio/CH pages 194-195 all Freeze Frame Studio/CH page 196 courtesy of Shaw page 197 top courtesy of Helios bottom courtesy of Unique Carpets, Ltd. page 198

courtesy of Mohawk page 199 all Home and Garden Editorial Services page 200 all left Home and Garden Editorial Services right courtesy of Mohawk page 201 top Home and Garden Editorial Services bottom courtesy of InterfaceFLOR pages 214-215 all Brian C. Nieves/CH page 217 top Jessie Walker pages 221-222 www.davidduncanlivingston.com page 223 courtesy of Rejuvenation page 224 top Mark Samu, designer: Kitchen Designs by Ken Kelly bottom Ann Gummerson page 225 Ann Gummerson, designer: Richstone Custom Homes page 227 Freeze Frame Studio/CH pages 228-229 all Freeze Frame Studio/CH pages 230-231 all except top right Freeze Frame Studio/CH top right Mark Samu page 232 top Mark Samu, design: Kitchen Design by Ken Kelly all bottom Brian C. Nieves/CH page 233 all Brian C. Nieves/CH page 234 left Jesse Walker right courtesy of Lindal Cedar Homes page 235 top Mark Samu, reprinted with permission from House Beautiful Kitchens/Baths, 1998/The Hearst Corporation, stylist: Margaret McNicholas bottom left Jessie Walker, designers: Kay McCarthy and Alfie McAdams bottom right www.davidduncanlivingston.com page 237 www.davidduncanlivingston.com page 238 top right courtesy of Alcoa pages 240-243 all Freeze Frame Studio/CH pages 244-247 all Brian C. Nieves/CH page 249 courtesy of Elmwood Reclaimed Timber

Have a home improvement, decorating, or gardening project? Look for these and other fine Creative Homeowner books wherever books are sold.

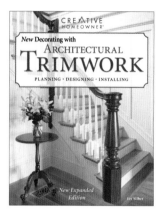

Transform a room with trimwork. Over 550 color photos and illustrations. 240 pp.; 8^1/$_2$" × 10^7/$_8$"
BOOK #: 277500

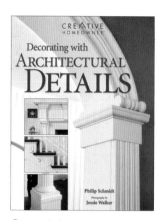

Covers design treatments such as moldings and window seats. 300+ color photos. 224 pp.; 8^1/$_2$" × 10^7/$_8$"
BOOK #: 278225

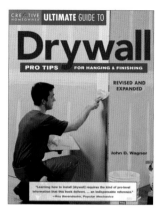

A complete guide covering all aspects of drywall. Over 450 color photos 160 pp.; 8^1/$_2$" × 10^7/$_8$"
BOOK #: 278320

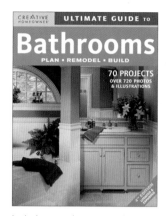

Includes step-by-step projects and over 630 photos.
272 pp.; 8^1/$_2$" × 10^7/$_8$"
BOOK#: 278632

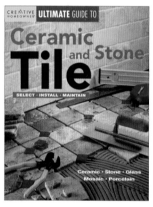

Complete DIY tile instruction. Over 550 color photos and illustrations. 224 pp.; 8^1/$_2$" × 10^7/$_8$"
BOOK #: 27753

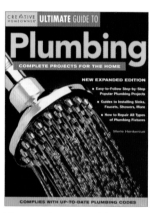

The complete manual for plumbing. Over 750 color photos and illustrations. 288 pp.; 8^1/$_2$" × 10^7/$_8$"
BOOK#: 278200

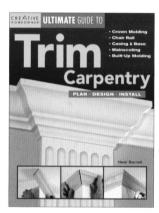

Best-selling trimwork manual. Over 500 color photos and illustrations. 208 pp.; 8^1/$_2$" × 10^7/$_8$"
BOOK#: 277516

The ultimate home-improvement reference manual. Over 300 step-by-step projects. 608 pp.; 9" × 10^7/$_8$"
BOOK#: 267870

Design inspiration for creating a new kitchen. Over 500 color photographs. 224 pp.; 8^1/$_2$" × 10^7/$_8$"
BOOK #: 279415

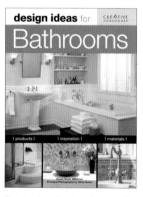

Design inspiration for creating a new bathroom. Over 500 color photos. 224 pp.; 8^1/$_2$" × 10^7/$_8$"
BOOK #: 279268

An impressive guide to garden design and plant selection. 950 color photos and illustrations. 384 pp.; 9" × 10"
BOOK #: 274610

Lavishly illustrated with portraits of over 100 flowering plants; more than 700 photos. 240 pp.; 9" × 10"
BOOK #: 274222

For more information and to order direct, visit our Web site at **www.creativehomeowner.com**